Supporting Teaching and Learning in Schools

In what ways can higher level teaching assistants effectively support the processes of learning in the classroom?

Supporting Teaching and Learning in Schools is an accessible, user-friendly handbook designed to provide practical guidance and ideas to support higher level teaching assistants (HLTAs). It covers the knowledge and skills needed by HLTAs to work effectively with pupils, teachers, parents and other professionals concerned with the well-being of children.

The book relates directly to the standards for HLTAs but also provides a deeper grounding in pedagogy and the role of the teacher and the HLTA in creating productive learning environments. The text is illuminated with examples of existing good practice, and a range of tried-and-tested strategies to help HLTAs develop in all aspects of their work. It provides essential background knowledge, together with a range of activities designed to support learning, examining:

- the roles of the HLTA and teacher respectively, and interactively;
- classroom management and interactions with pupils;
- pupil differences;
- the place of the HLTA within the school community;
- professional development.

The book can be used alongside the popular Routledge *Learning to Teach in the Secondary School* series, which gives detailed examples of theory and practice about teaching and learning for trainee teachers and provides an invaluable resource for current and prospective HLTAs across a wide range of subjects.

Sarah Younie is Principal Lecturer at De Montfort University with experience of teaching on the BA Honours degree in Education Studies, PGCE secondary and Masters programmes. **Susan Capel** is Professor and Head of the School of Sport and Education at Brunel University. **Marilyn Leask** is Professor of Education at Brunel University. She previously worked for the Improvement and Development Agency for Local Government and the Training and Development Agency for Schools.

Supporting Teaching and Learning in Schools

A handbook for higher level teaching assistants

Edited by
Sarah Younie, Susan Capel
and Marilyn Leask

Routledge
Taylor & Francis Group

LONDON AND NEW YORK

First published 2009
by Routledge
2 Park Square, Milton Park, Abingdon, Oxon OX14 4RN

Simultaneously published in the USA and Canada
by Routledge
270 Madison Avenue, New York, NY 10016

Routledge is an imprint of the Taylor & Francis Group, an informa business

Typeset in Bembo by
Pindar NZ, Auckland, New Zealand
Printed and bound in Great Britain by
TJ International Ltd, Padstow, Cornwall

British Library Cataloguing in Publication Data
A catalogue record for this book is available from the British Library

Library of Congress Cataloging-in-Publication Data
Supporting teaching and learning in schools : a handbook for higher level
teaching assistants / edited by Sarah Younie, Susan Capel and Marilyn
Leask.—1st ed
    p. cm.
  Includes bibliographical references and index.
  1. Teachers' assistants—Education (Secondary)—Great Britain. I. Younie,
Sarah, 1967- II. Capel, Susan Anne, 1953- III. Leask, Marilyn, 1950-
   LB2844.1.A8S87 2008
    373.114'1240942—dc22   2008028854

ISBN 10: 0-415-35884-1 (pbk)
ISBN 10: 0-203-00678-X (ebk)

ISBN 13: 978-0-415-35884-2 (pbk)
ISBN 13: 978-0-203-00678-8 (ebk)

Contents

Illustrations

TABLES

FIGURES

TASKS

Contributors

Diana Burton is Professor and Dean of the Faculty of Education, Community and Leisure at Liverpool John Moores University.

Susan Capel is Professor and Head of the School of Sport and Education at Brunel University.

Julia Lawrence is a Principal Lecturer and Subject Group Leader for Physical Education Teacher Education at Leeds Metropolitan University and contributes to both and primary and secondary initial teacher education courses at both undergraduate and postgraduate level.

Marilyn Leask is Professor of Education at Brunel University. She previously worked for the Improvement and Development Agency for Local Government and the Training and Development Agency for Schools.

Kath Lee is an educational consultant with 30 years' experience including as a deputy head in one of the country's largest secondary schools. She is a research associate with the National College for School Leadership.

Elizabeth Marsden works with Initial Teacher Education and postgraduate students at the University of Paisley.

Andrew Noyes is Associate Professor at the University of Nottingham where until recently he was the secondary PGCE course leader. He now directs a number of funded research projects.

Ken Powell is the Course Leader for secondary PGCE professional studies at Canterbury Christ Church University and the secondary PGCE ICT subject leader.

Andrea Raiker is Programme Leader for the BA Honours and Foundation Degrees in Educational Practice at the University of Bedfordshire.

Sarah Younie is Principal Lecturer at De Montfort University with experience of teaching on the BA Honours Degree in Education Studies, PGCE secondary and Masters programmes.

Paula Zwozdiak–Myers is Programme Leader for the BA Honours Degree in Childhood and Youth Studies at the University of Bedfordshire and leads the Professional Studies component of an ITE programme for secondary students.

Acknowledgements

We should like to thank our colleagues who have contributed to the book. We would also like to thank Jon Bird the cartoonist for giving permission for his work to be reproduced and Carrie Weston for the inclusion of her photograph. We wish to thank the Training and Development Agency (TDA) for permission to reproduce materials from their website regarding the set of professional standards for HLTAs and information on the career development framework. We should like to take this opportunity to thank Anna Clarkson from Routledge for providing continuing support.

We wish to thank Routledge for their kind permission to use extracts and adapt previously published work from M. Leask and N. Pachler (eds) (2005) *Learning to Teach Using ICT in the Secondary School: a companion to school experience*, 2nd edn, and from S. Capel, M. Leask, and T. Turner (eds) (2009) *Learning to Teach in the Secondary School: a companion to school experience*, 5th edn.

Introduction

This book is designed to help you develop the knowledge and understanding required to achieve the higher level teaching assistant (HLTA) professional standards for England.

HLTAs play a key role in the school workforce in England working alongside teachers to maximise the learning of pupils and this book covers the knowledge and skills you need to work effectively with pupils, teachers, parents and other professionals concerned with the well-being of children.

Each chapter is structured around key areas of knowledge required by the HLTA standards. The objectives for the chapter provide a way for you to check that your understanding has developed and a cross reference to the HLTA standards is made after the objectives. The words in *italics* in these sections are taken from the HLTA standards produced by the the Training and Development Agency for Schools. Each chapter has tasks for you to undertake which are designed to deepen your learning in the selected area and concludes with a summary and further reading. Professional websites are referenced as these provide further resources for you to use.

The appendices provide access to the HLTA standards, a map showing how the standards are covered in the text and a glossary of terms to help you develop your understanding of the education system.

If the HLTA standards are updated during the life of this book, then additional material to meet any new requirements will be put on the Routledge website.[1]

Whilst the role of the HLTA varies considerably from department to department and school to school, the basic principles of teaching and learning which are covered in this book apply across all subject areas. You will find however that whilst the content of the curriculum – what is taught to pupils – is outlined in National Curriculum documents, teachers have considerable freedom to choose the methods they use to teach. As an HLTA, you will see many different teaching strategies used and this text is intended to help you develop your own style. The effectiveness of any teaching strategy chosen depends on a number of factors, including the pupils' expectations and prior experience, the culture of the school and the individual approach of the teacher. Strategies that work well for one HLTA may not work for another, even with the same group of pupils, and may not work for you if you are required to take the class. You need to develop your own repertoire of professional skills which work for you in your school.

Likewise, there are different ways of supporting pupil learning. With the support of the teachers with whom you work, you will find your own way of supporting pupil learning and managing the learning of groups of pupils. Flexibility of approach is essential: in some subjects and in some contexts, learning through doing is most important; in other subjects, and in other contexts, rote learning might be appropriate. Sometimes it is appropriate for pupils to work alone: in other situations the teacher might judge that group work will achieve a deeper learning outcome.

Every teacher applies their professional judgement, drawn from theory and practice to the situation in the classroom. Likewise, every HLTA applies their professional judgement for supporting pupil learning and this book is intended to provide you with various tools for developing your skills, knowledge and judgement so that you can effectively support pupil learning.

The text is not intended to be read cover to cover in one sitting. It is intended to provide you with background information around key topics and tasks to undertake to develop your understanding of key elements of the teaching and learning process. With much (or all) of your work to achieve the standards being focused in your school, you may have limited access to a university library and to others working to achieve HLTA status. However, your local library provides an 'inter-library loan' service which gives you access to the texts suggested for further reading. Where possible, we suggest that you discuss the tasks and their outcomes with colleagues.

This book can be read in association with the popular Routledge 'Learning to Teach in the Secondary School' series of texts which are used for the training of teachers and which provide detailed examples of theory and practice about teaching and learning based on research. The core text for the series, *Learning to Teach in the Secondary School: a companion for school experience* (Capel, Leask and Turner, 2009), extends the material in this book and as your knowledge develops you may wish to read this. There are also texts for each subject area and practical texts in the 'Learning to Teach' series which may be of particular relevance to you in your work. These are listed in the front of this book.

We hope that you enjoy the book and that it encourages you to continue with your professional development.

Sarah Younie
Susan Capel
Marilyn Leask

NOTE

1   If you search by the title of the book on the Routledge website then you will find this material.

1 Your Role as a Higher Level Teaching Assistant

Marilyn Leask

INTRODUCTION

As an HLTA, you are in the position of having a major impact on the young people with whom you work – your attitudes to them, your capacity to help them learn, to help them develop self belief and understanding of what it means to be a citizen in our society, will affect their capacity to find their way in life. In this way your work has an impact not just fon the individual pupil but on society and the people your pupils come into contact with throughout their life.

In this chapter we outline the role of the HLTA, introduce basic principles of effective teaching and ask you to reflect on your values and beliefs and how these might impact on your professional practice and on the pupils, parents or carers and other staff with whom you come into contact. An introduction to your contractual and statutory duties is included.

OBJECTIVES

By the end of this chapter, you should:

- understand the variety of roles that HLTAs may undertake;
- understand the teaching process and the skills you need to be able to demonstrate;
- be aware of how your attitudes and values impact on your professional practice;
- have knowledge of your contractual and statutory duties with respect to child protection, special educational needs, equal opportunities (e.g. with respect to gender, race, disability), health and safety.

This chapter refers to the HLTA standards regarding your general role and responsibilities, particularly having *high expectations* of children and young people, demonstrating *positive values*; an awareness of statutory *frameworks* and understanding your responsibilities with respect to *keeping learners safe*. You can also refer to Appendix 2 to see how this chapter maps onto the standards at the time of publication; if these are revised then updated materials will appear on the website supporting this text.

BACKGROUND TO THE DEVELOPMENT OF THE HLTA ROLE

The HLTA role was introduced in England in 2006 and it recognises the value of schools drawing on the specialist skills of the whole school staff. The role builds on the teaching assistant role with key responsibilities normally including supporting pupil learning through collaborative planning and working with teachers as well as managing and leading the development of teaching assistants in schools.

The Training and Development Agency for Schools (TDA) is the government agency responsible for setting standards for teaching and for HLTAs and they describe the role of the HLTA as follows:

> Higher level teaching assistant (HLTA) status shows you have the ability to undertake complex tasks and can work independently. Under the direction of a teacher the sorts of tasks you'll be involved in are working with individual pupils and whole classes; planning and supporting learning activities; and guiding the work of other support staff. The exact nature of your HLTA duties will depend on the needs of your school. Your headteacher and school governing body will determine terms and conditions for your post taking into account any relevant agreements.
>
> (TDA, 2006, website: http://www.tda.gov.uk)

Agreement about what duties the HLTA may undertake was reached by government agencies and unions working together through the Workforce Agreement Monitoring Group (WAMG) and Table 1.1 provides examples of various tasks that WAMG identified as appropriate for HLTAs to undertake.

Subsequently, standards for HLTAs have been published on the TDA website together with a handbook providing more details about what the standards mean in practice. (See Task 1.1.)

THE HLTA ROLE

Under the 1988 Education Reform Act, schools in England have responsibility for implementing the National Curriculum and for the spiritual and moral welfare of their pupils, so most teachers have both a specialist academic role and a pastoral role. Both roles encompass administrative as well as teaching responsibilities in which you may be engaged as an HLTA. You may also have a management role – taking responsibility for managing teaching assistants and other staff. The HLTA role builds on the role of the teaching assistant as well as your role working with pupils.

You can expect to work alongside the teacher to support pupils' learning through the 'taught curriculum', i.e. specialist and cross-curricular subjects and out of school

Table 1.1 Examples of tasks undertaken by HLTAs

Tasks undertaken by HLTAs include:
• working as organisers of a transition programme for pupils from pre-school to school, infant to junior and primary to secondary school;   • devising learning plans for children with special educational needs to enable teaching colleagues to deliver more effective teaching, e.g. by devising plans with a kinaesthetic approach;   • working with pupils from different ethnic backgrounds and helping with the inclusion of children from very diverse backgrounds, thus creating positive relationships between home and school;   • being responsible for ICT management in collaboration with teachers, teaching whole classes on ICT and assessing pupils; giving information and advice on new ICT products, giving tailored ICT support to pupils with SEN;   • developing a peer mediation system to tackle and resolve conflicts between pupils, and training pupil mediators;   • putting together study guides on English novels for less able students in collaboration with teachers;   • acting as specialists in counselling and managing EBD, providing team-teacher training for colleagues working in people support centres.

Source: Workforce Agreement Monitoring Group, June 2006.

activities, as well as through the 'hidden curriculum' of the school. The term hidden curriculum is used to describe what pupils learn through the values and expectations of the school community. This learning can include respect for others, how to play a role in the school and wider community, interpersonal relationships, relationships with adults, and so on.

In your work with the teacher in the classroom, you are likely to be engaged in:

• Curriculum planning and development; assessment: supporting the planning and delivery of lessons and pupil assessment. Your responsibilities here will include preparation and management of resources (see Chapter 11: HLTA Standards 12, 21, 28) as well as teaching individuals (see Chapter 5 on pupil diversity: HLTA Standards 9, 27), small groups under the direction of a teacher or taking a whole class in the teacher's absence. Chapter 2 (HLTA Standards 6, 9, 14, 21, 23, 25, 32) provides further details about lesson planning; Chapter 6 on pupil behaviour and teaching strategies (HLTA Standards 2, 4, 9, 26).

• Administration and pupil performance monitoring, including updating records for assessment, tests, attendance and producing reports so that pupil progress can be monitored. Chapter 9 covers monitoring and assessment of pupils (HLTA Standards 10, 22, 23, 24, 25).

As well as your work alongside teachers in specialist curriculum areas, you can expect to be involved in cross-curricular and extra-curricular activities such as:

• planning educational trips and social events;

- work experience;
- liaison with other professionals with responsibilities for children;
- links with industry;
- liaison with other schools – perhaps arranging inter-school activities such as debates, sporting events, social events;
- careers advice;
- planning and implementing school policies;
- exam invigilation;
- lunchtime and after-school activities;
- cover for absent teachers.

You are likely to have or be developing a specialism where you make a unique contribution to school life, for example through your specialist knowledge in music, art, sport or other areas. Chapter 10 (HLTA Standards 10, 12, 13, 17, 18) provides advice about developing your specialist knowledge. HLTAs as well as teachers can expect to undertake ongoing professional development to keep their practice up to date. Chapter 13 (HLTA Standards 7, 10, 11) outlines opportunities for your further professional development.

Teachers, HLTAs and all staff have a role to play in supporting the school ethos by reinforcing school rules and routines, e.g. on behaviour, dress and in encouraging pupils to develop self-discipline so that the school can function effectively and pupils can make the most of opportunities available to them.

To plan your route to achieving HLTA status, you need to be familiar with the standards you are required to reach by the end of your course. Task 1.1 introduces you to these.

Task 1.1
The standards for HLTAs in England

The standards for HLTAs in England are available on the website for the Training and Development Agency for Schools (http://www.tda.gov.uk) and are included as Appendix 1. They are grouped under three headings:

1 Professional Attributes
2 Professional Knowledge and Understanding
3 Professional Skills (planning and expectations; monitoring and assessment; teaching and learning activities)

A handbook for HLTA candidates is available from the TDA website: http://www.tda.gov.uk/upload/resources/pdf/t/tda0420_candidate_handbook.pdf

Read through the standards and the handbook and work with your mentor to plan your route to achieving the standards.

The next section gives an overview of the principles underpinning the teaching process, as to be effective in working with the class teacher and in undertaking a teaching role from time to time, you need to understand the principles underpinning teaching.

UNDERSTANDING THE TEACHING PROCESS

To a large extent, *what* (i.e. the lesson content) pupils should learn in maintained (state) schools in England, Wales and Scotland is determined through legislation, and the requirements are set out in various National Curriculum documents. However, *how* the pupils are taught so that they learn effectively (i.e. the methods and materials used) is more often left to the professional judgement of the individual teacher/HLTA, department and school.

Teaching is a very personal activity and while certain teaching styles and strategies might suit one teacher or HLTA, they might not be appropriate for another. As an HLTA, you will need to be familiar and able to adapt to different ways of working in different classrooms.

There is no one way to teach. However, there exists a core of effective practice to which most teachers would subscribe. It is highly unlikely that you will see two teachers who teach identically. Provided effective teaching and learning takes place, a whole range of approaches from didactic (formal, heavy on content) to experiential (learning by doing) is appropriate – often in the same lesson. Chapter 6 provides more details about teaching strategies.

Supporting pupils in their learning in the classroom. Much of what many experienced teachers do to manage their classes has become part of their unconscious classroom behaviour. Their organisation of the lesson so that pupils learn is implicit in what they do rather than explicit, but careful observation will enable you to analyse what ways of working help teachers to be successful – things to observe are tone of voice, where the teacher stands in the room, how they move about, how they address the pupils, how pupils enter and leave the room, how the lesson is linked to previous lessons and the homework, how the teacher deals with latecomers or lack of equipment, how the activities with the pupils are structured. Chapter 12 (HLTA Standard 7) provides advice about undertaking effective lesson observation.

Undoubtedly some teachers and HLTAs have certain advantages such as a 'good' voice or organisational skills. Nevertheless, there are common skills and techniques to be learned that, when combined with an awareness of and sensitivity to the teaching and learning contexts, enable teachers and HLTAs to manage classrooms effectively.

As an HLTA, you may sometimes have small groups but sometimes have to manage the whole class. The transition from one way of working to the other requires you to adopt a different stance with the pupils. In working in groups, you are supporting learning; in managing the whole class you are leading the learning experience for the pupils.

Teaching is a continuously creative and problem-solving activity. Each learner or each group of learners has their own characteristics which experienced teachers and HLTAs take into account in planning the relevant learning programme. For example, if there has been recent controversy over environmental issues in the local area, or the school has taken refugees fleeing from civil war, an effective teacher/HLTA will adapt their approach to the discussion of such matters to make lessons more relevant and to allow the pupils to draw on their experience. Although lessons with different groups may have similar content, a lesson is rarely delivered in the same way twice. Variations in interactions between the pupils, the teacher and the HLTA affect the teaching strategy chosen. Chapters 5, 7 and 8 (HLTA Standards 5, 7, 8, 9, 15, 19, 20, 27) are intended to help you consider the need to personalise your approach to pupils in taking account of their backgrounds. For detailed information on special education needs we recommend Nick Peacey's chapter on Special Educational Needs in *Learning to Teach in the Secondary School: a companion to school experience* and the resources on the Teacher Training Resource Bank (http://www.ttrb.ac.uk) where you will find advice about working with pupils with the full range of special educational needs, for example dyslexia (related to letter recognition) and dyscalculia (related to number recognition) and including gifted and talented pupils who need demanding work.

Also see the SEN code of practice and disabilities legislation: http://www.tda.gov.uk/about/publicationslisting/TDA0202.aspx

The work in the classroom – the tip of the iceberg

On the surface, teaching may appear to be a relatively simple process – the view that the teacher stands in front of the class and talks and the pupils learn appears all too prevalent. (Ask friends and family what they think a teacher does.) The reality is somewhat different.

Classroom teaching is only the most visible part of the job of the teacher. The invisible foundation of the teacher's and your work in supporting teaching and learning is your *professional knowledge* about teaching and learning and *professional judgement* about the routines, skills and strategies which support effective classroom management. *Subject knowledge* comes from your previous education and experience and from your continuing professional development. (A quick way to get an understanding of the key work to be covered in any secondary subject area is through the GCSE and A-level revision guides which are available at most bookshops.)

An effective teacher or HLTA draws on these three factors in planning each and every lesson; and the learning for a particular class is planned ahead – over weeks, months and years – so that there is *continuity and progression* in the pupils' learning. Each lesson is planned as part of a sequence of learning experiences and pupils' individual needs are considered. Knowledge of the pupils and the existence of accurate records tracking their progress allow yourself and the teacher to provide a personalised and differentiated programme of learning for individual pupils or groups of pupils. Work for pupils or pupil groups may be differentiated by task or learning outcome. For example, consider a lesson where the learning objective is for pupils to learn the format of a formal letter. The learning outcome for some pupils may include a formal letter including material which has required them to undertake considerable research. For another pupil, perhaps a pupil who is new to the UK and for whom English is a second language, it may be more important to create a shorter letter using appropriate sentence structure.

The following analogy may help you understand what underpins the work in the classroom. Think of a lesson as being like an iceberg – 70 to 80 per cent of the base is hidden. The work in the classroom represents the tip of the iceberg. Supporting this tip, but hidden, are many elements of professional expertise. These include:

- evaluation of previous lessons;
- preparation for the lesson;

- planning of a sequence of lessons to ensure learning progresses;
- established routines and procedures which ensure that the work of the class proceeds as planned;
- personality – including the teacher's ability to capture and hold the interest of the class, to establish their authority;
- subject knowledge;
- professional knowledge about effective teaching and learning;
- professional judgement built up over time through reflection on experience.

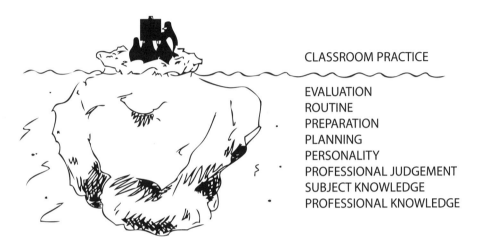

CLASSROOM PRACTICE

EVALUATION
ROUTINE
PREPARATION
PLANNING
PERSONALITY
PROFESSIONAL JUDGEMENT
SUBJECT KNOWLEDGE
PROFESSIONAL KNOWLEDGE

Figure 1.1 The work in the classroom – the tip of the iceberg

Chapter 2 (HLTA Standards 6, 9, 14, 21, 23, 25, 32) introduces you to lesson planning, schemes of work and assessment as well as two key concepts in lesson planning and teaching:

- *differentiation* i.e. providing different tasks or outcomes for pupils with different abilities which supports *personalization* of pupil learning; and
- *progression* i.e. ensuring the learning that is planned builds on foundations of earlier lessons and in turn provides a foundation for further learning.

Homework provides the opportunity for pupils to develop their skills in independent working but this can create problems for pupils in certain home circumstances. The respect you show to pupils by listening to what they see as the barriers to their achievement and helping them overcome challenges is one way of building relationships with pupils which support effective learning. You may find you are involved in consultation with parents, carers or other professionals when pupil progress is impeded. Since the government policy 'Every Child Matters' has been produced, professional links between all agencies concerned with child welfare have been strengthened and case conferences are regularly held to review the progress of pupils who give rise to concern.

Observing lessons

During your work, you will often see experienced teachers teaching. But what are you really seeing? You need to learn to 'read the classroom' – to train yourself to look beyond what is readily visible so that you come to understand the variety of skills and strategies which the teacher brings to bear in order to maximise the learning taking place. Some of these skills and strategies are easily identifiable; others require you to observe more carefully. Any classroom observation you undertake must have a purpose, be focused, generate information and should provoke thought. You can expect to have your work observed in turn and you can expect to be given feedback. We hope to sensitise you to what happens behind the scenes of the classroom so that you can build on that knowledge in your own work. Chapter 12 (HLTA Standard 7) provides advice about lesson observation.

Developing your own knowledge

You can expect to have to widen your knowledge base so that you can work more effectively with pupils and to give you confidence that you will be able to answer questions. Ways of developing your subject knowledge are covered in Chapter 10 (HLTA Standards 10, 12, 13, 17, 18) and Chapter 13 introduces ideas for your further professional development.

Teaching requires you to transform the knowledge you possess into suitable tasks which lead to learning. Acquiring appropriate up-to-date knowledge requires some effort on your part. The English National Curriculum (http://curriculum.qca.org.uk/) provides a useful starting point and most subject associations produce relevant materials and run annual conferences which help you keep up with developments. Subject associations provide help with resources and advice, much of which may be accessed online. Ask colleagues for details or search the Teacher Training Resource Bank (http://www.ttrb.ac.uk). Similarly, if you are undertaking extra-curricular activities, you will often find there is a professional association which can assist you with materials and advice.

From time to time, training may be provided which is particularly focused on government priorities for improvement and change in education. The National Strategies in England provide one example. Rob Batho's chapter on the National Strategies in *Learning to Teach in the Secondary School: a companion to school experience* provides you with the detail you need to know about the National Strategies work which is focused on raising pupil achievement.

To teach effectively, however, you need more than good subject knowledge. As already indicated, *personality and personal style* influence your effectiveness in the classroom, but many skills and strategies can be learned and practiced until they become part of your professional repertoire.

To summarise what has been said earlier in this chapter, *effective teaching* occurs where the learning experience structured by the teacher matches the needs of the learner, i.e. where tasks develop the individual pupil's knowledge, skills, attitudes and/or understanding in such a way that the pupil is applying past knowledge as appropriate and laying the foundation for the next stage of learning. A key feature of effective teaching is balancing the pupils' chance of success against the level of difficulty required to challenge them. Effective teaching depends on complex interrelationships of a whole range of factors, a major one of which is the teacher's understanding of the different ways in which pupils learn. Chapters 7 and 8 (HLTA Standards 7, 8, 9, 15, 20) provide further information about pupil learning. Understanding about the ways in which learning takes place is essential to your work and this understanding provides the foundations on which to build your professional knowledge about teaching and learning. The more closely the teaching method matches the preferred learning style of the pupils, the more effective the teaching will be.

YOUR PROFESSIONAL VALUES AND PRACTICE

The success of a school depends on the qualities and commitment of the staff as well as the pupils. Your expectations of pupils affect their self belief and their self esteem. Chapter 5 (HLTA Standards 1, 9, 27) provides examples of national benchmarks for pupil achievement and challenges you to help your pupils overcome stereotypes which create barriers to their achievement. In your relationships with pupils (Chapters 3 and 4: HLTA Standards 2, 4, 9, 30) you are providing a model of adult behaviour and appropriate relationships, including listening to the views of others, and sensitivity to diverse needs, which can shape the ways that pupils interact with you. Undertake Task 1.2 and reflect on the quality and impact of the relationships you have with pupils.

Task 1.2
Reflecting on your
relationships with pupils

Consider the poem below. What impact do you hope to have on the pupils in your care?

Children Learn What They Live
If a child lives with criticism,
    he learns to condemn,
If a child lives with hostility,
    he learns to fight,
If a child lives with ridicule,
    he learns to be shy,
If a child lives with shame,
    he learns to feel guilty,
If a child lives with tolerance,
    he learns to be patient,
If a child lives with encouragement,
    he learns confidence,
If a child lives with praise,
    he learns to appreciate,
If a child lives with fairness,
    he learns justice,
If a child lives with security,
    he learns to have faith,

(continued)

> If a child lives with approval,
>   he learns to like himself,
> If a child lives with acceptance and friendship,
>   he learns to find love in the world.
>
> Dorothy Law Nolta (date unknown)

Similarly, in your interactions with TAs for whom you are responsible, you should model appropriate behaviour – leading through demonstrating high standards in your own behaviour and ways of working.

Many HLTAs live close to the school. If this applies to you, you may find yourself in a position of acting as a bridge between the community and the school – creating opportunities for joint activities, for example, or drawing in adult or business support for in-school or out-of-school activities. You will need to be very careful about confidentiality – what happens in school should not be talked about outside of school. If you hear about activities in school or outside school which are adversely affecting children, e.g. bullying, then you must of course alert the school staff responsible for these matters.

YOUR CONTRACTUAL AND STATUTORY DUTIES

Appendix C of the TDA HLTA Handbook lists key statutory documents guiding the work undertaken in schools. You need to be aware of your responsibilities with respect to:

- child protection;
- equal opportunities (e.g. with respect to gender, race, disability);
- health and safety.

Support staff, like teachers, have various legally binding contractual responsibilities and statutory duties. In addition all staff have, as do all citizens, 'common law duties' which means, among other things, that you have a duty of care towards other people. Teachers and all school staff, again as citizens, are subject to criminal law. One aspect of criminal law you should note is that if you hit a pupil, or if a pupil hits you, this constitutes assault. It is also common sense to protect yourself against allegations by ensuring that you do not spend time alone in closed environments with individual pupils.

Contractual and statutory duties

Contractual duties are negotiated between an employee and their employer. So you may find that the duties set out in your contract are different to those of a HLTA in another school. Statutory duties are those which the government has established through legislation.

Your work is directed by the teacher and the school and you may find it interesting to read the document that sets out teachers' contractual duties. This is *School Teachers' Pay and Conditions* which is produced by the DCSF and updated annually. In *School*

Teachers' Pay and Conditions (http://www.teachernet.gov.uk/paysite), guidelines are laid down for the exercise of teachers' professional duties.

Additional conditions may apply in individual schools. There may also be 'implied terms' to your contract and to the teacher's contract, i.e. terms which are not written down, e.g. that you behave in a manner befitting your role. Some schools operate a dress code. You can obtain detailed advice from one of the teachers' unions.

Whenever you are working in a school, you are acting with the agreement and support of qualified teachers. When you take over their classes, you can expect to be accountable for the work in the classroom in the same ways they are.

Health and safety

School staff are responsible for the health and safety of the pupils in their charge. In working with pupils, you must take their health and safety into account through appropriate planning, e.g. identifying activities that do not endanger pupils, such as climbing on chairs; or for science and related subjects following the COSHH (Control of Substances Hazardous to Health) regulations. Working with your class teacher is an essential feature of your responsibility. If you have any doubts about what you are asked to do, ask for advice. If advice is not available, then take a conservative approach. There is a range of alternative lessons which you could undertake with pupils if the planned lesson has health and safety implications and qualified staff are not available, e.g. revision lessons, lessons in which pupils test each other on their understanding on the work undertaken to date, lessons where pupils prepare a short presentation on key aspects of the work and then give the presentation to their peers.

The school has a legal 'duty of care' towards you as well as pupils with regard to your personal health and safety. Your school should have a health and safety policy and member of staff and a governor with a particular remit for ensuring that your working environment is safe and suitable for the activities you undertake. You also have a legal responsibility to make sure that you do not put yourself or your pupils at risk of injury by practising or allowing unsafe behaviour, or failing to report damage which could cause an accident, e.g. a hole in stair covering.

Task 1.3
Health and safety – what should you know?

What should you know and be able to do with respect to health and safety matters if you are to discharge your duties? Find out who is responsible for health and safety in your school. Find the school and departmental policies on health and safety. Check the procedures you will be expected to apply – for example, in science, find the eyewash bottle and gas, water and electricity isolating taps/switches; in physical education check that you know how to test the safety of any apparatus pupils might use. How are *risk assessments* undertaken in the school? Find out the names of the first aiders in the school, where the first aid box is, what you are permitted to do if an incident occurs and what forms have to be filled in to record any accident. Discuss safety issues with your mentor and other HLTAs.

(continued)

> We suggest that you take a first aid course and find out how to deal with, for example, faints, nose bleeds, fits, asthma attacks, epilepsy, diabetic problems, burns, bleeding and common accidents. But you should not administer first aid yourself unless qualified and even then, only the minimum necessary. Subject associations may provide subject specific safety information and St John Ambulance produce a first aid text for schools and provide first aid courses for school staff.

Equally, you need to make sure that you look after your own safety. For example, it is not a good idea to agree to lift heavy boxes or furniture on your own and without making sure you are using the correct technique for doing so. The school site-manager and staff should be willing and able to deal with heavy lifting and it is reasonable for you to expect help. A common problem for teachers is voice strain (see Chapter 3: HLTA Standards 2, 4, 29, 30).

It is also advisable to take steps to protect your personal safety should you have reason to leave school, to attend a work-related meeting late at night, or to visit a pupil's home. You should always make sure someone, be it a family member, a friend or a colleague, knows the location of the meeting and your expected arrival home. It is wise not to be alone in a room with a pupil and not to text pupils.

SUMMARY

This chapter has introduced you to the different roles you may play and tasks you may undertake with the young people with whom you work. Support staff work is guided and regulated in different ways by national and local government, the school, school governors, parents and pupils – so support staff are accountable to a whole range of interested parties for the quality of their work.

In this text we aim to provide a basic introduction to what are complex areas and it is then up to you to develop systematically your professional knowledge and judgement through analysing your experience (i.e. through reflection) and wider reading.

Your attitude to and belief in the young people you work with is critical to them aiming high and achieving their potential. Do you have high expectations for them? A major factor limiting young people's achievement is the low expectations of those around them.

The following chapters provide more information and tasks to help you develop your knowledge and skills in order to achieve the standards required for HLTA status.

FURTHER READING

HLTA professional standards: http://www.tda.gov.uk/support/hlta/professstandards. The professional standards for higher level teaching assistants are available on the Training and Development Agency website and set out in broad terms the expectations of the standards which HLTAs will reach.

Induction materials for teaching assistants in secondary schools: http://www.tda. gov.uk/partners/supportstafftraining/inductionmaterial/induction_ta_secondary. aspx. These materials are intended for use in the training of teaching assistants.

They cover promoting good behaviour, inclusion, literacy, numeracy, science, and mathematics.

Voice Care Network. Their booklet *More Care for your Voice* and a copy of a guidance document, also titled *More Care for your Voice,* is available from the charity Voice Care Network (VCN), 25 The Square, Kenilworth CV8 1EF. Tel/fax: 01926 864000; web site: http://www.voicecare.org.uk. Email: info@voicecare.org.uk.

2 Collaborative Working with the Teacher

Susan Capel and Marilyn Leask

INTRODUCTION

As discussed in Chapter 1, key elements of your role as an HLTA are supporting the planning and delivery of lessons to individuals, groups or on occasion the whole class, and managing assessment and monitoring data so it can be used to support pupil learning and lesson planning.

This chapter focuses on collaborative working with the teacher in the classroom. There are two levels of planning used to guide the work in the classroom: the *scheme of work* and the *lesson plan*. This chapter covers both aspects.

OBJECTIVES

By the end of this chapter, you should:

- understand the planning undertaken by a teacher for each lesson;
- understand what is meant by schemes of work and lesson plans;
- understand the terms 'aims', 'objectives', 'progression' and 'differentiation';
- be aware of the structure of schemes of work;
- be aware of the structure of effective lesson plans;
- have an awareness of the different ways in which HLTAs and teachers might work together to maximise the learning of pupils.

This chapter refers to the HLTA standards regarding *professional attributes*, in particular demonstrating a commitment to collaborative and cooperative *working with colleagues*, alongside developing your *professional knowledge and understanding* of the *learning objectives, content and intended learning outcomes* for the learning activities in which you are involved; understanding the processes of *monitoring and assessment*; and an awareness of *keeping learners safe*. You can also see Appendix 2 for more information on how this chapter maps onto the standards at the time of publication; if these are revised then updated materials will appear on the website supporting this text.

Working together effectively in the classroom requires careful and shared planning for each lesson so that each adult with a role in the lesson (the teacher and the HLTA) understands their role and the role of the other. As an HLTA, you can expect to be given clear guidelines about your role in the lesson and the goals for pupils' learning in the lesson. Where you are not clear, you should be able to ask about, specifically, what you are expected to do/achieve in a lesson. You may be asked to prepare materials for a lesson and this might be an appropriate time to discuss specific learning objectives, the level of differentiation of learning possible to support personalisation of learning so as to meet individual pupil needs, and your role in helping the pupils learn in this lesson. You can expect to be given responsibility for particular activities. For example, in practical subjects such as science, design technology, physical education, music and drama, you might be given responsibility for preparation, distribution and guiding pupils' use of equipment and any subsequent written work.

PLANNING WHAT TO TEACH AND HOW TO TEACH IT

Ideas about what teachers should teach change regularly and the curriculum is under constant scrutiny by those responsible for education. The content of a curriculum – and therefore for any one lesson – is usually set out, at least in part, in documents from government (e.g. the National Curriculum documents – see Chapter 10), the school and syllabuses prepared by examination boards (see QCA for websites and further information on examination boards).

However constraining the guidelines are on content, the decision about which teaching methods to use is usually down to the teacher. A scheme of work gives an overall picture of learning over a period of time – usually between half a term's and two years' work. The content of each lesson is derived from the scheme of work. In planning a lesson, the teacher is working out the detail required to teach one aspect of the scheme of work. A lesson plan provides an outline of one lesson within a scheme of work. Hay McBer (2000, para 1.2.4) defines effective lessons as follows: 'Our lesson observations revealed that in classes run by effective teachers, pupils are clear about what they are doing and why they are doing it. They can see links with their earlier learning and have some ideas about how it could be developed further. The pupils want to know more.'

As pupils learn in different ways and different teaching methods are suitable for different types of material, teachers normally use a range of ways of structuring learning experiences in the classroom. For example, a teacher might choose to use discovery learning (through, for example, experimentation and investigation), rote learning (repetition), role play, discussion and so on to achieve particular objectives. Certain approaches with particular groups of pupils may be allocated to you as an HLTA. For each lesson you need to discuss with the teacher how they want you to work in the classroom to maximise pupil learning.

The factors influencing *what* should be taught (lesson content) are discussed in

Chapter 10, but how much is taught in each lesson and *how it is taught* (teaching methods) are the teacher's own decisions (see Chapter 6 on teaching strategies and Chapters 7 and 8 on learning theories).

Task 2.1
How do you learn?

Pupils learn in different ways and different areas of learning require different approaches. It would therefore be a mistake not to take account of this in planning periods of learning. Spend a few minutes making notes of the methods you use to help you learn and the methods of teaching used by teachers from whom you felt you had learned a lot. Then make notes about those situations from which you did not learn. Also, write a list of topics in class(es)/subject(s) you support where you can identify commonly used teaching methods. Compare these notes with those of other HLTAs on your programme. Teachers need to take account of such differences in planning lessons and you will need to demonstrate that you are aware of the range of teaching methods which can be employed to help pupils learn.

SCHEMES OF WORK AND LESSON PLANS

There are two main stages to planning for pupil learning:

1   Preparing an outline of the work to be covered over a period – *the scheme of work* (also known as programmes or units of work).
2   Planning each individual lesson – *the lesson plan*.

A number of formats for both schemes of work and lesson plans are in use. If you are interested in following this up in more detail, and are supporting pupils in a primary school, we suggest you look at *Learning to Teach in the Primary School* (Arthur, Grainger and Wray, 2006). If you are supporting specific subjects in a secondary school, we suggest you read the advice given for the teaching of your subject in the subject specific texts in the 'Learning to Teach' series. Whilst the level of detail may vary between different formats or approaches to writing schemes of work and lesson plans, the purpose is the same – to provide an outline of the work to be done either over an extended period (scheme of work) or in the lesson (lesson plan) so that the planned learning can take place. Different schools have established different expectations for the schemes of work and the kind of lesson planning which is expected of teachers.

The scheme of work

Different terms may be used to describe longer-term planning of work. In your school a scheme of work may be called a 'programme of work' or 'unit of work'. Whatever the name, the purpose is to devise a long-term plan for the pupils' learning. So, a scheme of work sets out the long-term plans for learning and thus covers an extended period of time. This could be a period of a year, a term, half a term or weeks, e.g. for a module of work. A scheme of work should be designed to build on the learning which has gone before, i.e. it should ensure continuity of pupil learning.

Schemes of work should be designed to ensure that the knowledge, skills, capabilities, understanding and attitudes of the pupils are developed over a particular period in order to ensure progression in learning. The term 'progression' means the planned development of knowledge, skills, understanding or attitudes over time.

What is included in a scheme of work

Schools/departments generally have well-established schemes of work. In putting this together, the following questions have been considered:

1   What is to be achieved? (Aims for the scheme of work and objectives for particular lessons – see the definitions in the numbered paragraphs below.)
2   What has been taught before?
3   How much time is available to do this work?
4   What resources are available?
5   How is the work to be assessed?
6   How does this work fit in with work pupils are doing in other subjects?
7   What is to be taught later?

In some schools/departments, schemes of work are very detailed and include teaching materials and methods as well as safety issues. In others the scheme itself may be quite brief. However, both will be based on the above information. Figure 2.1 shows one example of a proforma for writing a scheme of work. Each of the areas included in a scheme of work is now discussed in turn to help you start to think about what learning should be taking place.

1   *What is to be achieved?* The *aims* of a scheme of work are general statements about the learning that should take place over a period. On the other hand, *learning objectives* are specific statements which set out what pupils are expected to learn from a particular lesson in a way that allows school staff to identify if learning has occurred. Learning objectives are prepared for each lesson and further detail is included under lesson planning later in this unit. *Learning outcomes* specify the expected pupil outputs. For example, a learning objective might be for pupils to know how to write a formal letter. The learning outcome for the lesson may be a letter to an employer in application for an advertised post. In devising each scheme of work, a small aspect of the whole curriculum has been taken and a route planned through this, which provides the best opportunities for pupils to learn.
2   *What has been taught before? Progression* in pupil learning should be considered and built into schemes of work. It is important to know what pupils have been taught earlier in the school year and in previous years. This information should be available from school documentation and from staff. In primary schools when pupils move from one year to the next, the previous class teacher should provide this information. In the case of pupils in their first year of secondary education, there is usually a member of staff responsible for liaising with primary schools who may have this information.
3   *How much time is available to do this work?* The number and length of lessons devoted to a topic may be decided by the school or by the individual teacher. Homework

has a valuable role to play in enhancing learning. Supporting the teacher to ensure that all homework is completed, marked and recorded may be part of your role. Schemes of work also have to allow for the fact that some time is taken up by tests, revision, fire drill, special events, etc.

4   *What resources are available?* Resources include human resources as well as material resources and what is available depends on the school. There are many human resources outside the school to draw upon, e.g. parents and carers, governors and charities. Many firms provide schools with speakers on current topics. There may be field studies centres or sports facilities nearby. Making contact with these groups and organising their visits may well be part of your role. Checking if there are any safety issues to consider when choosing appropriate resources may also be allocated to the HLTA. With respect to material resources, the internet can provide a

---

Scheme of work for x topic

Area of work		Ref

Class	No in class	Age	Key stage
No of lessons	Duration	Dates	

Aims (from the National Curriculum programmes of study)

Objectives are listed in each lesson plan

Framework of lessons	NC reference

Assessment strategies

Other notes (safety points)

Figure 2.1 Scheme of work proforma

wealth of access to information, which you as an HLTA can access, review and select as appropriate for the lesson. You may even be required in your role to put any electronic resources you find or create onto the school's intranet (see Chapter 11).

5   *How is the work to be assessed?* Teaching, learning and assessment are interlinked. Most of the work you do with pupils is teacher assessed, although some is assessed by outside agencies. One purpose of teacher assessment is formative – to inform and check pupils' progress, e.g. in relation to lesson objectives. This may be called *assessment for learning.* Teachers are expected to have good records of the pupils' progress (homework, classwork, test results) and these have to be input into electronic databases in the form required by the school. You can expect to have a role in the recording of assessment outcomes. You may also have a role in aspects of assessment itself, for example marking multiple choice questions. Chapter 9 focuses in more detail on assessment issues.

Task 2.2
Record keeping and
assessment

Find out how HLTAs and teaching assistants across the school are involved in assessment and record keeping. If you are on a programme with a number of other HLTAs, compare this practice with that in other schools.

    Make sure you know how to input and interrogate pupil data using the systems in your school.

6   *How does this work fit in with work the pupils are doing in other subjects?* There are many areas of overlap where it is useful to consider the pupils' work in other subjects. For instance, if pupils are having difficulty with measurement in technology or science, it is worth checking if and when these skills are taught in mathematics and how they are taught. If you, as will many HLTAs, work across different subjects, you may find you have useful information about resources and approaches in different subjects which can benefit all subjects in which you work.

7   *What is to be taught later?* Progression in pupil learning has to be planned for and a scheme of work is drawn up for this purpose. From this scheme of work, school staff know what work is to come and the contribution to pupil learning that each lesson is to make.

Task 2.3
Reviewing a scheme of
work

Find a scheme of work which lasts about six to eight lessons and the lesson plans for one of the classes with which you are currently involved. Consider how they fit together to progress pupil learning. Work with other HLTAs if possible to compare the scheme of work and lesson plans for different age ranges and/or different subject areas.

The lesson plan

Lesson plans are constructed by teachers to take account of the requirements of the curriculum, the most appropriate methods of teaching the topic, how pupils learn, the resources available and the evaluations of previous lessons. Examples of lesson plans are available on websites such as the QCA, Teachernet and the Teacher Training Resource Bank (TTRB). An example of a detailed lesson planning framework is given in Figure 2.2. Experienced teachers probably have much less detailed lesson plans than newly qualified teachers. Newly qualified teachers are expected to plan their lessons in detail.

The following information is required for a lesson to be planned effectively.

1   *Overall aim(s) of the scheme of work, the specific learning objectives and learning outcomes for this lesson.* There are differences in terminology in use – some people refer to *learning* objectives and some to *behavioural* objectives. Whatever the name, defining objectives which clarify exactly what learning will take place is a crucial skill for the effective teacher. It helps the teacher to be clear about exactly what the pupils should be achieving and it helps the pupils understand what they should be doing. However, drawing up effective objectives requires thought.
    Listing objectives after the following phrase – *By the end of this lesson, pupils will be able to …* – helps the teacher to devise clear goals and to understand the difference between aims (general statements) and objectives (specific goals). This clearly states what it is that pupils are expected to have learned, not what the teacher hopes to have taught, irrespective of what the pupils learn.

Date: . . . . Class: . . . .

Area of work: . . . .

Aim:. . . . .

Objectives:. . . . .

. . . .

Time	Teacher activity	Pupil Activity	Notes/Equipment needed
0–5 min	Class enter and settle	Coats and bags put away	
5–10 min	Homework discussed/ recap of work so far/task set/new work explained		
10–25 min	Teacher supports groups/individuals	Pupils work in individual groups to carry out the task	
… and so on			
Ending	Teacher summarises key points/sets homework		

Evaluation: Were objectives achieved? What went well? What needs to be addressed next time? How are individuals responding?

Figure 2.2 Planning a lesson: one possible approach

Words that help the teacher to be precise in setting specific goals are those such as *state*, *describe*, *list*, *identify*, *prioritise*, *solve*, *demonstrate an understanding of*. These words force the teacher to write statements which can be tested. A test of good learning objectives is whether it is clear what the pupils must do to achieve them and what the pupils are required to demonstrate as learning outcomes. When pupils are told what the learning objectives are, do they understand what is expected of them? Learning objectives may be related to concepts, attitudes (behaviours), skills and knowledge – the CASK model.

Task 2.4
Being clear about
learning objectives

Learning objectives refer to the observable outcomes/learning outcomes of the lesson, i.e. to what pupils are expected to be able to do. Discuss with your tutor and other HLTAs and learn objectives which are written for lessons in which you are involved. Choose a particular lesson and, as a group, pay particular attention to the quality and type of objectives – are they focused on the pupils' learning or are they focused on pupils' behaviour? What learning outcomes might demonstrate that these have been achieved?

2   *Range of abilities of the pupils.* Teachers are expected to incorporate differentiation into their planning. This refers to the need to consider pupils' individual abilities when planning work so that all pupils, whatever their ability, are challenged and extended by the work, i.e. work is differentiated for each pupil. Differentiation can be achieved in different ways depending on the material to be taught. Differentiation may, for example, be achieved by *outcome*, i.e. different types or qualities of work may be produced, or by *task*, i.e. different tasks may be set for pupils of differing abilities. (See Chapter 7 for further information on pupil differentiation.) Continuity of learning for pupils is provided by taking account of and building on their existing knowledge, skills, capabilities and attitudes (scaffolding the learning).

3   *Time available.* On the example of a lesson plan provided, a time line is drawn on the left hand side. The teacher might refer to this in the lesson, so they are quickly able to see if it is necessary to adapt the original plan to fit the time available.

4   *Resources available.* HLTAs are often given responsibility for resources. This means checking in good time that resources are available for a lesson, that there are sufficient sets of resources, that any safety issues are considered and discussed with the teacher and that any equipment is returned to the appropriate location following the lesson – all in order and ready for use by the next class. Schools have different approaches to breakage or loss of equipment. In some cases pupils are expected to replace broken items. You need to know the approach and expectations of your school.

5   *Approaches to classroom management.* These should be suitable to the topic and subject. This is covered in more detail in Chapter 6, along with managing pupil behaviour.

6   *Teaching strategies and the learning situations.* These should be set up as appropriate to the work being covered. Explaining, questioning and modelling (see Chapters 3, 4 and 6) are three key skills which teachers use and which you use in individual work with pupils. Thus, you should work to improve your skills in these areas.

7   *Assessment methods.* There will be ongoing assessment of pupils in classes with which you are involved and you can expect to be involved in many assessment tasks that take place in classrooms. Much of this assessment will be formative – to inform and check pupils' progress, e.g. in relation to lesson objectives. You are likely to be involved in both the assessment itself and the recording of pupils' progress through assessment. Chapter 9 provides further information.

8   *Any risks associated with the work.* Safety is an important issue in schools. In some subjects, assessing the risk to pupils and incorporating strategies to minimise this risk are a necessary part of the teacher's planning. School, subject and national guidelines are provided to ensure the safety of pupils and should be followed. If you are in doubt about an activity, you must alert the responsible teacher to your concerns. Any accidents in classes should be formally reported and there will be procedures in the school for this. In some schools an HLTA or teaching assistant may be the named first aid person who is trained and responsible for administering first aid, recording accidents and liaising with parents and paramedics.

9   *What do the pupils know now?* In planning lessons, teachers consider what has been taught before as well as the experience outside school which pupils might have had. It is common to do some form of testing or analysis of knowledge, skills and understanding or to have a discussion with pupils to discover their prior experience and attitudes to the work in question.

Although lesson planning is important, it is also important to realise that planned activities do not have to be followed through rigidly and at all costs. Often the particular circumstances in which a lesson takes place makes it appropriate to change some of the plans.

Task 2.5
Observe a lesson

Develop a list of questions – some relevant to each of the points 1–9 above, which you need to answer to enable you to support a teacher in teaching the lesson. Ask a teacher if you can observe a lesson. In the observation, focus specifically on trying to answer the questions you have listed. Discuss the questions and answers with the teacher after the lesson.

Devise a new set of questions (some may be a repeat of the first list) which you need to know answers to and observe another lesson.

Constructing a lesson

Lessons that go well seem to unfold in a seamless way, and therefore it can be difficult to see exactly how teachers manage their classes. In order to help you see the underlying structure of a lesson, we have divided the lesson and its planning into five key stages: preparation, beginning, moving on, ending, evaluation. Each stage is discussed below.

1   *Preparation*. The most successful lessons are thoroughly planned and structured.

A key role of an HLTA can be to make sure there are enough of the necessary materials, equipment and resources available. It is important to know the exact number of the items you are using so that you know if something has been lost and you can take steps to find it immediately. For example, you need to count out the number of pieces of equipment handed out and count them back in. In primary school, you may have created a story sack as a resource to aid reading in the early years. If the props and aids to help illustrate the narrative are passed around the class during the story, you need to ensure they are all returned at the end of the lesson. In secondary schools, most departments have developed their own systems of stock control for resources, e.g. a useful technique for text books is to number them and when you give them to pupils, record the text book number in your personal record book.

If equipment is to be used then you should be familiar with this. Ensure that you know how to operate any equipment that is being used in the lesson (e.g. television monitors, videos, computers or subject-specific equipment) and that it is in working order. This enables you to anticipate problems pupils might encounter.

Pupils should always be given advance warning and preferably reminders of any books, materials, etc. that they need for the lesson. If they have been asked to collect particular items or materials, organise with the teacher what is to be done with those pupils who come without the required equipment.

2   *Beginning*. A good beginning is a crucial part of a successful lesson as it sets the tone, motivates pupils and establishes the teacher's authority. The teacher and the HLTA should be in the classroom before the pupils arrive and ensure any equipment and resources are ready. Undoubtedly, the school you are in has established rules about pupil movement around the school and entry to classrooms. However, in some schools or in some years in schools (e.g. in lower years in secondary schools), it is common to line up pupils outside the classroom and to usher them inside in an orderly manner.

The class should be settled as quickly as possible. Teachers do not normally begin the lesson when any pupil is talking – the HLTA has a role here in encouraging pupils to settle quickly. Class management is much easier when you know the pupils by name, so make a determined effort to learn pupils' names as quickly as possible. There are several strategies you could use here. For example, teachers use seating plans and in the early stages of getting to know a class may ask pupils to raise their hands when they are being registered. Although it might appear time-consuming, giving out exercise books to pupils individually quickly allows a teacher to put a face to a name.

There will be circumstances when you will be with the whole class, for example if the teacher is called away. If you find you are unable to address pupils by name, address them by their class/form designation. For example, 'Right 5R or 7G, I want everyone looking this way.' This is far better than 'Right girls/boys/ladies/lads etc.' Never resort to 'Oi, you lot!' or some equally unprofessional outburst. Similarly, an impersonation of a deflating balloon through continued 'Sshh-sshh-ing' does nothing to enhance anyone's authority.

Pupils like to know what is expected of them. They relax and have a far more positive approach if the teacher or yourself explains what you need them to do, for example, with respect to their *learning*, 'Re-read the passage below and identify the key words', and their *behaviour*, 'I need you to sit still and listen now'. Continuity of learning can be enhanced with a brief rationale of how it fits in with previous and future work and if you let pupils know what you want them to achieve in the lesson (the objectives). This provides a clear and contextualised start to the lesson.

Teachers are advised never to stand in one place in the room for more than a few minutes. Teachers use eye contact and vary the pace and tone of voice to exert control, and they monitor pupil reaction continually. Your role usually requires you to work to the direction of the teacher. So you may become used to expecting to be directed. But there will be times when you need to exert your authority in much the same way as the teacher does and you may need practice and help to achieve this. Coping with these changing roles may provide a useful discussion point if you are on a course with other HLTAs.

3   *Moving on*. A smooth, seamless transition between one part of the lesson and the next is vital if there is to be overall continuity and coherence. Having introduced the lesson, the teacher normally explains the purpose of the first (and thereafter any subsequent) pupil task. The teacher should be very clear about what they want the pupils to do and how much time they are to spend on the activity. Pupils then have an idea of the pace they need to work at and what quality and quantity of work is required.

Before pupils begin the activity, the teacher normally checks that all pupils understand exactly what they are expected to do, and you have a role here in reinforcing what the teacher has said – to ensure that pupils understand what they have to do. It is easier to deal with any queries before the class begins work as this saves endless repetition of the task to individuals.

Efficient teachers have a definite routine for distributing books, equipment and materials so the pupils know exactly what to expect and how to behave. Will the teacher or the HLTA give out equipment? Will pupils come out to collect it table by table or row by row? Will one pupil per table/row collect it? In any event, it is essential that this activity is carried out in a controlled and orderly manner in any classroom. Moreover, if you are teaching a physical education or science lesson, the safety aspect of this area of class management is of unequalled importance.

When the pupils are engaged in the activity, the teacher normally moves around the room monitoring pupil progress and dealing with questions. Effective class management depends upon the teacher's active involvement. Key skills are: circulation; monitoring progress; the use of proximity to pupils; and sensitivity to and awareness of, pupil needs. You should know what the teacher expects of you through discussion before the lesson starts. Your role will vary depending on the class and the requirements of the lesson. This must be agreed beforehand with the teacher.

At the end of an activity, the teacher again settles the class and expects all pupils to be sitting quietly, facing the teacher before proceeding to the next stage of the lesson. Again you have a role in reinforcing the teacher's expectation that all pupils are sitting quietly, facing the teacher and ready to move on.

4   *Ending* (sometimes called the 'plenary'). It is important that any learning experience is rounded off, that pupils experience a sense of completion. When pupils move from one lesson to the next they move from one topic/subject to another (indeed, depending upon the timetable, pupils in secondary schools may need to negotiate the conceptual intricacies of between four and eight subjects in a day). Every lesson, therefore, needs to be completed in an organised manner. Pupils need some mental space between lessons. They need to 'come down' from one lesson in order to prepare themselves for the next.

   Teachers normally plan enough time at the end of the lesson to: sum up what has been achieved; set homework where appropriate; give a brief idea of what the next lesson will comprise; and (if necessary) explain what pupils need to bring to it.

   As with the distribution of materials (see the section on beginning), the teacher will have decided on a definite, orderly routine for collection at the end of the lesson. You need to know what this is in order to be able to support the teacher.

   Before pupils leave, it is essential to make sure the classroom is neat and tidy and remember that the bell is a signal for the school staff, not the pupils. Normally a teacher dismisses the pupils by table or row and ensures that they leave the room in a quiet, controlled fashion. Enforcing a quiet orderly departure also adds to the pupils' experience of the standards expected, i.e. that the classroom provides an orderly and calm learning environment.

5   *Evaluation and planning future lessons.* Teachers are expected to evaluate their lessons as part of a continuous cycle of improvement and you too, as an education professional, are expected to reflect on what works well in your relationship with pupils and the teacher in the classroom and what could be improved upon. Did you and the teacher work as an effective team? If you develop the practice of reflecting on your work as a matter of course, then modifying future practice on the basis of this reflection becomes second nature. In this way, education professionals use their experience systematically to build up their professional knowledge and to develop their professional judgement.

Task 2.6
The sections of a lesson

Look at a detailed lesson plan. This may be for a lesson in which you are going to be involved or one from another school. Identify the different sections of the lesson: beginning; moving on; ending. Identify what an HLTA may be expected to do in each section and then discuss with the teacher concerned or other HLTAs what exactly you need to do to meet these expectations. If you have an opportunity to work with the teacher in this lesson, evaluate how the role was carried out and whether it can be improved in any way.

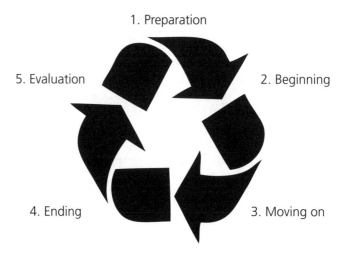

Figure 2.3 The structure of a lesson illustrates this rhythm

SUMMARY

You should now be able to explain the following terms: aims, objectives, progression and differentiation, and have considered how schemes of work and lesson plans are constructed. You should know what information should be included so that they are comprehensive and useful. You should also have some idea of the structure of the lesson so that if you are required to stay with the class in the absence of the teacher you have some understanding of what you need to do to carry on the lesson in a constructive way.

The next chapter explores how to develop your communication skills with pupils.

FURTHER READING

Hay McBer (2000) *Research into Teacher Effectiveness*, DfEE: London. This comprehensive report into effective teaching proposes a model of teacher effectiveness comprising teaching skills and professional characteristics. The early sections are particularly useful in relation to the preparation and planning of lessons.

Scottish Consultative Council on the Curriculum (1996) *Teaching for Effective Learning*, Dundee, http://www.claudius.sccc.ac.uk. The SCCC have produced a very readable booklet on the principles of effective teaching and learning. Discussion forums are available via the website.

3 Developing your Communication Skills: Non-verbal

Paula Zwozdiak-Myers

INTRODUCTION

Communication is a complex process that occurs in many different forms, e.g. written, verbal and non-verbal. It is a two-way process that involves the mutual exchange of information and ideas. We both send and receive written, verbal and non-verbal messages through eye contact, gesture, body language, posture, dialogue, written documents and texts. Your role is pivotal as you provide an important and complementary link between the pupils you support and the class teacher. This chapter examines the significance of non-verbal communication and explores how you can develop these skills.

OBJECTIVES

By the end of this chapter, you should:

- understand the importance of effective non-verbal communication skills;
- identify aspects of self-presentation, body language and paralanguage[1] that enable you to become effective within your role;
- be aware of the interdependence of effective non-verbal and verbal communication skills.

This chapter refers to the HLTA standards that cover establishing *supportive and constructive relationships* with children and young people; *communicating effectively and sensitively* with them, alongside the professional skills of advancing learning when working with *individuals* and *small groups*. You can also see Appendix 2 for information on how this chapter maps onto the standards at the time of publication; if these are revised, then updated materials will appear on the website supporting this text.

Much of your work will be with individual pupils or small groups, and since the introduction of the Five Year Strategy for Children and Learners in 2004 (http://www.

dcsf.gov.uk/publications/5yearstrategy), the predominant focus is to tailor education to suit the needs of individual pupils under the guidance of the class teacher. This process is referred to as personalisation of the curriculum or personalised learning. Whether working with pupils on a one-to-one basis, with small groups or with the whole class, the successful exchange of information and ideas using a range of communication channels enables you to help pupils better understand knowledge, concepts and skills and to respond sensitively, with sound judgement to their developmental needs.

In order to establish effective interpersonal relationships with pupils you need to develop a range of communication skills, e.g. the ability to listen to pupils attentively when they both answer and ask questions and to respond in an appropriate manner; the ability to carefully observe and interpret the meanings of pupils' behaviour in a range of learning situations; the ability to express yourself clearly and accurately using words and language that pupils can understand; the ability to follow up the questions and instructions presented by the class teacher. Providing feedback to the class teacher that is accurate, detailed and meaningful enables the next steps and stages of pupil learning to be identified and planned. You are an important part of this process as the nature of your role allows you to gain detailed insights about individual pupils and to establish positive and close working relationships with them.

NON-VERBAL COMMUNICATION

Much of our understanding of others is based on communication without words which involves reading the non-verbal cues and messages we both send and receive. Non-verbal communication includes your appearance, facial expression, gesture, mannerisms, stance and elements of paralanguage, e.g. a flicker of the eyes, shrug of the shoulders, a nervous twitch or a particular way of moving are messages we constantly send through our body language, yet seldom do we stop to think about their importance or significance. Also we need to be sensitive to the fact that these may mean different things in different cultures. Studies by Mehrabin (1972) indicate that 93 per cent of the meaning behind verbal messages is received through non-verbal channels: specifically, 55 per cent through gesture; 38 per cent through tone of voice and 7 per cent from the words actually used.

Non-verbal communication is important as embedded within the signals that we send and receive are clues to attitudes and feelings that might not be readily evident in the spoken word. Most children learn to respond to non-verbal cues and messages as they develop verbal language. As adults, much of our understanding involves reading the overt and covert messages from clues that are provided by the speaker behind the words spoken.

Self-presentation

This aspect of non-verbal communication relates to you as an individual and to your own unique set of characteristics. The clothes you wear, how you groom your hair, and the perfume and toiletries you use send messages to others about the kind of person you are and how you might be feeling. Pupils readily pick up on this kind of information and often place adults into certain stereotypes, e.g. a cleanly shaven, well-groomed and smartly suited male portrays a sense of purpose and commitment, whereas another, who arrives with a 'five o'clock shadow' at the start of the school day, shabbily dressed, with unclean hair and body, portrays quite a different message. Your personal appearance reveals a great deal about your personality, role and status.

Initial impressions are important. How you present yourself to a group of pupils when you meet them for the first time can influence the pupils and their learning over a period of time. Your appearance is an important part of the impression created, and by presenting yourself as a well-groomed individual you demonstrate both commitment and respect. Pupils do have expectations of adults in school and importantly 'value adults' (Sage, 2000a) that take pride in their appearance and who are well dressed.

Another factor that relates to a confident presentation of self is good planning in all areas related to organisation of the material you will present to the pupils you support. If you are unsure about what you need to do or how to organise a particular activity, discuss these concerns with the class teacher in advance so that when you present your well-planned activity or session to pupils it runs smoothly.

Body language

It is important that we gain awareness of an individual pupil's body language and of our own body language and its effects on the pupils we are working with. Some pupils, such as those with hearing or visual impairment and those on the autistic spectrum, may learn body language more slowly than their peers. They might have difficulty in 'reading' the people around them and in reproducing the appropriate body language themselves. This can skew our observations of what is going on and lead to ineffective communication. Therefore, when listening to pupils you need to observe their body language along with attending to what is being said; particularly if the two messages contradict one another. There is more on observation in Chapter 12. Also, when you interact with pupils be mindful that they will be observing you so it is important that what you say does match the non–verbal signals that you send.

Body language can be categorised into:

- gestures and body movements;
- facial expressions and eye contact;
- spatial proximity and touch.

Gestures and body movements

Gestures are used a great deal in learning situations to support pupil understanding of explanations, ideas and concepts. As an aid to expression, you can use specific gestures to emphasise the height, width, shape and size of something you are describing to pupils. Gestures help to convey the meaning of words and concepts that a pupil may have difficulty understanding, e.g. the relationship between narrow and wide, straight and curved, high and low, open and closed. Hand gestures are frequently used for this purpose and Ekman and Friesen (1972) distinguish between three types:

- *Emblems* – have a direct association with a particular word or phrase, e.g. 'wave' for goodbye; 'thumbs up' for okay; 'index finger to lips' for quiet. If you are working with individuals from multicultural backgrounds, ensure that they understand the meaning you give to the emblems you use to avoid confusion.

- *Illustrators* – have no specific association with a particular word or phrase but are used to reinforce their meaning, e.g. 'fingertips of both hands meet yet palms apart to form an arch' to illustrate the shape of a triangle or pyramid.
- *Adaptors* – are not associated to particular words or phrases but refer to the idiosyncrasies and mannerisms many people have, e.g. flicking hair from the face, rubbing the forehead or pulling an ear lobe. Such idiosyncrasies could be a distraction in learning situations as pupils might pay more attention to these non-verbal signals than to what is being said.

How you move when interacting with pupils demonstrates how relaxed and confident you are in particular situations. If you are confident, your movement is purposeful and related both to the context and task at hand, e.g. to reinforce a verbal message a person tends to stand still, hold an upright body stance and use arm gestures sparingly; to stimulate a small group working on a particular project a person tends to move freely between pupils, get down to their level and use arm gestures as a cue to emphasise a point or to reinforce something she is describing, e.g. by indicating the relevant shape or direction of an arrangement of apparatus. There is nothing agitated about the movement of a relaxed and confident person.

If, on the other hand, body posture is combined with certain gestures such as folded arms, clenched hands and hunched shoulders, this could suggest a lack of confidence, inner tension or even disinterest in a particular situation. This interpretation of body language is dependent upon the context in which it is used as folded arms in a meeting might suggest a relaxed demeanour, and clenched hands combined with hunched shoulders can indicate excitement.

You need to present an alert posture and accompany your speech with appropriate hand and arm gestures. If you are enthusiastic, all aspects of your posture and body movement should portray your interest, commitment and involvement. Enthusiastic people display overtly 'dynamic vigour … they show surprise, suspense, joy, and other feelings in their voices and they make material interesting by relating it to their experiences and showing that they themselves are interested in it' (Good and Brophy, 2002: 385).

Sign language is an important application of non-verbal communication that is used by deaf people. The British Sign Language (Scott-Gibson, 1992) is a well-developed system of communication that uses signing, finger spelling and gestures with an appropriate combination of lip reading and speech. 'Makaton' is another system that uses sign language to help some pupils that are autistic. To support the learning of a deaf or autistic pupil, the class teacher should provide you with guidance material that enables you to learn the signs and symbols of particular systems, how to use them and the meanings associated with each so that you can communicate effectively with the pupils.

Facial expressions and eye contact

Facial expressions such as smiles, pouts, bared teeth, raised eyebrows and frowns are used to accompany dialogue. The speaker uses facial expressions both to frame what s/he is saying and to convey what s/he feels about what s/he is saying. Robertson (1996: 86) describes an enthusiastic speaker as one who produces:

a stream of facial expressions which convey his excitement, disbelief, surprise or amusement about his message. Some expressions are extremely brief, lasting about one fifth of a second and may highlight a particular word, whereas others last much longer, perhaps accompanying the verbal expression of an idea. The overall effect is to provide a running commentary for the listener on how the speaker feels about the ideas expressed.

The listener responds to what is being said by producing 'a stream of facial expressions' that convey their agreement, surprise, amusement or puzzlement about the thoughts and ideas being expressed. This mutual exchange of facial expressions between speaker and listener provides feedback, one to the other, about how each feels about the message and, importantly, whether the listener has understood what was being conveyed or whether misconceptions are apparent.

By way of contrast, the speaker and listener who show little or no variation in their facial expressions give the impression that they are not involved in the subject, are disinterested and that the speaker has expressed the ideas rather automatically. This lack of engagement results in communication that is not effective between the two. The relationship described here between speaker and listener is highly appropriate to the context of teaching and learning.

Eye contact is an important non-verbal communication channel that can convey a range of messages. Clearly within your role it is important that you establish effective working relationships with individual pupils. (See also Chapter 6 on developing relationships with pupils.) Steady purposeful eye contact and the ability to stay alert to their reactions at all times, and to respond appropriately, will help you to achieve this objective. You might, for example, fix your eye gaze on a particular pupil longer than you would normally to indicate your awareness of her inappropriate behaviour or to indicate your attentiveness to another pupil who needs time and patience to deliver her response to a particular question.

A person who avoids eye contact may be perceived as one who has a nervous disposition and is unable to relate effectively to others. In response to a pupil's lack of eye contact, an exasperated adult might exclaim rather harshly 'Look at me when I am talking to you!' Perhaps s/he has perceived the situation as an act of avoidance or defiance but it could be related to something else. Some pupils avoid eye contact when they feel threatened, ill at ease or shy; those on the autistic spectrum might find eye contact painful (Diamond, 2002); and others could use 'gaze aversion' (Doherty-Sneddon, 2004) when you ask them to remember past events or to use their imagination.

Awareness and sensitivity as to how pupils, parents and caregivers from different cultures perceive the use of eye contact is also important. For example, pupils from some cultures will lower their head and avoid eye contact as a measure of respect or submission. This issue applies to other aspects of non-verbal communication, including gesture, touch and spatial proximity to another person (advice on cultural awareness can be accessed from http://www.multiverse.ac.uk). You should find out about the individual differences, needs and cultural sensitivities of pupils you work with and take these into account when you interact with them.

Spatial proximity and touch

Interaction with pupils involves working in close spatial proximity. The distance between you and how you position yourself in relation to them varies depending upon the task at hand and the individual nature and needs of each pupil. A pupil with mild hearing loss, for example, might benefit from being alongside you as would a pupil with a limited attention span who gets distracted easily. A circular arrangement of desks or of pupils seated around one large table enables you to establish proximity and contact with each of them which is important for managing behaviour, keeping them focused and to gain their attention.

The meaning of proximity differs from one culture to another. Some Latin Americans, Asians and Europeans stand close to one another whereas some Scandinavians and British are more distant. You should familiarise yourself with cultural backgrounds of the pupils you support so that appropriate boundaries can be established and to ensure that you do not intimidate nor threaten them by invading their personal space (refer to http://www.multiverse.ac.uk).

Studies undertaken by Wheldell et al., (1986) suggest that when accompanied by praise, touch can promote positive behaviour and reinforce the work of pupils. However, the meaning of touch also varies between cultures. A pat on the back or a high five are gestures that can convey approval, friendship or comfort in some situations within some particular cultural groups.

However, the current educational climate is imbued with legislation on children's rights and numerous cases of physical child abuse and paedophilia have been reported. You should therefore be mindful of these issues and consider carefully whether it is more appropriate to refrain from all forms of physical contact and touch with the pupils you support.

Task 3.1
Body language

Examining how children use and respond to body language can help you to reflect on how you use these aspects of non-verbal communication yourself. Observe the social interaction of a small group of pupils (three or four) as they work together on an activity for approximately 10 minutes.

- Identify and record what body language is evident under the headings: gestures and body movement; facial expressions and eye contact; spatial proximity and touch.
- How much body language is picked up and responded to by others?
- How can you use this information to enable pupils to be more receptive to the non-verbal cues and messages of each other?
- How has this informed your own use of body language?

Paralanguage: how you use your voice

How you use your voice to accompany speech in terms of pace, pause, intonation, pitch, volume, projection and enunciation reinforces the meaning of the message you want to convey. These 'verbal dynamics' are important elements of paralanguage and your voice, if sensitively tuned, can become a powerful agent of expression and communication. Your natural voice has certain fixed qualities that determine its unique character, yet there are many variations you can draw upon to add impact to what you say. Consider the phrase, 'I want you to work on this problem together.' If you stress the beginning of the phrase in a deep tone a command is indicated, but if expressed with a rise in voice pitch at the end, a suggestion is indicated. Crystal (1971) found that intonation is the most important aspect of verbal dynamics that we can draw upon to organise speech into units of meaning.

You can vary your voice by changing the volume, by speaking very quietly, moderately or loudly using the full range of the audible spectrum. In a one-to-one situation, the volume of your voice is likely to be at the quieter end of the spectrum unless you are interacting with a pupil who has mild hearing loss, in which case you should adjust the volume accordingly. When working with an individual pupil or small group in a noisy classroom environment and you need to be heard, this can be better achieved by altering the pitch of your voice rather than its volume. Voice projection depends on the careful enunciation and articulation of all sounds, words and phrases that you use which requires good breath control. You project your voice by ensuring that it leaves your mouth accurately and confidently. Good voice projection adds considerable volume to your natural voice and allows you to make a whisper heard from some distance.

Your voice may have a naturally high pitch or a naturally low pitch. In general, we tend to associate the sound of a high voice with liveliness and excitement and that of a low, deep voice with seriousness and a sense of importance. You can vary the 'natural' pitch of your voice to contribute to the meaning of the words, phrases and sentences that you speak. For example, you can drop the pitch to add weight to what you want to say or raise the pitch if you want to lighten the tone. A voice with a low pitch is often perceived by pupils as more confident and authoritative than one with a high pitch, and can be raised quite easily to gain their attention. If you speak with a monotone voice this can be perceived as a lack of interest on your part in the subject; it is not likely to convey enthusiasm or stimulate the pupils into wanting to learn more. The ability to alter the pitch of your voice is important for sustaining the interest and listening capacity of the pupils with whom you are working.

How you pace the delivery of your speech directly influences whether or not the pupils you support receive and understand the message. Sensitivity to the learning needs of individual pupils should guide how you pace your speech. If you speak too quickly and cover a lot of ground in a short space of time some pupils may not be able to process all of the information you impart. Conversely, if you speak too slowly and cover very little ground over a long period of time some pupils might 'switch off', because they are not being challenged and become bored. You must strike a balance between these two extremes and speed variations are important as they give contrast to your delivery. You can also use pause to good effect as it demonstrates confidence if you can hold a silence before answering a question or making a point.

Task 3.2
Paralanguage

Before I leave ...
Before I leave planet earth
There is somewhere I must go
To nests of leaves – atop the trees
In the land of Borneo
For me ...
There is no other primate
Quite like the orangutan
Whose doleful eyes – question the whys?
Of 'deforestation' man
Whose appendicular arms
Nurture and cherish their young
Yet hunters fire – orphans acquire
What then – extinction – all gone?
No more the distinct splendour
Of long sparse reddish-brown hair
Our herbivore – becomes folklore
Lumberjacks – hunters – beware!
And so ...
My quest is perfectly clear
This anthropoid ape to find
And so protect – from the neglect
Of perilous humankind

Paula Zwozdiak-Myers (2006)

- Read the above verse through a few times and experiment with the 'verbal dynamics' of:
    Voice intonation – pitch
    Stress – accent
    Timing – pace – pause – rhythm
    Volume – projection.
- Audio record yourself reciting the verse.
- Listen to the recording and identify parts of the verse where you feel the verbal dynamics were effective and parts where you feel they were less effective – explain why you have come to this view.
- Look again at the verse and identify where you could use particular gestures, facial expressions and body movements to complement the verbal dynamics.
- Combine these with your modified verbal dynamics and video record yourself reciting and performing throughout the verse.
- Identify aspects of body language and paralanguage that you would like to develop further and devise a plan of action of how and when you can try these out.
- Enjoy!

To use your voice effectively, each of the verbal dynamics considered above needs to be woven together appropriately. For example, you will not communicate successfully if the pitch of your voice is right, yet the volume is inappropriate or you fail to enunciate with clarity. Again for example, some pupils cannot hear your quiet delivery or pupils misunderstand the concept or your instructions, because they do not recognise important words and hence their meanings. It is also important to consider how you say what you say. If you need to discipline a pupil, sound firm; deal with a sensitive issue, sound empathetic; or, to motivate a small group, sound excited. A sensitively tuned voice should be a major advantage to you when interacting with pupils and you should practise altering each of the verbal dynamics in order to develop and use them more effectively.

Your use of non-verbal communication influences the interpersonal relationships you establish with pupils. Argyle (1978) distinguishes between 'affiliative' and 'dominant' styles of social behaviour. The former is exemplified through close proximity, eye contact and a warm, friendly tone of voice and the latter through speaking loudly, quickly, interrupting pupils, ignoring their contributions to the topic of conversation and using stern facial expressions. A caring approach when you interact with pupils is important for establishing effective interpersonal relationships and this can be developed by using various aspects of non-verbal communication in an appropriate manner. Your commitment to pupils' learning and well-being should be evident in all aspects of your self-presentation and manner which requires awareness, flexibility and sensitivity when you support their individual needs.

Task 3.3
Style of social behaviour

Video-record a lesson episode that involves you interacting with a small group of pupils to identify your style of social behaviour.

Ensure that you obtain the parent/caregiver's permission both to make a recording and to share it with your tutor.

After the lesson episode, watch the video and make notes on your interaction with pupils using the following headings:

- Eye contact
- Facial expression
- Proximity
- Touch
- Tone of voice
- Speed of verbal delivery
- Response to pupils

Discuss your observations with your tutor and record in your portfolio aspects of your social behaviour that you consider to be strengths and other aspects in need of further development.

Which of Argyle's (1978) styles, 'affiliative' or 'dominant', best describes your approach?

Identify strategies you could use to improve aspects of your social behaviour with pupils and try these out in future interactions with them.

SUMMARY

Good communicators express their meaning in a range of non-verbal ways. This chapter has aimed to increase your knowledge, skills and understanding of communication and has provided a range of activities to develop your use of non-verbal language, body language and paralanguage. As you gain experience and confidence, you should be able to: communicate sensitively and with sound judgement to accommodate the learning needs of the pupils you support; and help pupils to develop their communication skills and become more successful in social interactions to maximise their learning.

The next chapter considers how you can develop your verbal communication skills to help the pupils you work with.

FURTHER READING

Department for Education and Employment (DfEE) (1998) *The National Literacy Strategy*, London: HMSO.

Department for Education and Skills (DfES) (2002) *Supporting pupils learning English as an additional language*, DfES 0239/2002

Department for Education and Skills (DfES) (2004) *Five Year Strategy for Children and Learners,* London: HMSO. http://www.dcsf.gov.uk/publications/5yearstrategy

The National Curriculum online: http://www.nc.uk.net

NOTE

1 How you use your voice to reinforce the meaning behind verbal messages.

4 Developing your Communication Skills: Verbal

Paula Zwozdiak-Myers

INTRODUCTION

How you use language when you interact with pupils, either individually or in small groups, will shape the interpersonal relationships you establish with them and climate of the working environment. This chapter examines aspects of verbal communication that are important within your role to support pupil learning. You are encouraged to reflect on how you currently use these skills and to consider how you might develop them further. In exploring the significance of effective verbal interactions, this chapter illustrates how you can develop your use of language, explanations, modelling, questioning and listening. It also explores factors that influence discussions in small groups.

OBJECTIVES

By the end of this chapter, you should:

- understand the importance of effective verbal communication skills;
- use language, explanations, modelling, questioning and listening more effectively;
- recognise how social interactions influence small group discussions;
- be aware of the interdependence of effective verbal and non-verbal communication skills.

This chapter refers to the HLTA standards that cover establishing *supportive and constructive relationships* with children and young people; *communicating effectively and sensitively* with them, alongside the professional skills of advancing learning when working with *individuals* and *small groups*. You can also see Appendix 2 for information on how this chapter maps onto the standards at the time of publication; if these are revised then updated materials will appear on the website supporting this text.

VERBAL COMMUNICATION: DEVELOPING YOUR LANGUAGE SKILLS

When you speak to pupils, the language you use will vary according to the context and purpose of the verbal communication. In addition to language that is formal and specifically related to the subject areas of the curriculum, you use language in a more relaxed, informal manner during social conversations with the pupils. This social talk, or 'phatic' communication, allows you to get to know them (and allows them to get to know you) and to gather information about their personal interests, likes, dislikes, views and personality traits, which adds to the store of intuitive awareness that informs your communication and interpersonal relationships with them in the future. Pupils do respond well when you take an interest in them, greet them warmly, use their names, make regular eye contact with them and value their opinions and views. These are factors that contribute to creating a positive environment when you support their individual learning in more structured formal situations.

The National Literacy Strategy (NLS) explicitly states that 'good oral work enhances pupils' understanding of language in both oral and written forms and of the way in which language can be used to communicate' (DfEE, 1998: 3). The importance attached to your use of language during verbal communication cannot be emphasised strongly enough. You must ensure that you use language that the pupils you support can access readily and can understand. The class teacher, in most instances, will introduce pupils to the language associated with particular concepts in different subject areas, but you need to reinforce this language when you interact with pupils.

Language: developing pupils' skills

The rate at which language develops differs from one pupil to the next for several reasons, e.g. limited exposure to language; restricted opportunities to use language; some form of physical or cognitive impairment. The language development of a child with dyslexia typically shows a range of subtle impairments in speech, e.g. mislabelling, mispronunciation and word-finding difficulties. In addition to more common problems associated with spelling and reading, Miles (1993) identifies problems related to the acquisition of familiar sequences such as the months of the year; problems in repetition of polysyllabic words; accurately labelling left and right, and in learning tables. If you are supporting a child with dyslexia, this might involve using specific computer-based programmes (Fawcett and Nicholson, 1996) and books that use comic sans font and buff-coloured paper to help with pupils' component reading skills (for advice and guidance on how to support pupils with a range of learning difficulties refer to: http://inclusion.ngfl.gov.uk; QCA (2001); http://www.nc.uk.net).

Pupils need to acquire competence in four main areas of language:

- *Phonology* – rules associated with the sounds of words and their constituent vowels and consonants. Some words that share the same sounds, e.g. bow and bough, can cause confusion but you can help a pupil to understand their meaning by placing each within appropriate sentences.

- *Syntax* – rules associated with how words are combined to produce grammatical sentences.
- *Semantics* – rules associated with the meaning of words and utterances.
- *Pragmatics* – knowledge that relates to how language is used appropriately within different social contexts. A child who exclaims 'Sam is fat' in reference to a peer in the class may demonstrate an understanding of phonology, syntax and semantics yet lacks sensitivity to the feelings of others.

The rules and conventions embedded within language from different cultures may be, and often are, very different. This will have direct implications for you when working with individual pupils from different cultural, ethnic backgrounds – particularly when they use English as an additional language (EAL). The class teacher should alert you to any potential problems and provide structured guidance material that you can follow to support their learning of language (refer also to DfES, 2002 for additional guidance).

Learning the rules about how to structure sounds and form grammatical sentences provides an important foundation for language development, but this does not mean that a pupil has acquired the skills they need to use them. Developing narrative is concerned with 'putting language to work' so that a pupil can, for example, follow instructions, explanations, link information together and understand how different parts of a concept combine to make a whole. You can help individual pupils to develop narrative, and the associated thinking skills, through your use of explanations, modelling, questioning and listening.

Explanations

Explanations provide information about what, how and why. They are used to define, describe and clarify the meaning of words, phrases, terms, concepts and ideas and to provide reasons. When you are explaining something to pupils to support the knowledge and concepts introduced by the class teacher, it is important to:

- take account of their previous knowledge, experience and understanding;
- determine their existing familiarity with the information being presented;
- use terms that are not ambiguous;
- use language that they can understand and is within their capability and experience;
- describe (and define) the major terms and concepts;
- provide exemplars to illustrate these terms and concepts, e.g. use analogy and metaphor;
- relate new terms and concepts to work they are already familiar with;
- provide links where possible to other subject areas across the curriculum.

An explanation should be clear and well structured. To support the verbal content of an explanation, a range of visual aids can be used, e.g. maps, diagrams, pictures, task cards, photographs, models, apparatus, demonstrations and website-based programmes. By combining an explanation with activities, tasks, questions and visual aids, the pupils you support can become actively involved in their own learning.

Task 4.1
Explanations

Write down the key words and phrases the class teacher uses to introduce a particular topic. Consider how you might reinforce and explain these words and phrases to the pupils you support and provide opportunities for them to show that they understand. For example, what analogies or metaphors would help a pupil understand and remember what you are saying?

Video record your interaction with pupils when you explain the key words and phrases.

After the activity listen carefully to the recording and analyse your explanations using the following criteria:

- Clarity – was your explanation clear?
- Exemplars – were those used e.g. diagrams and task cards, effective?
- Language – was the verbal language appropriate?
- Structure – was the information presented logically?
- Pupils – did the pupils you support learn?

Discuss your observations with your tutor and set yourself three targets to develop your use of explanations in relation to the pupils you support.

Modelling

Modelling is a learning strategy used to reinforce verbal explanations and descriptions. It provides pupils with a visual demonstration, or model, of how to build or perform a skill and is frequently used when a new skill or complicated procedure is introduced. It is a particularly important strategy to use when you support a pupil who is a visual learner or one that uses English as an additional language (EAL). By modelling you can:

- think aloud, making skills, decisions and processes that would otherwise be hidden or unclear, apparent and explicit;
- expose pupils to the possible pitfalls of the task in hand, showing how to avoid them;
- demonstrate to pupils that they can make alterations and corrections as part of the process.

(DfES, 2003, Unit 3 – Modelling, p. 3)

This learning strategy enables a pupil to ask questions, at different stages, about the process as it is happening and to hear the verbal explanations that relate to each stage. Modelling resembles the technique referred to as 'scaffolding' that can be used to structure pupils' learning. Dillon and Maguire (2001: 145–6) explain the stages of this approach as:

1   learners are supported in carrying out a task by the use of language to guide their action;

2   learners then talk themselves through the task;

3   the learner's talk can, in turn, become an internalised guide to the action and thought of the learner.

Task 4.2
Modelling

To exemplify the process of modelling, consider how you can support a pupil who is learning to 'skip with a rope':

Verbal cues, e.g. hold one end of the rope in each hand, begin with the rope on the ground behind you, bend your knees, use you arms to circle the rope in an arch over your head, push your feet from the ground together and jump through the rope as it hits the ground in front of you ... whilst each action is taking place you talk the pupil through the process. The pupil talks him or herself through each verbal cue as they perform each action. The pupil can skip with the rope without using the verbal cues as he can perform the action without thinking through it ... s/he has internalised the skill.

Adapt this process to a skill or technique that you are helping a particular pupil to learn.

Questioning

An important technique for reinforcing the learning of pupils that you support is the use of questioning. Wragg and Brown (2001: 1) suggest that, 'Intelligent questioning is a valuable part of interactive teaching. Inept handling of questions, however, leads to confusion and misunderstanding.' Questions are asked for different reasons, e.g. to gauge whether a pupil has understood an explanation, the meaning of a concept or particular term; to develop problem-solving and thinking skills. Questions can be either closed or open-ended.

Closed questions are those that attract only one correct response, e.g. What is the capital city of Japan? How many sides are there in a rhombus? A pupil either knows the right answer or not, which s/he recalls or retrieves from memory. Closed questions can be used to monitor whether a pupil has memorised particular facts or pieces of information.

Open-ended questions are those that can attract several possible responses and it may not be possible to determine whether the answer is correct. For example, How could we tackle global warming? Can you explain the law of gravity? Should we invest in nuclear energy? Open-ended questions are used to develop thinking skills and to promote understanding, and these are more complicated than closed questions. When supporting pupils you can encourage them to think about a range of alternative responses to the open-ended questions posed by the class teacher and to synthesise this information in a variety of ways. In relation to the question posed above about gravity, for example, you might follow this up by asking:

- Can you give me an example?
- If I drop a brick and a tennis ball from the same height will they reach the ground at the same time?
- Why do you think this?
- Is this always the case?
- If I release a balloon from the same height what will happen?
- Why do you think this?
- What does this tell you about the law of gravity?
- Is gravity important?
- Why do you think this?

Asking questions is not a simple, straightforward process. The types of question you can ask pupils range from those that require descriptive answers based upon factual evidence to those that require more complex levels of thinking by encouraging discussion, debate, reasoning or to challenge values and different viewpoints. You need also to be mindful that the responses pupils give to questions require some form of feedback and comment. In order to support their learning, your comments should be informative and encouraging. It is therefore imperative that questions are pitched at a level that is appropriate to each individual pupil so as not to cause frustration, confusion or a sense of failure. The following table of Bloom's taxonomy of educational objectives illustrates how questioning has been classified in relation to six hierarchical levels of pupils' cognitive learning:

Table 4.1 Bloom's taxonomy of educational objectives

Level	Cognitive learning	Pupil should (outcomes)
1	Knowledge	describe; identify; recall
2	Comprehension	translate; review; report; restate
3	Application	interpret; predict; show how; solve; try in a new context
4	Analysis	explain; infer; analyse; question; test; criticise
5	Synthesis	design; create; arrange; organise; construct
6	Evaluation	assess; compare and contrast; appraise; argue; select

(in DfES, 2003, Unit 4: Questioning: 19).

The ability to ask questions effectively is a skill that you can develop throughout your training. It is important that you ask clear, relevant questions and use pause appropriately so that the pupils you support have time to think about an answer before they respond. Muijs and Reynolds (2001: 23) suggest that three seconds or slightly longer is a reasonable time for any such pause, although up to 15 seconds might be required for open-ended, higher level questions. You can use closed or open-ended questions or combine the two into a series of questions. You might for example begin with a few closed questions during a question and answer session and then move onto more complex open-ended questions. Devising a series of questions is an effective technique for extending a pupil's understanding of a particular topic that has been introduced by the class teacher.

Task 4.3
Questioning

Devise a series of questions that you can ask the individual pupils you support that relate to a theme introduced by the class teacher using the following guidelines:

Begin with a narrow focus that recalls existing knowledge; broaden the focus by introducing new ideas; build and extend on the pupil's response; return the focus to the original idea or stimulus; ask the same question in a different way to monitor pupil understanding.

Try your questions out and when you do so ensure that you balance the questions with your own comments in a positive and supportive manner, give pupils time to think about the answer, correct inaccurate responses sensitively and do not answer the questions yourself.

The above series of questions follows a linear pathway – you can create a circular pathway by repeating the three central stages for themes that require a more exploratory than factual approach.

If the pupils you support experience problems answering questions, you should find alternative ways to ask the same question. You can use a range of prompts to help them. Three types of prompts that have been identified by Muijs and Reynolds (2001: 22) are:

- *verbal prompts* – cues, reminders, tips, references to previous lessons or giving part of a sentence for the pupil to complete;
- *gestural prompts* – pointing to an object or modelling a behaviour;
- *physical prompts* – guiding a pupil through movement skills.

The latter two types of non-verbal communication prompts are important elements of questioning as they relate directly to the words that are used. By providing a range of prompts, your questions should be understood by pupils who are visual, auditory and kinaesthetic learners. Often referred to as VAK (visual, auditory, kinaesthetic) this way of viewing pupils' learning styles suggests that during any given learning activity each pupil will experience a range of different stimuli and, the way in which each pupil responds to these varies:

- *visual learners* – visual cues such as diagrams, pictures, gestures, task cards and models are the dominant trigger to stimulate pupil learning;
- *auditory learners* – auditory cues such as verbal prompts (above) and verbal explanations and questions are the dominant trigger to stimulate pupil learning;
- *kinaesthetic learners* – kinaesthetic cues such as physical prompts (above) in addition to using movements with phonics, as in the 'Jolly Phonics Scheme' (Lloyd, 1992) are the dominant trigger to stimulate pupil learning.

DISCUSSIONS IN SMALL GROUPS

Discussions can arise as a natural progression from the questions you ask pupils, particularly those that are open-ended. They can be used effectively to explore a theme that has been introduced by the class teacher and to broaden the understanding and perspectives of the pupils you support. Small group discussions are important as they provide you with insights about where individual pupils are in their learning and a platform for the pupils themselves to express their ideas, views and values on such controversial issues as the question raised earlier, 'Should we invest in nuclear energy?' You need to use your judgement about when to 'reel the pupils in' so that they don't wander too far from the central theme.

When handling a small group discussion you should be aware that some of the more confident, assertive pupils could try to dominate the discussion whereas others that lack confidence could be reluctant to speak for fear of being ridiculed in front of their peers. Group dynamics are complex and many pupils, particularly those with learning difficulties e.g. attention deficit hyperactivity disorder (ADHD) and emotional behavioural disorder (EBD), do not have the communication skills that enable them to cope within a group effectively.

It has been suggested that there are four critical stages or developmental sequences to effective small group work that incorporate the rhyming phases of: forming, storming, norming and performing (Bligh, 2000; Tuckman, 1965). Adjourning was identified as a fifth stage in 1977. Specifically, characteristics that influence how well a small group works together to achieve a common goal include: group size, group composition (pupil variables of ability, motives, personality traits, degree of participation), roles of group members (leader), task variables (activities that each individual needs to accomplish), group cohesion, structure and stability (how members support one another), the norms (rules and procedures established), and importantly, communication within the group.

An important aim of the Communication Opportunity Group Scheme (Sage, 2000b) is to teach group skills to children to enable them to learn more effectively. Some of your work might involve working with two pupils in pair situations to help them to develop communication skills they need for group work, e.g. taking turns to speak, not interrupting each other, listening carefully to their partner, rephrasing what their partner has said, recognising that others' views should be respected, using eye contact and appropriate body language.

Interactions that involve joint attention help individual pupils 'to learn much about the world around them, including things that are important to pay attention to and how these are valued by others in their community' (Gauvain, 2001: 86–7). Group work can help pupils to become more active in their learning (Ruel and Bastiaans, 2003). When working with peers in a group, pupils should be encouraged to articulate their ideas and to question the ideas of others. This social process can lead to the construction of ideas and development of possible solutions to a problem. When the group size involves three or more pupils, care must be taken to ensure that individual pupils do not become marginalised or that sub-divisions within the group do not occur e.g. 2 v 2, 2 v 3. You must encourage all members of the group to participate as this provides opportunities for them to increase their skills.

Task 4.4
Communication within
small groups

Observe the social interactions of a small group of pupils (three to four) as they work together on a joint task set by the class teacher for approximately 10 minutes. Identify and record:

- how roles were established within the group;
- how tasks were distributed within the group;
- whether individual pupils expressed their ideas clearly and others listened;
- whether ideas were responded to and built upon by others;
- whether individuals asked for clarification of others' ideas if unsure about them;
- whether pupils were actively engaged or marginalised;
- what communication channels were evident between individual members of the group;
- whether the group worked together cohesively to achieve the task.

What have these observations shown you about the nature of:

- group dynamics?
- individual personalities and characteristics of the pupils involved?

LISTENING

Well-developed listening skills can be used to reinforce verbal aspects of communication with pupils. The importance attached to listening attentively to individual pupil responses and being able to respond in an appropriate manner cannot be overemphasised. How a pupil responds to the questions you ask indicates different things, e.g. whether she knows the correct answer or not, and whether she has understood the question or not. Listening is a deliberate activity and by attending carefully to the words, phrases and sentences that an individual pupil uses, you should be able to recognise whether she has received the message accurately or has developed any misconceptions along the way.

Techniques that you can use to develop your listening skills include:

Attending to the key points, e.g. the event, time and place, individuals and subject matter involved. These provide you with a framework for linking and remembering the specific details and you might find it helpful to write these down. Paraphrase and mirror what the pupil has said to clarify points, e.g. 'You think that the film of Robin Hood is more exciting than the book?' Use non-verbal cues to respond to what the pupil is saying and provide positive feedback, e.g. use eye contact, facial expressions, nod your head and lean forward to establish closer spatial proximity.

If your communication with the pupils you support is not effective, you need to question why, e.g. perhaps the vocabulary you used was inappropriate or the question was not worded sequentially or clearly. You might respond by rephrasing the question; repeating the same question; or by using analogy to clarify the meaning. If your communication was ineffective, because some pupils within the group were not listening to you and have 'switched off' again, you need to question why this has happened, e.g. perhaps these pupils perceive that you are not interested in what they have to say as you have not been paying attention nor responding appropriately to their individual responses.

How you respond to each individual pupil is important. They need to know that you are listening and interested in their responses. Pupils receive this information in a range of different ways, e.g. when you provide verbal feedback that builds on and relates to their response and how you use your voice and body language to convey enthusiasm. Effective listening is an important interactive process that is conveyed through a range of communication channels, e.g. non-verbal cues such as establishing eye contact, thumbs up for 'okay' and verbal cues such as, 'That's right, well done, now can you give me another example of gravity and explain how it works?'

Pupils also need to develop their listening skills for interactions between themselves and between them and you to be effective. Revisit task 4.4 on 'Communication within small groups' and consider how effective or otherwise the group were in listening attentively to each other's ideas, views and perspectives in order to accomplish the joint group task.

SUMMARY

Good communicators express their meaning in a range of verbal and non-verbal ways. This chapter has aimed to increase your knowledge, skills and understanding of communication and has provided a range of activities to develop your use of verbal language, explanations, modelling, questioning and listening. As you gain experience and confidence, you should be able to: use communication sensitively and with sound judgement to accommodate the learning needs of the pupils you support; and help pupils to develop their communication skills and become more successful in social interactions to maximise their learning.

The next chapter examines pupil diversity and considers ways you can take account of the diverse backgrounds of your pupils in your work.

FURTHER READING

Department for Education and Employment (DfEE) (1998) *The National Literacy Strategy*, London: HMSO.

Department for Education and Skills (DfES) (2002) *Supporting pupils learning English as an additional language*, DfES 0239/2002.

Department for Education and Skills (DfES) (2003) *Teaching and Learning in Secondary Schools: Pilot Unit 3: Modelling*, London: Crown, Ref: DfES 0343/2003.

Department for Education and Skills (DfES) (2003) *Teaching and Learning in Secondary Schools: Pilot Unit 4: Questioning*, London: Crown, Ref: DfES 0344/2003.

Department for Education and Skills (DfES) (2004) *Five Year Strategy for Children and Learners,* London: HMSO. http://www.dcsf.gov.uk/publications/5yearstrategy

The National Curriculum online: http://www. nc.uk.net.

5 Understanding Pupil Diversity[1]

Andrew Noyes

INTRODUCTION

No two pupils are the same. Your role, along with the other staff in the school, is to enable the pupils to achieve as highly as possible and to maximise their life chances.

This chapter is intended to introduce you to the complex make-up of modern UK society, and to show how social diversity and educational opportunity and attainment are interrelated. You are then encouraged to consider ways in which you should take account of the diverse backgrounds of your pupils in your work.

OBJECTIVES

By the end of this chapter you should be able to:

- demonstrate an understanding of how pupil diversity can affect achievement;
- analyse evidence about the relative academic performance of pupils in relation to class, ethnicity and gender;
- discuss issues of discrimination and bias in relation to gender, ethnicity and class;
- consider school policies and critique classroom procedures in order to promote better opportunities for learning for all pupils;
- relate these skills and attitudes to the competences/standards expected for you as an HLTA.

This chapter covers the following aspects of the standards for HLTAs, which require you to know how to contribute to effective personalised provision by taking practical account of *diversity* and for you to *recognise and respond appropriately to situations that challenge equality of opportunity.*

The Standards for HLTAs make it very clear that you are expected to be aware of stereotyping pupils in ways which limit their aspirations and their achievement and to take steps to remove barriers to participation and achievement. Every child who leaves school without well-developed literacy skills – reading, writing, arithmetic and ICT skills and without GCSEs will struggle to make their way in the 21st century. Children from particular groups are particularly at risk. These children include 'looked after children' or children in care who because of their personal circumstances may move schools often and lack supportive home structures.

You have a professional obligation as do teachers with respect to diversity. The GTC's 'Code of Professional Values and Practice' states that: 'Teachers challenge stereotypes and oppose prejudice to safeguard equality of opportunity, respecting individuals re-gardless of gender, marital status, religion, colour, race, ethnicity, class, sexual orientation, disability and age' (GTC, 2002). This is easy to write but difficult to implement. It is important for you to recognise that you are part of that diversity and that your experiences of education and perspectives on a variety of complex social and cultural issues have a significant influence on the way in which you respond to diversity. This chapter focuses on issues around ethnicity, gender and social class and, although they are examined separately herein, they clearly overlap and intertwine.

A HISTORY OF DIVERSITY

The presence of people originating from other cultures, faiths and backgrounds has been a feature of British society for many centuries. The notion of 'other' suggests that British society is easily described, but 'Britishness' is neither a clearly defined nor a fixed concept. Immigration into the British Isles has come in waves and even now is a significant political issue both here and across the European Union. A few examples draw attention to the changing ethnic mix that contributes to present day society. The Roman conquest of England at the dawn of the Christian era lasted some six centuries, at the end of which came invasion by Germanic peoples. About two centuries later the Viking invasion brought Danes and Norwegians to the mix of peoples. In 1066, the Normans took over much of England and many French people stayed and were assimilated. In the 16th century many people fled mainland European countries to escape, for example, religious persecution.

The ethnic mix was added to by Jewish immigration following their persecution at the end of the nineteenth century. Two world wars saw a further migration of people in mainland Europe away from conflict. As many former colonial countries have gained independence, immigration from Africa and Asia has altered the ethnic mix in the UK. The important difference associated with this latter wave of immigration was the visibility of newcomers. Prior to 1948 there was only a trickle of black immigrants; the 1950s in the UK saw the active recruitment of Black and Asian families to fill the gaps in the work force (Briggs, 1983: 310–12). Through the last century the population of England grew steadily, from 35.5 million in 1901 to nearly 49 million in 1991. The 2001 census showed that the population of Great Britain was almost 57.1 million. It would appear that steady population growth has been supplemented by immigration. The minority ethnic population is expected to grow to some 10 per cent of the population by 2020. The freedom of movement of EU citizens and the widening of European Community membership has further increased the cultural mix. In some areas of the UK (e.g. farming regions that rely on seasonal manual labour) this has had considerable effect on the educational system with an increased number of children coming to schools with English as a second language.

Up to the early 1950s, immigration was largely white. Many immigrants prior to that date were assimilated into the host culture, although a few immigrant groups maintained their distinctive lifestyle, e.g. the Jewish community. At first, the host community adopted the same attitude towards the black and Asian immigrants and expected them to adopt the values and lifestyle of the host nation. That this policy did not work may be attributed to the influence of racism – black people were not accepted in the same way as white immigrants of the past. Such issues still exist in our society and far–right political parties such as the British National Party continue to find support in many parts of England.

EQUAL OPPORTUNITIES AND EDUCATIONAL EQUITY

For many people it is self-evident that the implementation of equal opportunities policies is a reflection of basic human rights, but how does the notion of equality of opportunity relate to a school's response to a diverse pupil population? Should the same curriculum, teaching styles, etc., be used consistently, or does such 'equality' in fact perpetuate inequality? Sociologists of education have argued for many years that if you assume that all pupils come to school equally prepared, and treat them accordingly, then in reality you advantage those who have been better prepared in their social milieu to succeed at school (Bernstein, 1977; Bourdieu, 1974; Willis, 1977). These authors were writing over a quarter of a century ago but their writing remains pertinent for 21st century Britain.

Concerns with equity have shifted between different groups over the years. In the 1980s and earlier there was concern about the under-achievement of West Indian pupils (Short, 1986). Now there is growing concern about the low performance of many white working-class boys and pupils from some minority ethnic groups (OFSTED, 2003a). Although much progress has been made in the last three decades as regards equal opportunities for men and women in the workplace and boys and girls at school, there remain substantial differences in the roles of men and women in society (EOC, 2006; Myers, 1987, 1990). These issues around gender, ethnicity and class are the foci of the remainder of the chapter.

In many cases, explanations of pupil under-achievement have focused on the shortcomings of the pupil or their families – the 'deficit model' explanation. More recently the focus has shifted to addressing the educational system as one of the factors contributing to under-achievement. This focus is not only at the level of government and school policy but also in the classroom where such policies are interpreted and implemented by teachers.

GENDER

The Equal Opportunities Commission (EOC), which is now part of the Equality and Human Rights Commission (http://www.equalityhumanrights.com), has regularly produced overviews of social differences in our society. These overviews include performance in Key Stage and GCSE examinations, through take-up and achievement at A-level and in further and higher education, to employment patterns and rates of pay and can be found online (EOC, 2006). There remains much difference in the ways in which men and women exist and move through our society. Focusing on secondary schooling, both boys and girls have been steadily improving their performance in school examinations over the past 20 years but there is now a clear gender gap, particularly in some subject areas. Table 5.1 compares the performance of boys and girls at GCSE gaining grades A*–C in many of the popular GCSE subjects in 2006.

Given the different performance at GCSE level, Table 5.2 shows student examination entries for General Certificate of Education (GCE) A-level courses in 2006. There is clear gender delineation in some areas (e.g. physics, English, psychology) between what might be considered masculine and feminine subjects.

The EOC reported that often children have very stereotyped ideas about the roles of men and women, and how these stereotypes are themselves linked to what might be termed class (EOC, 2001). There is much research on the different ways in which boys and girls are positioned by, and respond to, moving schools (Jackson and Warin, 2000), teachers (Younger et al., 1999), learning and the curriculum (Paechter, 2000), the use of physical space and so on. These different modes of being are not simply genetic but are socially constructed identities that gradually influence, and are shaped by, boys' and girls' responses to the opportunities and challenges of school (see also Task 5.2). Ruddock explores the challenges of developing and possibilities for gender policies in secondary schools in some detail (Ruddock, 2004).

Table 5.1 GCSE attempts and achievements in selected subjects in schools in 2006

Subject	Boys		Girls	
	Entries (thousands)	% passes at grade C or above	Entries (thousands)	% passes at grade C or above
Maths	310	55	305	57
English	307	55	305	69
English literature	255	61	255	73
Science (any)	298	54	294	55
French	94	58	116	69
German	40	63	45	74
History	106	63	102	69
Geography	104	63	83	69
Art and design	77	59	112	78
Design and Technology (any)	180	52	159	67
Physical education	91	60	61	61
Religious studies	63	63	82	75

Source: DCSF, January 2007, http://www.dcsf.gov.uk/rsgateway/DB/SFR/s000702/index.shtml.

Table 5.2 GCE A-level examination take-up for men and women in 2006

Subject	Entries (thousands)	
	Women	Men
English	53.9	24.2
Mathematics	19.1	30.6
Biological sciences	27.3	19.3
Physics	5	18.7
Chemistry	16.8	17.7
French	8.3	3.9
Psychology	36.2	12.4
Sociology	18.6	5.7
Art and design	25.8	11.6
Business studies	12.1	17.8
History	20.1	20.5
Geography	12.8	15.5

Source: DCSF, January 2007, http://www.dcsf.gov.uk/rsgateway/DB/SFR/ s000703/index.shtml.

So far in this section we have been looking at the relationship between sex and performance, whereas the notion of gender is more nuanced, including different masculinities and femininities. Traditional stereotypes are being broken down and at the same time are more fragmented. Such differences are increasingly celebrated and this includes children's sexuality. As we said at the outset, teachers' responses to this level of diversity are influenced by their personal views and experiences. (The EOC (2006) reports that there were an estimated 2.3–3.2 million gay, lesbian and bisexual adults in the Great Britain earlier in the decade). However, whatever your views, many issues in this area require a thoughtful, professional approach: e.g. homophobic bullying, see the advice on the Intercom website (http://www.intercomtrust.org.uk (accessed 12 June 2008)).

ETHNICITY

A report in the mid-1990s showed that considerable progress had been made by many, but not all, groups of minority ethnic pupils (Gillborn and Gipps, 1996). That situation remains today. Two reports at the turn of the century identified the serious under-achievement of Afro-Caribbean pupils and that these pupils have not shared in the rise in standards and achievement shown by many other pupils, especially white pupils (Fitzgerald *et al.*, 2000; Gillborn and Mirza, 2000). For example, many pupils of Pakistani background failed to keep up with the improvements of most pupils. As a consequence, the gap between the high and low achievers widens with time. The under-performance of many white, working-class boys serves to emphasise the importance of taking into account how class and gender effects are embedded within the data showing attainments of ethnic groups. (Gillborn and Mirza's report is well worth reading and is available online.)

The 2004 Youth Cohort Study (DCSF, 2005) was the twelfth survey of its kind and presents interesting findings about the education, training and employment of young people in England and Wales. It includes data on how performance and participation in education varies across ethnic groups, for example:

- 'Attainment varies considerably according to ethnic group. According to the YCS there was a marked increase in the attainment of 5 or more GCSE A*-Cs by Indian respondents, from 60 to 72 per cent between 2002 and 2004, with Bangladeshis and Whites also showing increases (from 41 per cent to 45 per cent, and 52 per cent to 55 per cent respectively). Achievement of 5 or more GCSE A*-Cs by Pakistani young people fell from 40 per cent in 2002 to 37 per cent in 2004, and for black young people attainment fell slightly to 34 per cent over the same period.'
- 'White 16 year olds are much less likely than any other ethnic group to be participating in full-time education, with just seven out of ten doing so, compared to over nine tenths of Indian respondents. However, white respondents are more likely than any other group to be in employment or government supported training (12 per cent and 10 per cent respectively).'
- Beyond 16 'Over nine out of ten Indian young people were studying for a qualification of some sort, and over three quarters were studying for a level 3 qualification. Black and Pakistani respondents were more likely to be studying than whites (80 per cent, 78 per cent and 73 per cent respectively), but were less likely to be studying for a level 3 qualification (46 per cent, 45 per cent and 51 per cent respectively).'

The YCS also includes a lot of data on gender and the achievements and activities of students with parents in different occupational groups. Research shows that although achievement has been raised for most pupils, under-achievement persists and is very much linked to class and ethnicity.

If you are working with pupils from a range of ethnic backgrounds, the issue of supporting those for whom English is an additional language is important. The issue of language goes far wider than classroom oracy. Many classroom resources are heavily text-based and their use of language requires not only a level of literacy but also cultural awareness. One area impacted by pupils' non-English home language is homework and coursework tasks. As is pointed out above, the increased use of home-learning resources, and indeed homework, relies to some extent upon the knowledge and support of parents or other family members. If language provides an extra hurdle only for some pupils, then homework will have a differential effect. You should consider carefully the language requirements made by textbooks, classroom talk and homework tasks.

The above discussion reminds us that the performance of pupils is related to many factors including ethnicity, gender and class. The variables used here – class, ethnicity and gender – are not causes; these variables hide causative factors which contribute to under-achievement. Table 5.3 shows considerable variation in the performance of pupils from various ethnic groups in 2006 GCSE examinations but the data does not include class. It is however evident that gender is a factor across ethnic groups.

Table 5.3 Achievements at GCSE/GNVQ in 2006, by ethnicity and gender

Ethnicity	% of pupils gaining five or more A*–C		
	Boys	Girls	Total
White	53.0	62.3	57.5
White British	52.9	62.2	57.5
Irish	57.2	65.0	61.3
Traveller of Irish heritage	14.0	23.2	19.0
Gypsy/Roma	9.3	11.8	10.4
Any other white background	55.0	65.3	60.1
Mixed	50.7	61.2	56.1
White and black Caribbean	39.9	54.2	47.3
White and black African	51.8	61.5	56.8
White and Asian	65.6	72.1	68.9
Any other mixed background	54.0	63.3	58.7
Asian	55.5	66.9	61.0
Indian	67.1	76.6	71.7
Pakistani	45.4	57.9	51.4
Bangladeshi	50.9	62.2	56.6
Any other Asian background	57.8	72.4	64.6
Black	41.0	55.1	48.1
Black Caribbean	36.5	52.9	44.9
Black African	45.2	56.7	51.0
Any other black background	39.4	55.7	47.1
Chinese	75.5	84.8	80.0
Other	51.0	62.3	56.3
Unclassified	47.5	57.1	52.1
All pupils	52.6	62.2	57.3

Source: DCSF, February 2007, http://www.dcsf.gov.uk/rsgateway/DB/SFR/s000708/index.shtml.

Under-achievement in school may be a factor in the higher unemployment rate suffered by many minority ethnic adults. In 2005, 9.1 per cent of women and 10.7 per cent of men from minority ethnic groups were unemployed in Great Britain compared to 3.7 per cent female and 4.6 per cent male white adults (EOC, 2006). This relatively high level of unemployment has an impact upon the future economic status of those groups and therefore, in some complex way, the chances of their children in school. This is not to say that such inequality of attainment cannot be addressed, or is somehow cyclical, but rather to highlight the limitations of schools' ability to affect social change.

CLASS

Gender is perhaps considered to be the most straightforward category for grouping and analysing pupil performance. This means that it is easy to communicate variability in outcomes and therefore to set targets related to gender attainment. Ethnicity, although considerably more complex, also allows us to analyse the attainments of ethnic categories and see which groups are performing above or below what might be expected from national datasets. Class is far more complex but the effect that pupils' economic circumstances have upon their education is very real. Connolly (2006) makes a convincing argument from statistical analyses of performance data that pupils' social class and ethnicity have a far greater effect on GCSE performance than gender. Understanding social class goes beyond simply looking at economic capital (e.g. measures like free school meals) but relates to other 'capitals' that pupils' families possess. This might be *social capital* or the *cultural capital* that includes having well-educated parents and ready access to books, computer media or other learning and cultural experiences. There is much evidence to signal the relationship between culturally rich homes and pupil attainment. This chapter has repeatedly referred to the way in which gender, ethnicity and class effects are overlapping and intertwined. In that sense Table 5.3, which shows the performance of different ethnic groups, might have as much to do with class as it has to do with gender. Table 5.4 uses the rather crude measure of free school meals to show how socio-economic status relates to GCSE performance. The relative under-performance of these 80,000 pupils is striking.

In the same way that our response to gender issues needs to become more nuanced, so here we should include the increasing number of children in care and the needs of refugee and asylum seeker children. The challenge for school staff is of course that we cannot necessarily see who these pupils are, but they might well require different kinds of support. Class works in many subtle ways to disadvantage those already disadvantaged. Through language, manners, cultural awareness, etc. the middle classes have a better sense of the 'rules of the game' and so can capitalise better on their educational opportunities.

Another aspect of this class discussion is poverty, the effect of which has been described graphically by Davies (2000: 3–22) and can be seen in the GCSE attainments data in Table 5.5. It is worth noticing in the table the difference in proportional decrease of 5 A*-C when including English and maths from high to low deprivation

Table 5.4 Achievements at GCSE/GNVQ in 2006, by free school meals and gender

	No. of 15-year-olds		% Achieving five or more grades A*–C at GCSE	
	Boys	Girls	Boys	Girls
Free school meals	39,498	38,589	28.7	37.4
Non-free school meals	261,971	252,545	56.2	66

Source: DCSF, February 2007, http://www.dcsf.gov.uk/rsgateway/DB/SFR/s000708/index.shtml.

Table 5.5 Achievement at GCSE (and equivalents) in local council wards at the end of Key Stage 4 in 2006 by Indices of Multiple Deprivation band

	Percentage of pupils at the end of Key Stage 4 achieving GCSE and equivalents	
	5+A*–C grades	5+A*–C grades including English and mathematics
ENGLAND		
0–10% most deprived areas	47.6	29.2
10–20%	50.1	34.3
20–30%	52.0	37.4
30–40%	52.8	39.3
40–50%	56.3	42.6
50–60%	57.5	45.0
60–70%	60.1	47.9
70–80%	61.6	49.1
80–90%	64.8	53.1
90–100% least deprived areas	68.1	57.6

Source: DCSF, January 2007, http://www.dcsf.gov.uk/rsgateway/DB/SFR/s000702/index.shtml.

areas. The second-term Labour government (2001) had a commitment to eradicating child poverty by 2020, but many commentators suggest that the gap between rich and poor is increasing (Gold, 2003; Woodward, 2003). This division is happening partly as a result of legislation aimed at the marketisation of education by Conservative and Labour governments. Typically, more well-educated, middle-class parents have a better understanding of the school system (Power *et al.*, 2003), where to get information from (Hatcher, 1998), how to best support their children's schooling and so generally stand a better chance of maximising the opportunities afforded by the new educational markets (Ball, 2003). Class remains the main factor in educational disadvantage and yet possibly the most difficult factor to define, identify and respond to in a way that will precipitate meaningful and long-term change.

SCHOOL POLICY AND CLASSROOM PRACTICE

In this section we ask you to examine both your school policies and your classroom practice, in the light of the earlier discussion. If schools play a role in the ongoing structuring of inequality in society, albeit not deliberately, then you need to reflect critically upon your practice. This involves examining how your own position and action in a diverse society both help and hinder you from challenging inequity in the classroom. See Task 5.1.

No matter how concerned the school is to promote equity through good policies, implementing them in the classroom is not an easy matter. As you develop as an HLTA, you will be able to consider wider issues of inclusion and diversity. These issues might be regarding language or the textual materials used by pupils. They, like us, are heavily influenced by words and pictures, particularly moving ones. Access to the Web has opened up all sorts of material to pupils, and not all of this is helpful for their academic or social development.

Task 5.1
The school's EO policy

Obtain a copy of the EO policy in your school. Read it and try to identify:

- Who wrote the policy and were parents or pupils involved?
- How old is it?
- Are there any later documents, e.g. working party reports?
- What areas of school life does it cover? Is it the curriculum, playground behaviour, assembly or other aspects of school life? Are any areas of school life omitted from its brief?
- What is the focus of the policy? Is it gender, ethnicity, social class or disability?
- Who knows about the policy?
- Who is responsible for EO in the school?

Task 5.2
Bias and stereotyping in teaching resources

Interrogate a resource used in teaching in your school for bias and stereotyping. Resources include books, worksheets, wall charts, CD-ROMs, video recordings and internet material. Some questions you could use to address this issue include:

- How accurate are the images shown of people and of places?
- Are women and girls shown in non-traditional roles?
- Are men in caring roles?
- Who is shown in a position of authority? Who is the employer, the decision-maker, the technologist? Is it always men? What are the roles of women?
- Are people stereotyped, e.g. black athletes, male scientists, female social workers, male cricketers?
- How and why are people in the developing world depicted? Is it to illustrate malnutrition or their living conditions or the technology employed? Are the images positive or negative?
- What assumptions, if any, are made concerning minority ethnic citizens in the UK?
- What assumptions, if any, are made concerning under-development in the developing world?

Read 'Printed and published materials in schools' in Klein, 1993: 167–80, for further discussion of teaching resources and equal opportunities.

Task 5.3
Who is recruited to
post-16 courses?

If your school has a sixth form, compare the number of pupils in the first year academic and vocational courses, by gender and ethnicity and then compare those numbers with the numbers in the previous years' Year 11 cohort. Identify the subject preferences.

How many pupils left school to carry on education in another institution and what are their gender and ethnic characteristics?

RESPONDING TO DIVERSITY IN THE CLASSROOM

Much of what goes on in the classroom has its origins outside the classroom. These origins include the cultural background of the pupils, the school staff's expectations of pupils, the externally imposed curriculum and the school's ethos realised through its policies and practices.

Expectations of academic performance are often built upon both evidence of what the pupil has done in the past and their social position: male/female; white/black; Irish/Afro-Caribbean; working/middle class; stable/unstable family background. A perceived social position is sometimes, if unconsciously, used by teachers to anticipate pupils' progress and their capacity to overcome difficulties (Noyes, 2003). For example, 'Jimmy is always near the bottom of the class, but what do you expect with his family background?' Or, 'The trouble with Verma is her attitude, she often seems to have a chip on her shoulder and doesn't respond well to discipline even when she is in the wrong. She never gives herself a chance; I'm always having a go at her.' You might have found yourself thinking these things, or even making assumptions about pupils from the time you first saw their names on the register.

You need to consider whether you subconsciously favour asking boys, rather than girls, to answer questions. Similar questions can arise about the way you respond to pupils' answers. Whereas one pupil might make a modest and partly correct response to a question to which your response is praise and support, to another pupil, offering the same level of response, a more critical attitude may be adopted by the teacher.

Are these different responses justified? Is the pupil who received praise gaining support and encouragement from praise; or is the pupil being sent a message that low-level performance is good enough? It is your expectations that direct and control such responses. If, as has been documented in the past about the performance of girls, the praise is implicitly saying, 'You have done as well as can be expected because you are a girl', and the critical response is implying, 'Come on now, you're a boy; you can do better than this', then there is cause for concern.

Such interpretations depend very much on the context.

SUMMARY

In order to promote equity in educational contexts you need to 'understand how children and young people develop and that the progress and well-being of learners are affected by a range of developmental, social, religious, ethnic, cultural and linguistic influences' (TDA, 2007). But this is only the first step! Beyond 'understanding' needs to come action and this involves noticing, critiquing and changing your own practices if necessary, in order to create learning environments in which all pupils can thrive and succeed, and where prejudice is rooted out. Some of the developments that need to take place might involve changing resources, grouping procedures, developing other teaching styles. Through such actions school staff can begin to challenge some of the inequalities in our society. Alternatively, teachers can simply maintain the status quo and, although discourses might welcome diversity, practices might just as easily be maintaining inequity.

Sometimes you may hear someone say, 'I didn't notice their colour, I treat them all the same'. Learning opportunities are enhanced by *not* being 'gender blind' or 'colour blind'. We suggest that not recognising pupil differences, including culture, is just as inadequate a response to teaching demands as the stereotyping of pupils. Pupils learn in different ways and a key part of the differentiated approach to learning is to recognise those differences without placing limits on what can be achieved. This brings us back to your expectations, preconceptions and even prejudices (however unintended). If you expect most Asian girls to be quiet and passive and good at written work, then that is not only what they do, but also perhaps all they do. Individuals respond in different ways to different teachers; you should try to treat each person as an individual and respond to what they do and say, making positive use of your knowledge of the pupils' culture and background. This chapter has addressed inclusion in relation to class, ethnicity and gender. Special educational needs is another dimension of inclusion.

The next two chapters cover learning theories and how you might use these to understand how pupils learn and how to create an effective learning environment.

FURTHER READING

Department for Children, Schools and Families (DCSF). http://www.dcsf.gov. uk (accessed 12 June 2008). The Resources and Tables and Statistics sections of the DCSF website contain extensive information that helps you to consider pupil diversity. The Youth Cohort Study (DCSF, 2005), which can be accessed through the lists of selected keywords, offers longitudinal data over a number of years.

Equal and Human Rights Commission (EOC). http://www.equalityhumanrights. com (accessed 12 June 2008). This site brings together three commissions: the Commission for Racial Equality (CRE), the Disability Rights Commission (DRC) and the Equal Opportunities Commission (EOC). The site is a wealth of information and includes many easily downloadable statistical summaries of social life in Britain. From these reports you can examine the changing nature of the society in which you live and teach. Many reports are repeated on an annual basis.

Gillborn, D. and Mirza, H.S. (2000) *Educational Inequality: Mapping Race, Class and Gender; A Synthesis of Research Evidence*, London: OFSTED. http://www.ofsted. gov. uk (accessed 12 June 2008). This report says that black children failed to share in the dramatic rise in attainment at GCSE, which took place in the 1990s, to the same degree as their white peers. Black and ethnic minority youngsters are disadvantaged in the classroom by an education system which perpetuates existing inequalities.

Differences in the achievements of boys and girls and children of professional and working-class parents are compared and contrasted.

NOTE

1   Adapted from Noyes, A. (2009) 'Responding to Diversity' in Capel, Leask and Turner (2009, 5th edn) *Learning to Teach in the Secondary School.*

6 Pupil Behaviour and Teaching Strategies

Julia Lawrence

INTRODUCTION

Pupil–teacher relationships are a vital part of the effective teaching/learning cycle. The quality of the relationships you establish relates to how you act as a role model in front of pupils, the way you interact with pupils and how you plan and organise learning. Closely connected with the interactions you have and relationships you build with pupils are issues regarding behaviour management. Where relationships are positive, behavioural problems are less likely, but also where there are issues with behaviour they are more likely to be dealt with efficiently and effectively.

OBJECTIVES

By the end of this chapter, you should:

- have a deeper understanding of how to develop and maintain relationships with pupils;
- have an overview of strategies that can be employed to build and develop meaningful relationships with others;
- be able to identify strategies that can be used to manage pupil behaviour;
- be able to identify a range of teaching styles that can be employed within the classroom setting.

This chapter covers the following aspects of the HLTA standards, which are pertinent to *establishing relationships* with children and young people that are respectful, trusting, supportive and constructive; these include being able to *communicate effectively and sensitively* with them, as well as an awareness of effective strategies to promote *positive behaviour.* You can also refer to Appendix 2 to see how this chapter maps onto the standards at the time of publication; if these are revised then updated materials will appear on the website supporting this text.

According to the Training and Development Agency for Schools (TDA, 2007), in order to be effective within the classroom setting HLTAs should 'build and maintain successful relationships with pupils, treat them consistently, with respect and consideration, and [be] concerned for their development as learners'. Whilst it is possible to suggest a range of strategies that can be employed to achieve such an end, it is important when working in schools that you are aware of the policies, expectations, rules and routines that staff and pupils are expected to conform to. It is important that the approaches you adopt conform to the school policy and are consistent with those of the members of staff with whom you work. A lack of consistency may result in pupils being unclear about what is expected of them, which can result in behavioural problems.

Task 6.1
School policy

Obtain a copy of the current policies within your school regarding interactions with pupils and approaches to teaching. These will include behavioural policies, discipline policies, reward policies. Discuss with your class teacher how such policies are reflected in the practices adopted within the classroom and their individual expectations in relation to each of these policies. Discuss the nature of your role in relation to these policies and expectations so that you and the class teacher act consistently. Note any practical examples of these for future reference.

BUILDING POSITIVE RELATIONSHIPS

The development and maintenance of positive relationships both with peers and significant others (including teachers and adults other than teachers (AOTTs)) may impact on pupils' achievement, behaviour and the attitudes they demonstrate towards specific activities (Green, 2002).

The basis for the relationships you develop with pupils is related to the way in which they perceive you. You are in a position of power, and as such you are a role model. As you have expectations of pupils, they also have expectations of you. Consequently, the way your pupils perceive your actions impacts on the way they respond to you (see Chapters 3 and 4 for more information about 'self presentation', which affects pupils' perceptions of you, in particular, through your use of language and appearance, as well as your actions).

Whilst you may be seen as an authority figure, this does not guarantee respect and the development of a positive relationship. A positive relationship between an HLTA and pupil or a teacher and pupil develops as a result of trust, respect and understanding. The relationship you develop with your pupils impacts upon the way they respond to you and consequently how effective you are in the classroom. Pupils want to know where they stand, what the boundaries are, what is acceptable and what is not, but most of all they want consistency. By completing Task 6.1 you should have started to develop such consistency between yourself and your class teacher.

'Teachers' beliefs about students' potential academic achievement become their goals for the students and shape their daily classroom decisions and action including what they believe to be appropriate curricula and instructional practices' (Timperley and Phillips, 2003, p. 3). Teacher expectations have been found to link closely to pupil achievement, with high expectations leading to high achievement when compared to achievement when expectations are low (Green, 2002). Thus, if a teacher or HLTA identifies a pupil as being unlikely to achieve a task, the pupil's behaviour towards the task is likely to result in them being unable to achieve it. The expectation therefore becomes self-fulfilling, with pupils perceiving themselves as failures before they have completed the task. This impacts on pupils' emotional development; in particular, their perceptions of themselves and consequently their self-esteem; an issue covered in more depth in Chapter 7. Thus, it is important that you have high expectations of all pupils with whom you work.

Establishing clear, challenging and achievable expectations is important if positive relationships are to be promoted. The expectations of pupils are reflected in the classroom climate created by the teacher and yourself. Pupils should be made to feel secure, and that their opinion is respected and valued. They should feel confident that if they answer incorrectly they will not be ridiculed, but that it will be seen as part of their own learning process. The way you communicate with your pupils is important in developing relationships with them and is covered in more detail in Chapters 3 and 4.

One aspect of developing relationships with your pupils is the use of names. Pupils need to feel that you know them. We have all been frustrated when someone has called us the wrong name. Pupils feel the same. As well as feeling that you are taking an interest in them, by learning pupils names you can improve your effectiveness by being able to give directed praise and feedback and manage behaviour of individuals.

Task 6.2
Learning pupils' names

When you start working with a new class obtain a class list from the teacher. Each day try to learn the names of three or four pupils in the class. Your school may have pupil photographs that will help you to identify pupils. Aim to have learnt all the pupils' names by the end of your first half-term.

However, communicating with pupils is not just about being able to say their name. It is how you use your voice to encourage, praise, and show interest (see Chapter 4). It is therefore important to understand when praise should be given, the tone you might use to praise a pupil, as opposed to a reprimand, and how you encourage.

Task 6.3
Motivating pupils

Observe a number of members of staff in your school (or if possible in other schools) teaching across a range of subject areas. Using the proforma opposite, record when the teacher used praise, showed encouragement, or reprimanded a pupil. Record how this was done, e.g. use of voice, body language.

Use of voice	Times used	Examples of use
Praise		
Encouragement		
Interest		
Others		

Praise and encouragement can be used to shape pupils' behaviour and therefore assist in managing behaviour effectively. However, it is important that praise and encouragement are used appropriately and consistently, in order that their effectiveness is not undermined. Thus, it might at times be necessary to use sanctions. It is important that as an HLTA your use of praise, encouragement and sanctions is consistent with the class teacher's.

STRATEGIES FOR MANAGING BEHAVIOUR

Effective behaviour management policies and practices prevent much poor behaviour, but also enable you to address any behaviour management issues that do occur. As has already been discussed, pupils need to understand where they stand in terms of acceptable and unacceptable behaviour and much of this is reflected in the relationships you establish with your pupils. How you plan and manage the learning environment impacts on the relationships you develop with pupils and on pupil behaviour.

Misbehaviour can occur as a result of pupil boredom, ability or effort. If pupils find activities over- or under-challenging, they may withdraw from the activity, resulting in off-task behaviour occurring. It is the responsibility of the teacher to plan effectively to ensure that pupils remain actively involved throughout the lesson. The level of difficulty of the tasks set, time allocation and resource organisation all need to be considered carefully. If you as an HLTA are clear of the outline of the lesson you can concentrate more on the pupils and their learning. It is therefore important that you take time to discuss with the class teacher what is planned for the lesson and your role. You may also be encouraged to joint plan with the teacher based on your observations. Some schools provide opportunities for such discussion and joint planning to occur outside of the normal day, so it is worth discussing with your school what provisions they have.

Once the lesson has been planned, effective management is required to ensure that pupils remain on-task. However, some pupils may be off-task. You can support the teacher and pupils by actively observing pupils during lessons, picking up on any off-task behaviour as quickly as possible. You can achieve this through patrolling the classroom, interacting with groups or working with individuals to support pupils in achieving the task set, to reinforce appropriate behaviour and identify and deal with inappropriate behaviour. It is worth noting that at times some pupils may actively seek attention by behaving inappropriately. Although they are clear about what is expected of them, such 'attention seeking' pupils may actively disrupt lessons in order to increase the number of interactions they have with you. You should therefore think carefully of how to react to such situations, which may include limiting your interactions with that pupil.

Many schools adopt report systems where comments are made on pupil behaviour during individual lessons. Alternatively pupils whose behaviour is known to be poor receive rewards if their behaviour is above that which is routinely demonstrated, for example, primary school pupils may receive additional play time.

Task 6.4
Managing behaviour

Obtain a copy of the lesson plan for one lesson you are supporting. Check that you are clear about what is planned. Discuss with the teacher any aspects about which you are not clear. Also, discuss your role in relation to supporting the teacher, particularly in relation to pupils' behaviour. After the lesson identify any aspects of the lesson plan about which you were not clear and how this affected your support of pupils and/ or pupils' behaviour. Also evaluate how effectively you worked with the teacher to manage pupils' behaviour and identify any changes you need to make for the next lesson. Discuss with the teacher concerned.

Developing and maintaining a purposeful learning environment is important for managing behaviour and is the focus of the next section of this chapter.

A PURPOSEFUL LEARNING ENVIRONMENT

As an HLTA, it is your responsibility to work with the class teacher to provide a learning environment appropriate to the learning needs of the pupils. Research suggests that learning is most effective when the learner takes a level of responsibility for their own learning. For example, if a pupil is consistently told what to do, but never has the opportunity to practice or to take responsibility for their learning, they are unlikely to learn effectively. Further, research shows that the way pupils learn most effectively varies between individuals. Thus, an effective teacher uses a range of strategies to improve learning. The teaching models and strategies adopted by the teacher to deliver the lesson content must reflect the learning needs of the individuals. As an HLTA you may be required to work with small groups of pupils. It is therefore important that you understand the learning needs of the pupils with whom you work. As you become more knowledgeable about the pupils in your class, this will become easier. However, you should liaise with the class teacher during the planning stage in order to address any potential issues.

MODELS OF TEACHING

Models of teaching relate to the approaches adopted by teachers and others to allow learning to take place. A range of models of teaching can be identified. Table 6.1 provides a description of two of the main models used within teaching.

The model, or pedagogical approach adopted, is reflected in the lesson objectives, and in the teaching strategies adopted as appropriate to achieving these objectives.

TEACHING STRATEGIES

Teaching strategies or methods are the approaches adopted by teachers to promote pupils' learning. Whilst a range of approaches can be identified, all are based on movement along a continuum, from teacher-focused, where the teacher is in control of the decisions made, to pupil-focused, where the pupil is in control of the decisions, or from a direct approach, where information is transferred, to an indirect approach, where understanding is encouraged.

One frequently used categorisation of teaching strategies is that of Mosston and Ashworth (2002). A summary of the teaching strategies they identified, along with examples, is in Table 6.2.

Task 6.5
Teaching strategies

Observe teachers you support or staff in your school teaching across a range of ages/subject areas.

*   What teaching strategies are adopted by each teacher?
*   Does the teacher use a range of strategies within the lesson?
*   How do the strategies link to the learning objectives of the lesson?
*   How do pupils respond to the strategies adopted?
*   What other strategies could be used to deliver the same lesson content?
*   What does each of these strategies mean for the way you work with pupils in lessons?

Table 6.1 Models of teaching

Approach	Description	How the approach works
Direct/teacher-focused	The focus is on the transmission of knowledge focused on skill development.	The teaching approach is authoritarian. The pupils copy the teacher and each other to develop basic skills, which they can subsequently adopt and adapt within other contexts. Guidelines regarding expectations are clear. The teacher controls the class and therefore can monitor safety.
Indirect/ teaching for understanding/ pupil-focused	The focus is on pupils developing their understanding based on their own experiences. Approaches reflect the need for pupils to develop conceptual understanding.	Pupils use knowledge they already have and apply this to different contexts, allowing for the development of understanding. Pupils are active in their learning allowing them to become more independent in their learning. Differentiation is encouraged.

Table 6.2 Mosston and Ashworth's teaching strategies (adapted from Mosston and Ashworth, 2002)

Strategy	Focus	Examples
Command	The teacher is autocratic and controls the learning experience.	The teacher relays a large amount of information to pupils. Pupils respond to these instructions.
Practice	Whilst the teacher sets the task pupils are given the opportunity to practice, allowing the teacher to circulate around the class and provide feedback where appropriate.	The teacher explains how to solve a mathematical problem. The teacher then sets a series of problems for the pupils to solving using that technique and monitors the performance of the pupils.
Reciprocal	The teacher provides resources that allow pupils to observe themselves and others and give feedback based on the activities undertaken.	In physical education the teacher may provide a resource card identifying the key teaching points of a skill against which pupils assess each other's performances and provide feedback as relevant.
Self-check	The teacher provides a checklist for pupils against which they can assesses themselves and identify targets for further development.	In science the teacher provides a checklist regarding the structure of an experiment. The pupils check their experiment against the checklist, identify where they have/ have not met the requirements and set targets regarding how they need to change their experiment to improve.
Inclusion	The focus is on individual learning with pupils provided with activities differentiated to their needs.	In English pupils are looking at composition but different groups have a different focus according to their level of attainment.
Guided discovery	The teacher provides a series of activities/questions aimed at guiding pupils to achievement of the intended learning outcome.	In science pupils conduct an experiment with prompts provided by the teacher regarding things they should consider. The solution is the same for all pupils.
Divergent	Whilst the achievement of an intended learning outcome remains the focus of the task, the pupils are encouraged to find alternative ways of solving a problem.	In design and technology pupils are provided with the opportunity to find, through trial and error, the most appropriate design for a children's toy.
Learner's design	Using an agreed framework, and with support from the teacher, pupils design and carry out defined task.	Pupils plan and complete a piece of coursework. The pupils use a framework provided either by the teacher or exam board. The teacher monitors progress.
Learner initiated	Pupils identify a learning experience and develop a programme through which their own defined learning outcomes can be achieved. The teacher remains involved but only if support is needed.	Pupils identify an area of development and identify a series of activities which will allow them to achieve development in this area. The pupils provide a log of the activities they have undertaken and reflect on how they have achieved their learning objectives.
Self-teaching	The teacher is not involved. The pupil works independently.	A pupil may engage in independent study for which they have received no guidance or monitoring.

Factors influencing the adoption of teaching strategies

Whilst there are a number of possible teaching strategies that can be used, the selection and use of strategies is influenced by a range of factors. These include:

1   *Time.* A more direct teaching strategy may be employed when time is short or where there is a need to deliver large amounts of information in a short time period or where deadlines need to be fulfilled.
2   *Teacher preference.* Teachers tend to adopt strategies they are most comfortable with or have greater experience of. For example, they might adopt strategies they experienced as a learner, or ones through which they learnt best. Some teachers model themselves on other members of staff, for example, their training mentor.
3   *Behavioural control.* Where pupil behaviour is an issue, the teacher may adopt a strategy that is perceived to allow greater control to be exerted – normally a direct or teacher-centred strategy.
4   *Safety.* Where activities have a high safety risk, for example, throwing events in physical education or some science experiments, the teacher may adopt a more teacher-centred than pupil-centred approach.
5   *The ability of the pupils.* The level of pupil development may impact on pupils' ability to work effectively. For example, some pupils may find it difficult to interact with other pupils during a problem solving activity, limiting the effectiveness of the learning achieved. Consequently, the movement towards pupil-centred approaches should be integrated gradually into the pupil experience.
6   *The focus of the activity.* Within the planning of a lesson, the learning objectives will be closely linked to the strategies adopted. For example, if an objective is to develop problem solving skills, an approach that allows pupils to interact with each other is needed.

SUMMARY

From reading this chapter you should have started to reflect on the impact of your interactions with pupils on the relationships you develop and hence on both their learning and behaviour. Reflecting on the needs of the pupils in your class is an important aspect of your work with pupils to support their learning and to support the work of the teacher. The teaching strategy adopted reflects the planned learning activity. However, paramount to any planning is what it is intended that pupils learn from the activity, i.e. the objectives and the most appropriate ways to achieve this. You should seek out opportunities to observe and implement a range of strategies, related to both behavioural management and teaching, and reflect on their effectiveness.

The next chapter examines how pupils learn by introducing you to the key theories of learning and outlines the processes of cognitive development in children.

FURTHER READING

DfES (2003) *Key Stage 3 National Strategy Key Messages: Pedagogy and Practice.* London: HMSO (downloadable from http://www.standards.dfes.gov.uk). This document provides an overview of the Key Stage 3 National Strategy identifying key aspects of learning and teaching. It provides definitions and practical applications of a range of approaches to teaching.

DfES (2004) *Pedagogy and Practice: Teaching and Learning in Secondary Schools, Unit 2: teaching models.* London HMSO (downloadable from http://www.standards.dfes.gov.uk). This unit encourages reflection on how different teaching approaches can be utilised within classroom settings to fulfil differing teaching aims.

Muijs D. & Reynolds, D. (2005) *Effective teaching: Evidence and Practice,* 2nd edn. London: Sage Publications. This book provides evidence-based practice regarding teaching. It covers in detail the main teaching approaches adopted within the school setting.

7 Understanding how Pupils Learn

Julia Lawrence

INTRODUCTION

All pupils are individuals. You will be aware from observations in school that pupils differ greatly in their development. As an HLTA, it is important that you have a knowledge and understanding of the processes of child development to enable you to provide an effective learning environment, with learning experiences designed to meet the individual needs of pupils with whom you work.

Whilst the stages of development are similar for all pupils, the time and speed of development vary. It is therefore important that you not only have an understanding of the developmental stages appropriate to the age of the pupils with whom you work, but also those stages prior to and post that stage.

Child development can be looked at in a number of domains: physical, intellectual, linguistic, social and emotional. Whilst the school is one influence on a child's overall development, the environment in which the child is reared, in particular the home and socio-cultural environment, is also very influential.

OBJECTIVES

By the end of this chapter, you should:

- have an overview of key theories and processes of learning and development;
- have a deeper understanding of the processes of learning and development;
- be able to identify pupils who may not necessarily be developing in line with other children of their age.

This chapter covers the HLTA standards that refer to understanding the *key factors that affect children and young people's learning* and knowing about the need to support learners in accessing the curriculum in accordance with the *special educational needs* (SEN) code of practice; also those that refer to understanding factors affecting motivation so that you are able to *motivate* learners and advance their learning, and planning for *inclusion*. You can also refer to Appendix 2 to see how this chapter maps onto the standards at the time of publication; if these are revised then updated materials will appear on the website supporting this text.

THEORIES OF DEVELOPMENT

The main theories of development refer to cognitive development, with behavioural and constructivist theories. In addition, consideration will be given to language development, socio-emotional development and physical development.

PHYSICAL DEVELOPMENT

Physical development is not just associated with growth and development, but includes a range of fine and gross motor skills that the child develops over time. For example:

- locomotor skills – walking, running, jumping, hopping, skipping, climbing;
- manipulative skills – throwing, catching, writing, cutting, kicking;
- stability skills – bending, stretching, rolling, balancing.

A child's physical development impacts on and is reflected in the motor skills the child is able to perform.

Whilst many of the skills identified above are performed in a physical context (e.g. in physical education lessons), they develop through play and, in the case of some of the manipulative skills, through activities undertaken in a classroom environment. Thus, it is important for opportunities for developing physical and motor skills to be included in a range of lessons.

Task 7.1
Physical development

From the list of motor skills identified above, choose one from each sub-group (locomotor, manipulative, stability). (You may want to choose the specific activities in light of the development needs of pupils with whom you are working.) For each skill, describe the key characteristics of that skill (see further readings at the end of the chapter).

Using your descriptions as a guide, observe three children performing the skill (this may be in a classroom lesson, a practical lesson or in the playground). For each child describe how they perform the skills and compare this to how the skill should be performed. Identify what the child needs to do to improve each skill and plan a learning activity to assist in this.

Use this information to help plan opportunities for the child to improve that skill in the next and future lessons.

COGNITIVE DEVELOPMENT

There are a number of theories of how a child learns and develops knowledge and understanding. These include theories which view learning as a modification of behaviour (behavioural theories), theories which view learning as constructed (constructivist theories) and theories which view the mind as a machine (information processing theories). Whilst other theories exist, the next part of this chapter looks at behavioural, constructivist and information processing theories as these are the most common theoretical practices evident in schools. Additional literature sources are provided at the end of the chapter should you wish to further your understanding of other theories.

Behavioural theories

Behaviourists view learning as the modification of behaviour. Examples of behavioural theorists include Skinner and Bandura. Skinner, whose work came to prominence in the 1950s, developed the concept of operant conditioning in which a central focus is reinforcing appropriate behaviour. Thus, correct behaviour is reinforced through rewards and incorrect behaviour is punished. An example in a classroom setting would be when pupils receive commendations or merit points for good behaviour and detentions for poor behaviour. Bandura (1989) argued that learning is a result of behaviour modification. He developed a more learner-centred approach. His social learning theory suggests that children model their behaviour on what they see and hear around them, modelling behaviours they identify as positive in respect of desirability. The concept of self-efficacy emerged from his work. Self-efficacy is 'beliefs about one's own effectiveness and competence that guides one's ability to cope with particular situations such as academic problems at school … [developed] through observations, watching others comment on their own behaviour and developing standards based on these experiences' (Kennan, 2002, p. 25). Thus, the individual learner bases their behaviour on that of role models. In practice, this type of learning may be seen through some pupils copying behaviours from others. Such behaviours may be physical (for example how they react to situations), affective (for example their attitudes), or social (for example the way they interact with others). More specifically, a normally well-behaved child may act inappropriately if they feel that will make them more accepted by the rest of the group. Alternatively, pupils may use pupils in higher school years as role models.

Constructivist theories

Constructivist theories are based on children being active in their own learning, with learning being constructed as a result of the child's experiences. Whilst some (e.g. Piaget) believe these experiences occur between the child and the environment and are therefore solitary interactions, others (e.g. Vygotsky) believe that learning occurs as a result of interactions between the environment and other individuals. However, learning requires a level of interaction between the learner and an external influence.

Piaget

According to Piaget (1976), a child constructs learning through exploration and manipulation, which results in the development of schema, that is 'interrelated sets of actions, memories, thoughts or strategies which are employed to predict and understand the environment' (Keenan, 2002, p.119–20). This is a staged process of learning, whereby a child adapts prior knowledge in light of the changing environment. The efficiency by which this is achieved is reflected by a child's ability to organise and apply existing knowledge to different situations. For Piaget, such development occurs as a result of four key stages: the sensorimotor; preoperational; concrete operation; and formal operational (see Table 7.1).

For those HLTAs working at the Foundation stage or Key Stage 1, most children are likely to be in the preoperational stage. At this stage, development occurs rapidly and predominantly in the areas of language, number, pictorial and spatial representations, and the ways in which children play. Children focus only upon themselves and may be viewed as egocentric. As a result, they do not take on board the views of others. Further, their general understanding limits their ability to focus on more than one activity at a time. Their understanding is limited to what they have experienced. Thus, for example, a child given a container of sand and asked to pour it into another container of a different size and shape cannot understand that although the physical appearance of the sand has changed the amount of sand is still the same. This is known as the principle of reversibility.

For those HLTAs working at Key Stage 2, most children are likely to be in the concrete operational stage. In this stage a child begins to be able to link situations to previous experiences and therefore starts to be able to predict and suggest reasons for events. Consequently, links should be made to prior learning as much as possible.

For HLTAs working at Key Stages 3 and 4, most pupils are at the formal operational stage. They have greater conceptual understanding and as a result are able to hypothesise and predict outcomes to situations. The development of thinking skills should be encouraged.

Table 7.1 Piaget's stages of cognitive development

Age	Stage	Behaviours
Birth – 18 months	Sensorimotor	Learn through senses Learn through reflexes Manipulate materials
18 months – 6 years	Preoperational	Form ideas based on perceptions Can only focus on one variable at a time Over generalise based on limited experience
6 years – 12 years	Concrete operational	Form ideas based on reasoning Limit thinking to objects and familiar events
12 years and older	Formal operational	Think conceptually Think hypothetically

(Adapted from Smith, Cowie & Blades, 1998, p. 336).

Task 7.2
Cognitive development

Using your understanding of models of teaching from Chapter 6, observe a lesson and reflect upon how the model adopted linked to the theories of development.

Discuss with your class teacher how the principles of theories of learning can be applied within the classroom.

When planning your next learning episode, reflect on which theories you are applying.

Vygotsky

Vygotsky (1994) believed development to be an interactive, constructive process between an individual and their environment, reflecting both social and cultural influences. Development occurs on two levels: the interpersonal level (between the individual and others) and the intrapersonal (within the individual). Whilst Vygotsky acknowledged stages of development, for him these were not specifically age related; rather, they occur in what he referred to as periods of sensitivity (see Table 7.2), re-inforcing the individual nature of learning.

Whilst Vygotsky saw development occurring progressively through periods of sensitivity, he also proposed that for learning to take place an individual must work within a zone of proximal development (ZPD) that is 'the distance between the most difficult task a child can do alone, and the most difficult a child can do with help' (Garhart-Mooney, 2000, p. 83). Scaffolding learning experiences helps with this. Scaffolding is 'an interactive process in which the adults adjust the amount and type of support they offer to the child, leading to the eventual mastery of the skill being taught' (Keenan, 2002, p. 134). Effective scaffolding requires the provision of learning opportunities that are towards the limits of the learner's ZPD. Where the learner is able to cope with the new demands of the task, the level of input from the teacher/HLTA should be reduced. Where the learner is unable to achieve the task, the activity should be modified and the level of input increased. This results in clear differentiation in the learning environment to meet the needs of individual pupils in the class. As an HLTA, it is likely that you will work with pupils who need greater input to help them scaffold. However, it is important for you to know when you need to have greater input.

Table 7.2 Vygotsky's periods of sensitivity

Period of sensitivity	Learning experienced	Behaviours demonstrated
1	Discovery learning through trial and error	Enhancement of spatial awareness Tendency to talk to oneself
2	Learning through direct experiences	Concept development Able to group and link situations more appropriately Internalisation of speech
3	Learning through association	Application of concepts and generalisations Application of rules and regulations

The social and environmental aspects of Vygotsky's theory also raise important issues regarding the teacher and HLTA. Vygotsky believed that learning occurs as a result of social interactions with experts who possess a greater level of knowledge than the child. Such experts may be teachers, HLTAs or children at a higher level of development. However, it is conceivable that children of a similar developmental age may respond differently to instruction. Thus, within the learning environment, and in particular the classroom setting, peer support has been used to provide enhanced learning opportunities. In practice, this may be demonstrated by pupils of differing abilities working together on a task or by pupils working across year groups with older pupils providing support and development – for example in reading.

Approaches to teaching vary according to the objectives of a lesson and the content, as well as to individual beliefs about approaches to learning (see Chapter 6). From a socially constructive perspective, strategies such as differentiation may be adopted. Differentiation involves adapting or differentiating activities to allow all pupils to access the learning experience. For example, more able pupils may be given more challenging activities, the equipment pupils use to complete the activity may vary or pupils may be given different amounts of time to complete a task. Other strategies include collaboration, which involves pupils working together in small groups to achieve the task, and reciprocal teaching, whereby pupils act as the teacher by observing and giving feedback to another pupils based on criteria identified by the teacher.

> **Task 7.3**
> **Supporting differentiation, collaboration and reciprocal teaching**
>
> Select three learning activities – one each in which the following strategies are used specifically:
>
> * Differentiation
> * Collaboration
> * Reciprocal teaching
>
> Discuss with the teacher how you are going to support the teaching method. After the lesson, evaluate the effectiveness of your role. Discuss with the teacher and consider how you might improve your effectiveness in future.

Information processing theories

Information processing theories are based on the premise that information is taken in by the senses and transferred to our working memory. The working memory, also referred to as the short-term memory, has a limited capacity for storage and therefore unless information is rehearsed or practiced it is lost. Storage capacity can be enhanced by organising the information entered into it, e.g. by 'chunking' bits of information together into manageable pieces. Thus, at the early stages of development, the ability of a child to link and recall information is limited. As a child matures and develops, their ability to store information increases as they develop the ability to link situations to previous experiences and are able to transfer the information into their long-term memory. A child's ability to encode and retrieve information develops with age until retrieval from long-term memory becomes automatic. See Chapter 8 for further discussion on this theory.

LANGUAGE DEVELOPMENT

Language development is associated with sound (phonology), meaning (semantics), grammar (syntax) and the effective use of language (pragmatics). The inclusion of subjects, verbs and objects is common among languages. Consequently, it is assumed that a child learns naturally the language to which they are exposed, provided that they are at what is deemed the 'critical time', that being the time/age when they learn the language most effectively; predominantly during early to middle childhood (ages 6 to 10).

EMOTIONAL DEVELOPMENT

Erikson (1995) identified a number of stages of emotional development: changes in how a person feels about themselves and others. He referred to these as the eight stages of man. As children mature, they become more aware of themselves and their environment and start to compare themselves to those around them, therefore becoming more self-conscious. For Erikson, emotional development occurs as a result of the resolution of 'crises'; a crisis being a situation that the individual must experience and resolve before moving on. Table 7.3 shows Erikson's eight stages.

Most pupils you are working with are likely to be in the stages of autonomy vs. shame; initiative vs. guilt; industry vs. inferiority; or identity vs. identity diffusion. For example, in the industry vs. inferiority stage the crisis may manifest itself through pupils attempting increasingly complex problems. Where they are successful, they become more industrious – as evidenced by their level of motivation. Where failure occurs, they may become withdrawn. The development of self-identity is manifested in their social characteristics, friendship groups and general behaviour. However, it is important to acknowledge that during crises pupils may seek to develop attachment relationships. Such relationships reflect the need of a child to form a close attachment with a person they perceive can provide them with support and security. It is therefore important that clear boundaries are established within relationships formed.

Linked to the need for security and support is the formation of friendships amongst pupils. The role of friendship varies across ages. At Foundation and Key Stage 1, friendships are play related and therefore relate to the activities undertaken. At Key Stage 2 and early Key Stage 3, friendships are associated with social acceptance and trust. During late Key Stage 3 and Key Stage 4 friendships become more intimate and based on mutual understanding. However, friendships are fragile, particularly during Key Stage 2 and early Key Stage 3, resulting, at times, in the natural breakdown of established friendships as they no longer fulfil the individual's needs. As an HLTA, you should look to develop strategies that allow you to support children during this time. Keenan (2005) provides further detail on friendship formation.

Table 7.3 Erikson's eight stages of man

Stage of development	Age	Crisis
Trust vs. mistrust	Birth to 1 year	Developing a sense of trust in caregivers, then environment, oneself
Autonomy vs. shame and doubt	1 to 3 years	Develop a sense of autonomy and independence from the caregiver
Initiative vs. guilt	3 to 6 years	Developing a sense of mastery over aspects of one's environment, coping with challenges and assumptions of increasing responsibility
Industry vs. inferiority	6 years to adolescence	Mastering intellectual and social challenges
Identity vs. identity diffusion	Adolescence (12 to 20 years)	Developing a self-identity, that is, a knowledge of what kind of person one is
Intimacy vs. isolation	Young adulthood (20 to 40 years)	Developing stable and intimate relationships with another person
Generativity vs. stagnation	Middle adulthood (40 to 60 years)	Creating something so that one can avoid feelings of stagnation
Integrity vs. despair	Old age (60 years plus)	Evaluating one's life by looking back; developing a sense of integrity through this evaluative process

(From Keenan, 2005, p. 23).

PLAY AS A TOOL FOR CHILD DEVELOPMENT

The various theories of development suggest that a range of learning opportunities need to be provided. These opportunities may occur at home, at school or in out-of-school activities. Play can be included as one of these opportunities. As with friendships, the type and role of play vary across ages, although its key aims remain consistent in relation to concept development, exploration of roles and interactions, and the development of social competence.

Between the ages of two and five, play reflects conflict between right and wrong, the development of reciprocal relationships, and the development of hierarchies amongst children. Between the ages of six and 12, play becomes more structured as the involvement of adults is reduced. The focus at this time is peer relationships. With an increase in the number of relationships developing between a child and others, for example in school, at clubs, or as members of voluntary organisations, an increase in the peer group (number of friends) occurs. This results in the development of a hierarchy of relationships dependent upon their role and social/cultural significance. However, as a result of linguistic development, verbal aggression becomes more prevalent. Ages 12 to 18 see a restructuring of the relationship between an adolescent and their parents/caregivers. Relationships between peers become more intimate, with the formation of cohesive cliques and much larger groups.

Throughout, the importance of peer acceptance is paramount. Such acceptance may be related to a person's name, attractiveness (particularly amongst girls), gender and age. A person's ability or inability to become an accepted member of the group impacts upon their overall emotional development. Pupils who are not accepted may see themselves as marginalised, resulting in them withdrawing from situations as well as developing strong attachments to members of authority. Further, in order to be fully accepted, they may demonstrate behaviours that do not correspond with what is normally expected of them, for example they may become rude when normally polite, or demotivated when normally motivated. As with the breakdown of friendships, as an HLTA you should discuss with your class teachers the strategies and support employed within your school. Where possible look to attend continuing professional development courses (CPD) to support you in this.

Task 7.4
Play

Observe a group of children during a lesson and/or at break or lunchtime. Identify:

- the different roles the children take;
- the presence of any hierarchies within the group;
- how roles are assigned between the children;
- the dominant individuals within the group and how they interact with the other children;
- those children who do not become involved.

Discuss your findings with the class teacher. Identify any potential issues which may arise and suggest appropriate strategies to limit their impact.

Children, like adults, suffer stress and anxiety as they develop. A child's emotional development is directly related to their physical and cognitive development. Where development is not occurring, a child may become depressed, which slows development. Associated with this may be low self-esteem and a lack of motivation.

Coopersmith (1967, pp. 4–5) defines self-esteem as, 'The evaluation which the individual makes and customarily maintains with regard to himself: it expresses an attitude of approval or disapproval, and indicates the extent to which the individual believes himself capable, significant, successful and worthy. In short, self-esteem is a personal judgement of worthiness that is expressed in the attitudes the individual holds towards himself.'

Self-esteem is multi-dimensional, varying across contexts and situations. Thus, self-esteem is higher in an activity which children enjoy and perceive themselves to be good at than in an activity which is not enjoyable and in which they perceive themselves to be poor. However, it is important to note that much of a child's perception of ability is based on the responses they receive from those around them. For example, if a child is told that they are no good at something, they perceive themselves as poor and therefore have lower self-esteem. Related to this is the phenomenon referred to as 'the self-fulfilling prophecy' (see Chapter 6), which in part can be linked to the expectations of teaches and HLTAs, as well as the child's perceptions of your actions and manner towards them (see Chapters 3 and 4 for more detail on communicating and interacting with pupils). The issue of self-esteem and performance then has clear implications for how assessment is recorded (this is covered in more detail in Chapter 9).

Self-esteem varies between genders and ages. Boys generally demonstrate higher self-esteem than girls; in secondary schools this reflects to some extent the earlier onset of puberty experienced by girls. This may be demonstrated in the classroom setting by the reluctance of individuals to become involved in situations which they feel are a threat to their self-esteem, for example when reading out loud or having to give a demonstration or explain an answer. It therefore becomes important that as an HLTA you look at the strategies employed by yourself, the class teacher and other members of staff to promote learning environments that value the contribution of all pupils.

One time at which fluctuations in self-esteem are particularly evident is during the transfer from primary to secondary school, as a result of a change in friendship groups, the environment in which they work and the teaching approaches. As children mature, their self-esteem becomes more stable and as a result the impact of their peers on their self-esteem lessens. Clear links can therefore be seen between self-esteem and the emotional development profile developed by Erikson in respect of the crises of mastery of intellect and social challenges as well as the development of one's self-identity.

Henry (2004) views the teacher as a facilitator of learning and, hence, a developer of self-esteem. If a teacher has an authoritarian approach, children may become dependent on the teacher. This results in low self-esteem and is reflected in either obedient or deviant behaviour. This links to the work of Vygotsky in respect of the need to adopt strategies in the classroom which encourage the development of confidence in one's own ability, resulting in higher self-esteem.

Motivation is closely linked to self-esteem. A child who perceives themselves as capable and enjoys the activity undertaken is likely to have a high level of motivation to continue with that activity. Bouffard and Couture (2003, p. 19) suggest motivation to be 'a construct that is built out of individual learning activities and experiences, and varies from one situation to another'. Thus, as with self-esteem, motivation is multidimensional and therefore varies according to the activity undertaken. It has been suggested (e.g. Gage and Berliner, 1984) that an individual's motivation is associated with the factors identified in Table 7.4. These should therefore form the basis of your reflective reasoning for the inclusion of all activities within your work as an HLTA.

The premise of interest and enjoyment supports the work of Dewey (1938) who identified that children learn best when they are engaged in a meaningful activity. He concluded that learning needs to have a purpose and be highly organised. Central to his philosophy were the following questions, which you could consider when organising a learning activity:

- How does it expand children's knowledge?
- How will it help children grow?
- What skills are being developed?
- How will it help children's understanding?

Task 7.5 Observing pupil motivation
Using Table 7.4 and the four questions identified by Dewey, evaluate a learning activity you have recently undertaken with pupils with whom you work. You should think about what the intended learning outcomes were and the extent to which these were achieved. Use you evaluation to inform your next learning activity.

So far, this chapter has outlined some key aspects of child development relevant to you as an HLTA. Emerging from the information provided and the tasks set should be an understanding of how different children progress at different rates. However, it is important to understand that some children may not progress in line with other children of their age in one or more domain. Some of these pupils may have special educational needs.

SPECIAL EDUCATIONAL NEEDS

It is likely that within the classes with which you work there are a number of pupils who are defined as having special educational needs (SEN), i.e. they have 'learning difficulties which call for special educational provision to be made for him/her' or 's/he has a significantly greater difficulty in learning than the majority of children his/her age' (Education Act, 1981). Indeed, it is likely that as an HLTA you are supporting some of them. Table 7.5 shows the areas of need as outlined by the Code of Practice (DfES, 2001).

Table 7.4 Factors to consider regarding motivation

Factor	Explanation	Questions to ask self
Interest	The activity must hold some form of interest for the individual	Does the activity interest the participant? Is the activity challenging?
Need	The activity must satisfy a need within the individual	Does the activity link to the learning needs of the pupils?
Value	The activity must have attached value, and therefore be seen to be beneficial	What value does this activity have to the individual?
Attitude	The activity must instil a positive attitude	Are the pupils positive about the activity?
Aspiration	The activity must be seen to be important and part of a wider plan	How is the activity linked to the overall scheme of work?
Incentives	Rewards must be available from the activity	What rewards will the pupils receive if they complete the activity?

Table 7.5 Areas of need: code of practice (DfES, 2001)

Specific need	Sub-groups	Example
Cognitive and learning needs	Specific Learning Difficulty (SpLD) Moderate Learning Difficulty (MLD) Severe Learning Difficulty (SLD) Profound and Multiple Learning Difficulty (PMLD)	SpLD – Dyslexia
Behaviour, emotional and social development needs	Behaviour, Emotional and Social Difficulty (BESD)	Attention Deficit Hyperkinetic Disorder (ADHD)
Communication and interaction needs	Speech, Language and Communication Needs (SLCN) Autistics Spectrum Disorder (ASD)	English as an Additional Language (EAL) Asperger's Syndrome
Sensory and / or physical needs	Visual Impairment (VI) Hearing Impairment (HI) Multi-Sensory Impairment (MSI) Physical Disability (PD)	VI – total blindness HI – partial deafness

As an HLTA you need to ensure that wherever possible all pupils are able to access the work you provide. Whilst specific strategies for the inclusion of pupils with SEN have been developed, these strategies are appropriate for all pupils due to their generic nature. Key questions that you may consider when planning for the inclusion of all pupils are shown in Table 7.6.

Using the learning activity from Task 7.5, reflect upon the extent to which you have planned for inclusion. Modify your plan in light of your evaluation. Once you have completed the learning activity produce an evaluation of the success of your inclusion strategies.

Additional, more specific information regarding individual learning needs can be found in the suggested further reading section of this chapter.

SUMMARY

From reading this chapter you should have begun to understand some aspects of children's physical, intellectual, linguistic and social/emotional development and the

Table 7.6 Questions to consider when developing an inclusive classroom

- How do you communicate with the pupils?

- How do you ensure that they understand?

- How do you plan for full participation?

- What strategies do you employ to manage pupil behaviour?

- How do you plan to deal with issues concerning pupils' emotions?

- How have you planned to ensure that all pupils can and will complete the tasks you have set?

- What skills are pupils developing during your lesson?

predetermined stages of development in the majority of children. Whilst developmental stages may be similar, the age at which development occurs varies according to the individual child. Further, you should understand that social and cultural factors impact on this development. Play and social interactions form an important role in children's development.

Your understanding of the theories of learning should also have developed, allowing you to reflect on the approaches adopted in your classrooms to ensure that pupils learn effectively and efficiently.

The next chapter continues to examine more recent theories of learning and introduces you to learning styles and strategies.

FURTHER READING

Association of Teachers and Lecturers (2002) *Achievement for All: Working with Children with Special Educational Needs in Mainstream Schools and Colleges*, London: Association of Teachers and Lecturers. This publication, which is free to members, gives some strategies that can be employed to ensure the inclusion of pupils with special educational needs. However, the strategies identified are equally applicable to all pupils.

Gallahue, D.L. and Ozmun, J.C. (1995) *Understanding Motor Development: Infants, Children, Adolescents, Adults*, 3rd edn, Iowa: Brown and Benchmark Publishers. This text provides detail regarding children's development, focusing more specifically on their motor development, although reference is made to other developmental domains.

Kennan, T. (2005) *An Introduction to Child Development*, London: Sage. This provides an introduction to the field of child development.

8 Understanding Learning Theories and Strategies

Diana Burton, Kath Lee and Sarah Younie

INTRODUCTION

This chapter builds on Chapter 7, introducing theories of learning in more detail and exploring your role in supporting learning and teaching. As you work through this chapter and as your knowledge about learning and teaching increases, you will feel confident to try out and evaluate different approaches. Theories about learning and teaching provide a framework for you to use in the analysis of learning situations and a language to describe the learning taking place. As you become more experienced, you develop more insight into how pupils learn and you can place these theories in the wider context. This chapter is adapted from Burton (2009) and we recommend you read her work for greater detail.

OBJECTIVES

By the end of this chapter you should:

- demonstrate your knowledge and understanding of how pupils make progress in their learning and their learning styles and strategies;
- be aware of the ways pupils learn;
- consider the latest theories about what learning involves;
- be able to use a range of strategies to create a purposeful learning environment;
- be able to reflect on your own learning preferences.

This chapter covers the following aspects of the standards for HLTAs which are pertinent to the management of the learning process. First, you must demonstrate sufficient knowledge and understanding to be able to help the pupils you work with make progress with their learning. Specifically, you are required to know the *key factors that can affect the way pupils learn* as well as a range of strategies to establish a purposeful learning environment. You can look at Appendix 2 to see how this chapter maps onto the standards at the time of publication; if these are revised then updated materials will appear on the website supporting this text.

The primary aim of your work is to support pupils in their learning. The interaction between the activities of teaching and the outcomes of learning are critical. In order to facilitate effective learning, you must first have an understanding of how pupils learn. There are a number of theories of how children learn and a selection is discussed in the next section.

LEARNING THEORIES

There are a range of theories about learning drawn from the field of educational psychology that have been influential in shaping pedagogy. These include Piaget's theory of *cognitive development*, which holds that learners acquire knowledge through active exploration of their world (Piaget, 1932, 1954) and *social constructivism,* derived from Vygotsky's work (1978), which explains knowledge acquisition through social interaction, with learners actively constructing their individual meanings as their interactions with others help them to make meaning. See Chapter 7 for further detail on these theories. A further key theory is *information processing*, in which knowledge is viewed as pieces of information that are analysed within the short-term memory and stored in the long-term memory alongside other related concepts. It is this theory that we now turn our attention to.

When information is received, short- and long-term memory work together dynamically. Information is processed in short-term memory, where information and retrieved existing knowledge are used together to make meaning of new situations. This meaningful learning can then be stored in long-term memory. The more pupils are able both to take in the information and to link it to existing knowledge, the greater the probability that it is processed rather than disregarded. So a teacher's role is to link new knowledge with existing knowledge the learner might have. However, as McCormick and Leask (2005) explain, learners can only take in a certain amount of information in a set time. There is limitation of capacity and bottlenecks can occur when a lot of information is transmitted. When bottlenecks occur, not all of the transmitted information is received in the memory. Therefore it is important that you do not deliver too much information too quickly or digress too much.

It is also important to develop a teaching strategy in which information is provided in small amounts and key features are signalled so that pupils can concentrate on what is important and feel secure when seeking clarification.

Using information processing theory, the following task will help you to reflect on developing your support strategies for learning and teaching in the classroom. You can begin with your scheme of work to identify where you may use different approaches as identified in the task. In partnership with your teacher, you can go on to develop your ideas in individual lessons and, when you analyse your work, to consider the effectiveness of the approaches used.

Task 8.1
Helping pupils process new information

Consider one area of work your class will be covering soon. How might you apply information processing theory to help pupils learn? For example:

• What method of presentation of information could you use to identify and stress key information so that it is processed?
• How will you link the new material to pupils' existing knowledge?
• How will you use patterns and mnemonics to help pupils remember?

In addition to the learning theories discussed so far, there are newer theories, such as situated cognition. This depicts knowledge as shared, ongoing interactions between people, and is associated with communities of practice (Lave and Wenger, 1991; Davis and Sumara, 1997). The first three referenced theories, however, cognitive developmentalism, social constructivism and information processing, have been the most influential theories in the UK in developing understanding of how pupils learn.

When you are talking of learning with others, it is easy to assume everyone has the same understanding of the term. However, there are many notions about what learning is. Sometimes it is used to mean what the learner does in response to teaching – 'If you don't listen to me, you won't learn this' which equates learning with memorisation. This is a simple way to describe what the process of learning involves. West Burnham (2004, 2007) offers the following model of learning, which attempts to capture the range of our understanding about what is involved in learning (see Table 8.1).

This model is not hierarchical, but descriptive of the characteristics of different modes of learning. In some contexts, it is entirely appropriate to engage pupils in shallow or single loop learning, for example when learning mathematical times tables by rote. Deep or double loop learners know how to create knowledge; they are reflective about what they learn and how they learn. Profound or triple loop learning is not only about 'the what' and 'the how', but also 'the why'.

Table 8.1 Model of learning (after West Burnham, 2007, p. 25)

Learning is …	Shallow (What?)	Deep (How?)	Profound (Why?)
Means	Memorisation	Reflection	Intuition
Outcomes	Information	Knowledge	Wisdom
Evidence	Replication	Understanding	Meaning
Motivation	Extrinsic	Intrinsic	Authentic
Attitudes	Compliance	Interpretation	Creativity
Relationships	Dependence	Interdependence	Independence
	Single loop	Double loop	Triple loop

West Burnham (2007) describes it thus: as a visitor to Italy, you may have a small vocabulary and some knowledge of grammar, which is sufficient for a tourist's needs. This would be classified as shallow learning. Whereas, deep learning of Italian would allow you to converse with locals in their language and have a sound grasp of the language and understanding. Profound learning means that the level of engagement in the Italian language would enable you to consume and contribute to Italian culture. West Burnham (2007) maintains there is a clear incremental shift akin to the progression from novice to expert. This can be likened to Lave and Wenger's (1991) understanding of learning whereby a learner moves from the periphery to the centre in a community of practice. For example, a newly qualified teacher (novice) becomes more expert in their practice through engagement with experienced/expert others. So, whilst West Burnham (2007) offers an individualised model of learning from shallow to deep to profound, Lave and Wenger (1991) offer a collaborative/practice based model. However, both models of learning share the understanding that deep learning or situated learning is the creation of meaning.

It is the responsibility of the teacher and you, as the HLTA, to enable pupils to access all levels of learning by involving them in a variety of teaching and learning strategies.

LEARNING AND TEACHING STRATEGIES

A key way of developing your understanding of learning and teaching strategies is to plan lessons with a teacher and discuss decisions about how to approach a particular lesson with a particular pupil or group of pupils. As Burton (2009) stresses, when introducing a new concept, the reasons a group of pupils may fail to understand could be associated with any one of the following:

- their levels of attention;
- their interest and motivation;
- their physical and emotional state of readiness to learn.

Other factors to be considered would be:

- the relevance of the new material to the pupils;
- how well the new concept fits into the structure of the topic;
- the level of difficulty of the concept;
- the clarity of speech and explanation;
- the accessibility of any new terminology used;
- the questioning and summaries given at intervals during the explanation.

It is also important to consider the knowledge pupils already possess when helping them to progress their learning, which is a key requirement of your role as an HLTA. Unfortunately, identifying this knowledge is not as simple as recalling what was taught to the pupils last time as each pupil will vary in how they process and gain knowledge. Where accessing prior knowledge is most effective, the pupil is questioned about what was learned last lesson or given a brief resume of the point reached in a topic. Such strategies are very important because, if previous learning has been effective, information is stored by pupils in their long-term memories and needs to be retrieved.

Using effective and well–structured schemes of work supports more effective learning, i.e. learning that is retained and develops understanding. Psychologists explain that this is due to the material being introduced to pupils according to the inherent conceptual structure of the topic (Ausubel, 1968; Gagne 1977; Stones, 1992). This allows the information to be stored using a logical structure, which is easier to recall because the brain can process it more easily in the first instance, linking the new ideas to ones which already exist in the memory.

Burton (2009) explains that teaching in the context of information processing theories stresses the application of knowledge and skills to new situations. The teacher's role is to help pupils find new ways of recalling previous knowledge, solving problems, formulating hypotheses and so on. Montgomery (1996) advocates the use of games and simulations, because they facilitate critical thinking and encourage connections to be made between areas of subject knowledge or experience. One strategy that can help pupils to develop their thinking is 'pupil talk'. For further information on this see the work of Mercer (2000) and further discussion on pupil talk in Chapter 4.

Task 8.2
Developing pupils'
learning through talk

Consider how often opportunities are made for pupils to talk in lessons, to each other, and to you. Listen to how the talk develops the learning of each member of a small group of pupils. Notice how well-timed and focused intervention from you moves the learning on.

One of the most popular commentators on how people think is Gardner (1983, 2006), who has developed a theory of multiple intelligences. Some people find this a helpful framework for thinking about the way pupils learn. See Table 8.2.

For instance, in a science project about the processes involved in the formation of volcanoes, pupils might be given the opportunity to explain the process in a number

Table 8.2 Gardner's forms of intelligence

Gardner's work is well worth reading. He identifies core intelligences as:
• linguistic intelligence: the ability to work with words;
• logical-mathematical intelligence: related to mathematics and logic;
• musical intelligence: musical abilities;
• spatial intelligence: the ability to visualise space accurately;
• bodily-kinesthetic intelligence: the ability to understand how to use one's body effectively;
• interpersonal intelligence: the ability to understand people;
• intrapersonal intelligence: an understanding of oneself, emotions and impact on others;
• naturalistic intelligence: an ability to categorise and recognise differences between plants and other artefacts.

of ways, such as drawing a flow-chart (spatial intelligence) or setting the words to the tune of a well-known song (musical intelligence). In this way the types of expression pupils could employ were extended so that each child had greater access to the curriculum and could tackle a task at the relevant level of complexity depending on the strength of a particular intelligence. This approach might have application in terms of differentiating tasks in the classroom.

Each of the key theories of cognitive development, social constructivism and information processing considers how learning occurs as an internal process. However, you also need to consider what is known about pupils' *learning styles* and complementary *learning strategies*, as this equips you to further understand pupils' individual differences.

LEARNING STYLES, AND STRATEGIES

As Bartlett and Burton (2007) note, there is often confusion about what constitutes learning style as distinct from learning strategy. Psychologists argue that a cognitive or *learning style* is considered to be a fairly fixed characteristic of an individual, which may be distinguished from *learning strategies*, which are the ways learners cope with situations and tasks. Strategies may vary from time to time and may be learned and developed. Styles, by contrast, are static and are relatively in-built features of the individual (Riding and Cheema, 1991).

Learning styles

There is currently a great deal of interest amongst teachers in identifying whether learners are predominantly visual, auditory or kinaesthetic learners (*VAK*, Dryden and Vos, 2001), i.e. they learn best through seeing, hearing or doing. However, there are a huge number of such classifications based on different psychological constructs and using a range of measurement tools. Some of these ideas, such as the VAK construct and preferred environmental conditions or stimuli for learning, have been incorporated, along with a range of other ideas, such as neuro-linguistic programming, into accelerated learning programmes such as that of Alastair Smith (Smith and Call, 2002). See Burton (2007) for a critique of these ideas.

It can be attractively simple to feel that we can categorise pupils into fixed learning approaches or styles and then teach to a formula that such a categorisation suggests, but we know that learning is complex and context-dependent, with pupils employing different approaches in different settings. It is important that you take a careful approach to the growing industry of learning style classification and do not readily pigeonhole pupils and fail to provide a range of media and activities to maximise access for all to the curriculum. Influential government agencies have lent a spurious validity to the over-used VAK construct. They tell us that the majority of pupils are not likely to be auditory learners (DfES, 2003). This implies that you should consider an alternative *strategy* to talk or use talk in conjunction with visual aids, for example, a PowerPoint presentation. For a full overview of the range of research into individual learning styles consult Riding (2002) in the further reading section of this chapter.

It is important to understand how innate features may affect how learners' process information. Many researchers have worked in this area, but Riding and Rayner (1998) have proposed that the various conceptualisations may be grouped into two principal cognitive styles:

- *Wholist-analytic style* – whether an individual tends to process information in whole sections (wholist) or in parts (analytics);
- *Verbal-imagery style* – whether an individual is inclined to represent information in words (verbalist) or in mental pictures (imagers).

The two styles operate as dimensions so a person may be at either end of the dimension or somewhere along it (see Bartlett and Burton 2007 for further details).

Task 8.3
Reflecting on your own learning style

Think about what your own learning style might be. Do you:

- approach essay or report writing incrementally, step by step, piecing together the various parts or do you like to have a broad idea of the whole document before you start writing?
- experience lots of images when you are thinking about something or do you find yourself thinking in words?

Discuss your style with other HLTAs. In doing so you are developing your meta-cognitive knowledge, i.e. 'knowing how you think and learn', about your own way of learning.

Riding and Rayner (1998) explain that these styles are involuntary so it is important to be aware that pupils' habitual learning styles vary. Both teachers and HLTAs need to ensure they provide a variety of media in which pupils can work and be assessed. It would not be sensible to present information only in written form; if illustrations are added, this allows 'imagers' easier access to it. Similarly, 'wholist' pupils are assisted by having an overview of the topic before starting whilst 'analytics' benefit from summaries after they have been working on information.

Learning strategies

Pupils bring personal attitudes and motivation to their learning and these shape their approach to learning.

Entwistle (1981) described different orientations to learning, such as being oriented towards discovering the meaning of a topic or being oriented simply to scratch the surface. Combinations of these orientations with extrinsic factors, such as the need to pass examinations or the love of a subject, were thought to lead to learning strategies which characterised certain approaches to study, from 'deep' to 'surface' levels of thinking.

Biggs (1993) explained that a pupil's motivation influences the learning strategies they adopt. For example, a pupil with an instrumental (surface) motivation is likely to adopt reproducing or rote-learning (surface) strategies. For example, the need to pass exams will motivate a pupil to develop learning strategies which include well-ordered resources, time management and efficiency. Deep motivation results from an intrinsic desire to learn and can inspire the use of deep strategies wherein understanding and meaning are emphasised.

Pupils whose motivations and strategies are compatible with the demands made by learning tasks are likely to perform well. Pupils are likely to be less successful where motivation and strategy are incompatible with task demand. For example, a pupil with a deep approach to learning is constrained by superficial task design such as a requirement for short answers whilst a pupil with a strong motivation to achieve may be deterred if he/she is set very long-term, vague objectives.

Burton (2009) argues that successful learning, if defined in terms of understanding and permanence, is linked with deep and deep-achieving approaches, which can be taught. The achievement-driven context within which school pupils in England currently learn, however, could militate against the possibility of teaching deep approaches because of time constraints. An important development in this regard is the UK government's emphasis on personalised learning and the use of interactive technology to this end (Leadbeater 2004).

SUMMARY

After reading this chapter, you should have an understanding of learning theories and the different learning and teaching strategies you can adopt to progress pupil learning. You should be aware that pupils have different preferred learning styles and that you should provide learning experiences that enable them to access subject knowledge and make meaning of it. You should appreciate that the learning process continually draws on the interaction between your knowledge of the pupils, of the subject and of how learning happens. You should have gained an awareness of your own preferred learning style and an appreciation of your own predilection to use learning strategies that complement this style. However, you will now know it is important to employ a range of learning strategies that cater for all the different learning styles of your pupils.

The next chapter covers monitoring and assessment of pupils' progress.

FURTHER READING

Bee, H. and Boyd, D. (2006) *The Developing Child*, 11th edn, London: Allyn and Bacon.

Child, D. (2007) *Psychology and the Teacher*, 8th edn, New York, London: Continuum. Both of the above excellent books will take you further into theories of learning and child development.

Riding, R. (2002) *School Learning and Cognitive Styles*, London: David Fulton. Riding incorporates recent psychological developments on individual learning differences with practical classroom applications. He presents new approaches in three key areas: processing capacity, cognitive style and understanding the structure of knowledge. These are central to the understanding of pupil differences and address our perception of how pupils can be helped to learn, why pupils find some aspects of their school work difficult, and why pupils behave as they do.

Shayer, M. and Adey, P. (eds) (2002) *Learning Intelligence: Cognitive Acceleration Across the Curriculum from 5 to 15 Years,* Buckingham; Philadelphia: Open University Press. This edited collection describes how children's general ability to process information – their 'intelligence' – can be improved by appropriate cognitive acceleration methods. Through examples of cognitive acceleration in a variety of contexts, from Year 1 to Year 9 and in science, mathematics and arts subjects, each chapter draws on research or development experience to describe effects of cognitive acceleration programmes. The book also looks at the psychological theory that underlies cognitive acceleration.

9 Monitoring and Assessing Pupils

Andrea Raiker

INTRODUCTION

This chapter outlines your role in relation to the monitoring and assessment of pupils under the direction of the teacher(s) that you work with. Your role is to support the teachers in evaluating pupils' progress through a range of assessment activities. This chapter outlines the differences between formative, summative and diagnostic assessments and considers the need for monitoring, recording and reporting, and your role in supporting these.

OBJECTIVES

By the end of this chapter, you should:

- have an understanding of the nature of and need for assessment;
- understand the ranges of assessment;
- be aware of the nature of and need for monitoring;
- be clear about feedback and the construction of knowledge;
- understand the relationship between assessment, monitoring, recording and reporting.

This chapter addresses the professional standards for HLTAs that refer to the monitoring and assessment of pupils' progress. You can also refer to Appendix 2 to see how this chapter maps onto the standards at the time of publication; if these are revised then updated materials will appear on the website supporting this text.

According to the standards, HLTAs must show that:

they can work effectively with individual pupils, small groups and whole classes under the direction and supervision of a qualified teacher, and that they can contribute to a range of teaching and learning activities in the areas where they have expertise. *They require all HLTAs to demonstrate skills in planning, monitoring, assessment* and class management.

(TDA 2006: 5, my italics)

This quotation, from the Training and Development Agency's Professional Standards publication for higher level teaching assistants (2006), comes under the heading Teaching and Learning Activities. A clear link is made between learning/teaching and monitoring/assessment. By reading this chapter, and working through the practical tasks, you will come to an understanding of how these different aspects of classroom activity interlink to form a holistic approach to educating our young people.

In the first part of this chapter we consider the HLTA Standards, which state that you must be able 'to support teachers in evaluating pupils' progress through a range of assessment activities'. This will involve considering the nature of assessment, and its essential components. You are invited to complete a task that will increase your awareness of assessment, in the classroom and in life outside. It is crucial for your role as an HLTA that you understand the reasons for effective assessment for learning. Only then will it become incorporated into your view of learning and teaching as an essential element. Finally we look at the differences between formative, summative and diagnostic assessments.

The second part of this chapter discusses the requirement stated in the standard that HLTAs will 'monitor pupils' responses to learning tasks and modify their approach accordingly'. This involves considering what is meant by monitoring, how tasks become learning tasks and ways in which you can change your teaching style in light of the information you gather. This means thinking about your part in the planning process through considering the impact of Assessment for Learning (AfL). AfL is introduced in terms of the 10 principles identified by the Assessment Reform Group, on whose work the government's current approach to classroom assessment is based. You will be introduced to putting AfL into practice through the techniques of sharing learning goals, using effective questioning techniques, and peer and self-assessment. You will be invited to take part in an activity whereby you link AfL techniques to a case study.

The next part of the chapter reflects upon the standards that HLTAs will 'monitor pupils' participation and progress, providing feedback to teachers, and giving constructive support to pupils as they learn'. Observation techniques will be discussed in more detail in Chapter 12. However, as observation is an essential part of monitoring to provide feedback, it will also be considered here.

The latter part of the chapter addresses the standards that require you to 'contribute to the maintenance and analysis of pupils' progress through the keeping of records'. This last section presents different ways of recording assessments, both formal and informal. There is an increasing emphasis on using electronic means for information management and transfer, so the concept of e-portfolios is introduced. The chapter concludes with a discussion on reporting.

Although monitoring and assessment is considered in four different parts, as identified above, it must be remembered that this is done to highlight their distinctive features as defined in the standards. In the classroom you will find that monitoring and assessment interweave and interact. It is a case of identifying the parts so that there can be greater understanding of the whole.

UNDERSTANDING ASSESSMENT

As an HLTA you are expected to be able to support teachers in evaluating pupils' progress through a range of assessment activities.

What is assessment?

Assessment is the means whereby the structured learning that occurs at school through teaching is measured. A more formal definition is that assessment is a means of measuring ability at a particular point in time in a specified learning area or areas. By ability we mean the mental capacity to learn and to reason. Every pupil has this capacity. Gardner (1993) has argued that individuals have multiple abilities or, as he terms them, intelligences, each contributing in varying degrees to an individual's performance in a particular area. For example, a pupil's ability in mathematics and science will determine to some degree his/her attainment in technology.

It follows that assessment of a pupil's ability in any of the subjects studied at secondary school is going to be difficult, and it certainly is not going to provide a complete and accurate representation of what the pupil knows. However, by carefully considering what is to be assessed and for what purpose, collecting the right information and considering it alongside other records on pupil performance, reasonable judgements can be made about the learning that has taken place.

> **Task 9.1**
> **Understanding assessment as reflection and evaluation**
>
> Think of an activity in which you have been involved that has enabled you to learn something new, for example to drive, to cook a new recipe for friends, to put up shelves. Consider the process in which you engaged to complete the activity.
>
> This process would have involved an objective, maybe some instruction from an 'expert', some trial and error learning, an outcome, and some reflection and evaluation of that outcome. The 'reflection and evaluation of that outcome' is a form of assessment of something that has happened to you. Assessing the learning of others is more difficult.
>
> Think of a classroom activity at school, again in terms of the process outlined above. Write down the learning that occurred. Now consider:
>
> * How do you know?
> * How sure can you be?
> * What other evidence might you need to be able to make an informed judgement?

This is important because learning in secondary schools is structured according to assessment schemes laid down by external examination boards in schemes of work.

The resulting programmes progress by lessons building on those that came before. If the pupil's learning has been faulty, or incomplete, their subsequent learning will be adversely affected.

Why assess?

We assess because assessment enables analysis of learning aimed at raising standards. You will have heard of such tests as the Key Stage SATs, GCSEs or even the QCA tests. This kind of assessment is called *summative assessment* and usually takes place at the end of a school year or key stage. These are assessments *of* learning, and have well-established grading and reporting procedures linked to them. The results of summative testing informs not only teachers, but parents, members of the senior management team, governors, the local authority and government.

In this section we are talking about assessment *for* learning, or *formative assessment*. In the classroom, formative assessment of individual pupils is made to ascertain the degree to which learning objectives have been met. Future teaching can then be tailored to the learning needs of each pupil. In the past this kind of assessment was undertaken solely by teaching professionals. However, research has shown us that pupils are not empty vessels into which adults pour knowledge and understanding. Each individual has to construct his/her own view of the world based on reasons that have meaning for him/her. This cognitive view of how pupils learn means recognition has been given to pupils having an understanding of what they do and do not know. So they too must be brought into the assessment process so that teaching activities can be modified to stretch them towards fulfilling their potential. The teaching professional and the pupil both give feedback on the assessment with the teacher taking the lead as the 'expert' on what is needed to meet the learning objective. It is the pupil's task to achieve the learning objective. Research by the Gillingham Partnership Formative Assessment Project 2000–2001 (2003) and the Assessment Reform Group (2003) has demonstrated that this approach increases pupils' learning.

The government has acknowledged the importance of assessment in its adherence to AfL. It sees effective assessment as essential, not only in terms of individual pupils' achievement, but also of its own success in hitting its published targets, particularly the percentages of pupils attaining Level 4 in literacy and numeracy in the Key Stage 2 SATs. This level is seen as the key to successful study in secondary school and future job prospects.

So assessment in the classroom has several functions:

- It enables each pupil to learn more effectively, because s/he is given feedback that is targeted on individual needs and is meaningful.
- It enables the teacher to teach more effectively because focused information is produced on each pupil. Those that need extra support are identified as well as those that need more challenging work.
- Teachers are able to give parents detailed information on their child's progress.
- Should a pupil move school, accurate records of progress and attainment can be forwarded to ease transition and prevent regression in learning.
- School management teams will have evidence on which to base targets aimed at whole school improvement.

- Government, both local and national, will be able to assess the performance of individual schools and identify where the best of good practice is to be found. This practice can then be disseminated with the aim of increasing overall school improvement.

FORMS OF ASSESSMENT

Formative assessment. Much formative assessment will be *informal.* For example, you might be working with a group of pupils on adverbs. Each pupil has a small whiteboard and a marker pen. You ask your pupils to write down an adverb that can be used with the verb 'run'. When the pupils show their whiteboards, you will be able to assess quickly whether individuals or the whole group are firm in that knowledge, or that adverbs should be revisited.

Diagnostic tests. It is part of the HLTA's role to focus on individual pupils' needs and abilities. Many pupils will be enabled by having individual targets within the structure of class lessons based on learning objectives and differentiated activities and tasks. More of this in the next section. However, there will be some pupils who need more than differentiated tasks. The following quote from the Primary Strategy is equally applicable to secondary education: 'Increasing the focus … will be the single most important force in mainstreaming (without diluting) the support that is given to pupils with special educational needs' (Primary Strategy, 2003, 4.5).

When individual assessment reveals that further assessment is needed to identify a particular educational need, *diagnostic tests* are carried out. These tests are summative in the sense that the results from them will inform stakeholders outside the classroom, for example parents, the senior management team, etc. However, they are also formative in that strategies will be put into place to enable the pupil to close the gap between his/her achievement and class learning objectives.

Mock and graded tests. Occasionally teachers administer interim tests to their classes. Examples are table tests, spelling tests, end of project/half-termly/termly tests and past test papers for SATs and QCA tests. These are not formal tests in that the results will not be published. The results will be used to identify areas of development for individual pupils, a group of pupils or the class as a whole so that gaps in knowledge and understanding can be addressed before the pupils sit their *graded tests.* These are summative tests on which pupils will be graded.

Task 9.2
Identifying different forms of assessment in your context

Consider the assessments that you would carry out with your pupils during a working day, a working week, a term:

- Which types of assessments did you carry out, and how often?
- Which type of assessment was most useful to you?
- Which assessments were of most use to the wider society?
- Can you draw any conclusions?

MONITORING PUPILS' PROGRESS

The standards outline that HLTAs are to monitor pupils' responses to learning tasks and modify their approach accordingly.

What is monitoring?

Monitoring is the process whereby you collect information for a particular purpose. This information can be termed *evidence*. The standards require monitoring so that individual pupils' needs can be identified in terms of meeting learning objectives. Learning tasks are created by your teacher, and on occasion by yourself, so that the pupil can learn to meet the learning objectives. Giving an individual pupil the greatest opportunity to learn means that you have to tailor the learning task, the information you give and the questions to ask to meet those needs. By monitoring individual pupils' responses to current learning tasks, the information you give and the questions you ask, you will be able to plan future tasks, information and questions to enhance learning for each particular child.

Monitoring is always linked with evaluation. There is no point in monitoring and collecting evidence about an individual pupil unless you do something with it to improve his/her learning chances. This means that judgements have to be made. Why did that strategy not work? Is this a behavioural or cognitive issue? What could I have done better? How will I know that this change has helped him to learn? These are the types of question you must ask yourself in order to make effective decisions on what aspects of your teaching and the lesson plan to change.

With a moment's thought you will link this to the discussion on assessment above. Monitoring is very much formative assessment. As you will see in Figure 9.1, which links assessment with planning and record keeping, monitoring feeds into all aspects of the learning/teaching cycle:

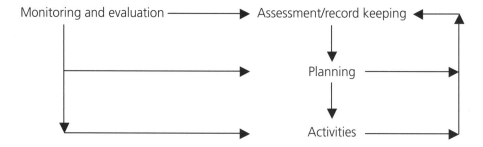

Figure 9.1 Learning/teaching cycle

You will see by the following quotation from the Assessment Reform Group's 1999 publication, *Assessment for Learning: Beyond the Black Box,* that monitoring, or collecting evidence, for a purpose is very much at the heart of AfL:

> 'Assessment for Learning is the process of seeking and interpreting evidence for use by learners and their teachers to decide where the learners are in their learning, where they need to go and how best to get there.'
>
> (Assessment Reform Group, 1999: 3)

The purpose of AfL is to raise achievement. As discussed earlier, it is now recognised by government that pupils construct their own learning. Therefore they need to be included in the assessment of their learning and take ownership of it. If pupils understand what it is they are learning, and how far along that learning journey they have travelled, with help from you and their teachers they will be able to complete the journey.

The Assessment Reform Group (1999) identified 10 principles for AfL, all based on outcomes from their research. The 10 principles are:

1   *AfL is part of effective planning.* Planning, including assessment, should be focused on learning objectives, but should not be rigid. There should be opportunities for emerging ideas and skills to be fostered and assessed. How pupils and teachers are to assess learning should be fully integrated into lesson planning.

2   *AfL should focus on how pupils learn.* Pupils should be encouraged to understand that how they learn is as important as what they learn.

3   *AfL is central to classroom practice.* Teachers should become aware that much of what they do is assessment. Activities, observation and questioning are all directed towards providing information on which teachers can make informed judgements about the learning that is taking place.

4   *AfL is a key professional skill.* The analysis and interpretation of verbal and visual information and the feeding back of resulting judgements are research techniques. Opportunities must be given to trainees and teachers to develop these important skills.

5   *AfL recognises the emotional aspect of learning.* Feedback, whether marks, grades or comments, can result in feelings of confusion, anxiety, guilt and failure that will affect a pupil's confidence and enthusiasm. Therefore teachers should devise means of giving constructive and sensitive feedback wherever possible.

6   *AfL recognises the importance of motivation.* The research by the Assessment Reform Group on which AfL is based demonstrated that pupils' motivation was raised when they felt in control of their learning and could choose how to improve their work. Assessment methods should embrace pupils' enthusiasm for learning and need for autonomy by promoting progress and achievement rather than failure.

7   *AfL recognises the importance of shared understanding of goals.* If a pupil does not know where they are going, how do they know how to get there and when they have arrived? Understanding and commitment to learning occurs when pupils and teachers have goals that are mutually understood, when a way to achieving them has been mutually understood and clear criteria of success in achieving the goals are mutually understood.

8   *AfL recognises that learners need to know how to improve.* Teachers should give pupils direction in how to build on their strengths and address their area for development, and provide opportunities for them to do so.

9   *AfL develops pupils' capacity to self-assess.* This is an essential life skill. As adults we are independent learners of knowledge, skills and understanding. Pupils must be given the opportunity and guidance to reflect on their work and develop skills of self-assessment to move from being dependent to independent learners.

10   *AfL acknowledges the range of possible achievements.* Achievement in all areas of education, within school and outside, should be recognised and celebrated.

AfL in practice

To put AfL into practice in the classroom, the 10 principles can be concentrated into the following four areas. Observance of the first three will enable you to meet the requirement that you know how to monitor pupils' responses to learning tasks and modify their approach accordingly, whilst adherence to the last, will enable you to meet the requirement that you can monitor pupils' participation and progress, provide feedback to teachers, and give constructive support to pupils as they learn. The four areas are:

1   Sharing learning goals.
2   Using effective questioning techniques.
3   Peer and self-assessment.
4   Using marking and feedback strategies.

Sharing learning goals

The learning objective (sometimes called a learning intention or learning goal) is what a teacher plans pupils will know, understand or be able to do at the end of a lesson or project. The activities created will enable the pupils to fulfil that learning objective. By the teacher sharing the learning objective, the pupils know the point of the lesson. As pupils are the ones doing the learning, much of the responsibility for its achievement is passed to them. The objective also gives direction as to where most effort should be made. For example, if the learning objective is to 'apply the use of tables to everyday problems', most effort should not be placed on the use of description of the settings to these problems. However, it would be different if the learning objective was 'to use adjectives effectively to describe settings'. Lastly, the learning objective generates key points that the pupils need to understand as steps towards its successful achievement, known as success criteria. This encourages the self-evaluation of a pupil's learning.

To share learning objectives effectively with the pupils the following must be observed:

- The learning intention should be written where all the pupils can see.
- It should be shared with the pupils, using pupil-friendly language.
- You should talk with the pupils on what they will be able to do as a result of the lesson.
- You should summarise the key points (success criteria) that will enable the pupils to ultimately achieve the learning objective. Involve the pupils in producing them.
- You must ensure that pupils know what these criteria are by writing them down.
- You must tell the pupils the reasons for the learning objective. This should be related to everyday life or further learning. This is sometimes termed an 'aside' and is given verbally, as it would be too time-consuming to write down.

Language should be kept simple and focused. Use such phrases as, 'We are learning to ... ', 'Remember to ...' or 'What you need to do to achieve this is ...'.

It is important to remember that the aim of AfL is the promotion of a learning culture where learning can be transferred to solve problems. This means that learning

Table 9.1 Learning intentions and success criteria

Learning intention	That materials can be classified as solid, liquid or gas, and that some are difficult to classify.
Success criteria	• That you *know* why some materials are difficult to classify. • That you can describe solids, liquids and gases. • That you can design a key to classify materials as solid, liquid or gas.

must not be identified with activities. Activities are the vehicles of learning, not the learning itself. Therefore we should be using language such as that given above, e.g. 'Today we are learning how water gets into the sky to fall as rain', rather than 'Today we are going to investigate the water cycle'. Effective AfL strategy demands that learning intentions and success criteria should be closely linked. The language used for both should refer to learning, thinking, knowing and using skills. There are some examples in Table 9.1 to clarify what we mean.

A learning intention for art might be, 'We are learning to record and analyse first-hand observations'. The success criteria for this would be the production of a sketchbook containing studies and other information based on the pupil's experience, organised so that ideas can be followed by other people.

Task 9.3
Learning goals

Consider the following:

• Are learning goals/intentions/objectives being used in the classroom where you work? Are the pupils being encouraged to use success criteria?
• If they are, assess their effect on the pupils' learning.
• If they are not, what would your success criteria be to judge the effectiveness of the lesson? Assess the work of some pupils by your success criteria. Would the pupils' learning have been enhanced if your success criteria had been used?

Using effective questioning techniques

Research by the author (Raiker 2002) as well as others has shown that most questions asked by teachers are closed. The teacher has one answer in her mind when asking a question and she is looking for pupils to confirm her own thinking. AfL encourages teachers and you as an HLTA to move away, where possible, from closed questioning to open-ended questions that require pupils to respond after having thought more deeply about the way they construct knowledge and understanding. In doing so, pupils will have to demonstrate their use and understanding of subject specific language. For example, the research by the author discussed above demonstrated that problems in the teaching and learning of mathematical concepts in part arise from, and are compounded by, the spoken language involved.

Open-ended questions you can ask to encourage higher level thinking could be:

- How do you know ... ?
- How would you describe ... ?
- What would you mean if you said ... ?
- What are the similarities you can see in ... ?
- Give me an example from your own experience of ... ?

This list is not exhaustive. Such questions can be applied to any subject area.

It is interesting to note that the average response time to a question before choosing a pupil is about a second. This is not enough for most pupils to have understood the language in which the question has been given, or to have related the question to their prior learning, selected the prior learning which is going to enable them to formulate their reply, structure their reply and put their hands up. You may find difficult the silence that occurs between a question being asked and a response being given, and will make that span of time as short as possible. However, there are various strategies that can be used to keep the quick thinkers engaged whilst giving others the time they need.

The thumbs-up-close-to-the-chest strategy for pupils who have the answer works well. By children showing that they know the answer to your question by quietly placing their raised thumbs on their chests, slower children are less likely to be distracted or intimidated by waving hands and such exclamations as 'I know!' or 'Easy!' Slowly counting to five before asking for hands up is another. Research has demonstrated that about five seconds is a reasonable length of time for most pupils to construct responses to questions. See Chapter 4 for further information on the use of questioning to aid learning.

Peer and self-assessment

Self-assessment tackles pupils' feelings of failure, which we have seen is a significant inhibitor to learning. It does this by encouraging the pupils to judge their own work and not compare its quality, and hence themselves, with that of others. An integrated aspect of the concept of ranking is failure.

AfL's approach includes introducing the pupils to the inevitability of finding difficulty in learning and giving them strategies to overcome these difficulties. We have already met the principal strategies – shared success criteria linked to shared learning goals. With self-assessment, a pupil applies these to judge the quality of their own work. QCA has recommended that pupils need to:

- reflect on their own work;
- be supported to admit problems without risk to self-esteem;
- be given time to work problems out (http://www.qca.org.uk).

Then, with feedback from the teacher or yourself as an HLTA, the pupil decides what has to be done to improve the quality of his/her work to meet the success criteria, which will lead to the learning objective. Sportsmen and women use this approach regularly when they train to achieve 'personal bests', known as PBs.

One method of increasing pupils' understanding of how to use success criteria to improve work is to give them examples of other, unknown, pupils' work that does or does not meet learning objectives. The pupils are then asked to decide what they would do to improve the work. Another advantage of this peer assessment is that pupils become aware that there is more than one way to improve work.

Of course, you must ensure the pupils know the meaning of self-assessment, or self-evaluation as it is sometimes termed. They can do this by having a list of self-help questions on display and referring to it throughout their lessons. This list could contain the following:

- Don't worry or panic.
- Solving problems = learning.
- Read again, think it through.
- Ask a friend.
- Use class resources – number squares, dictionaries etc.
- Ask an adult.

Another important aspect of counteracting the fear of failure is sympathetic use of language. The Formative Assessment Project (2001) revealed that teachers became aware that, as a result of using explicit language to help pupils see difficulty as part of the learning process, their pupils stopped being afraid of making mistakes and were more able to admit to finding work difficult. In particular, pupils with special needs demonstrated increased confidence.

PROVIDING FEEDBACK

You are expected as an HLTA to monitor pupils' participation and progress, provide feedback to teachers, and give constructive support to pupils as they learn.

Using marking and feedback strategies

You will have realised by now that the different parts into which this chapter is organised interlink and are part of a whole approach. Feedback has two elements, oral and written. The written element is more commonly known as marking. Both oral and written feedback should be closely linked to learning goals and give clear direction to improvement. Giving a mark of 6 out of 10, or writing 'Good work!' on a piece of writing is no longer appropriate.

Feedback can be given to individuals, groups or to the class as a whole. However, it is not a one-way process. AfL needs pupils to respond to the feedback with positive comments on how that feedback reflects on their work and with suggestions for its improvement. This means that time must be built into the activities and plenaries of lessons for pupils to be encouraged to be reflective, communicative and responsive *whilst the feedback is still relevant.* For pupils to able to reveal themselves in this way means that there has to be mutual trust between teachers, HLTAs and their classes. This will be embodied in the school's ethos, but takes time to become established between the teacher, yourself and the pupils. The following guidelines applied systematically by yourself will enable effective feedback to be embedded in your practice:

- Find the positives about a pupil's work. Discussions on improvement are more likely to succeed if the pupil believes that s/he is on the way to achieving the learning objective.

- AfL is not about giving a pupil the complete solution as soon as s/he meets difficulties. 'Scaffolding' the pupil whilst s/he reflects and finds his/her own way forward will promote independent learning.
- If a pupil continually makes the same mistake following feedback, s/he should be encouraged to consider alternative solutions. Being repeatedly 'stuck' invites feelings of frustration and failure leading to decline in motivation.
- In working towards meeting individual success criteria, pupils should not be allowed to lose sight of the learning objective. Learning must not be compartmentalised. The results of this approach can be seen in the lack of transfer of skills learned in literacy lessons to creative writing. A pupil can know what an adjective is, having completed a worksheet, but then not be able to use adjectives in writing a story.
- Oral feedback is more effective than written feedback. Oral feedback allows for further discussion and clarification. Written feedback does not.

RECORD KEEPING AND REPORTING

The standards outline that HLTAs are expected to contribute to maintaining and analysing records of pupils' progress.

Recording

Although much formative assessment is made and kept in your and your teacher's minds, formal records will have to be kept for various reasons and purposes. Firstly, there is a legal requirement for individual pupil attainment targets to be kept in each curriculum subject. Records of formative assessment inform the planning of future lessons based on individual pupils' learning. These provide evidence of what a pupil knows, understands and can do, and the progress s/he has made. Analysis of formative records gives information for reports to parents and the pupil's next teacher and/or school, enable judgements to be made on target setting, and form the bases of discussion with parents at consultation evenings.

Records of formative assessment also enable teachers to make summative judgements for their teacher assessments. It is useful to remember that formative and summative assessments are closely connected. Summative assessment should be used formatively to support future learning. Your records of formative assessments will eventually be given to the class teacher so that his/her records on work covered and progress made can be updated. So you can see that your records of formative assessment have a summative element too in that they record work completed at whatever standard.

Different schools have different record keeping systems that you and all teachers in the school are expected to use. This ensures that all teachers and HLTAs are recording evidence in a similar way. This is essential if reliable judgements are to be made on progress from year to year. In some cases, teachers will supplement these with their own systems. You may be given a record format to complete, or you may be expected to produce your own. Whatever, it is worth remembering that since the Freedom of Information Act (2000) was passed, parents can ask to look at any records kept on their sons or daughters. We now consider the following forms of record keeping:

1   Field diary.
2   Annotating lesson plans.
3   Tables.
4   Spreadsheets.
5   Portfolios and e-portfolios.

1 Field diary

A very useful and simple tool for recording the formative assessment that we do instinctively is a notebook, known as a field diary in research terms. As you are teaching or working with the pupils, you will notice something. Formalised 'noticing something' is the simplest form of observation (Chapter 12 discusses observation in more detail). During the oral/mental starter of a numeracy lesson you notice that Simon is consistently adding up a two and three number mental calculation incorrectly. In PE, Anne shows surprising eye/ball/hand control when practising netball throws. In Science, Toby's written work does not reflect his subject knowledge. All these observations can be noted down during lessons and added to a more formal record later. Through such means you will achieve greater depth of understanding of individual pupils and be able to tailor more effectively your teaching to their needs.

2 Annotating lesson plans

Another simple record of assessment is the lesson plan itself. Very quickly you will note points that have surprised you about individual pupils' learning. Most pupils will learn as the planning indicates, because the lessons have been differentiated according to their prior learning and abilities. However, there will be pupils who perform better than, or not as well as, you anticipated. Noting down at the time ensures that these important pointers towards effective future planning and learning are not lost.

3 Tables

Records vary according to the nature of the learning goals. For example, a record presented in a table can be straightforward:

Name		7/9	14/9	21/9	28/9	5/10	12/10
James	ABBEY	5 X 6	8	10	6 X 3	5	8
Eliza	BISHOP	8 X 9	10	9 X 8	10	M	M
Michael	CARTER	6 X 7	9	10	7 X 3	7	10
Nasreen	SINGH	6 X 4	7	9	10	7 X 5	6
Alicia	WHITE	M	M	M	M	M	M

Here the number followed by an X is the table being learnt. Single numbers are marks out of 10. M stands for 'mixed'. When pupils have shown they know all their tables, they have a weekly test of mixed tables to keep their skills sharp.

Simple tables like these can be created in any word processing package and can be easily adapted for different purposes.

4 Spreadsheets

A more sophisticated record can be created using a spreadsheet. Much detail can be stored on a spreadsheet. Also, with a spreadsheet information can be manipulated and extracted according to purpose. For example, the spreadsheet in Figure 9.2 has been created using Excel. The record charts the progress of a Year 7 class of pupils during a week working on fractions/decimals and percentages.

Group			DOB	SEN	Recgnise e 04-Jan	Identify 2 fr 05-Jan	Link simple 06-Jan	Identify 2 07-Ja
C	Joseph	Abbott	03/10/1993		A	A	A	A
A	Susan	Andress	06/06/1994	School Action Plus	Abs	Abs	R	R
C	Tracey	Anson	26/09/1993		A	A	A	A
C	Neil	Barton	11/12/1993		A	A + ext	A	A
D	Lewis	Cocklow	15/12/1993		A + ext	A + ext	A + ext	A + ext
A	Diana	Collins	31/05/1994	Statement	R + TA	R + TA	R + TA	R + TA
D	Kurt	Geenlea	11/06/1993		A	A	A + ext	A + ext
B	Desmon	Hall	15/09/1993		A	A	A	WT
B	Reese	Handma	28/01/1994		A + TA	A + TA	A	A
A	Christop	Jefferies	06/05/1994	School Action Plus	WT	WT	WT	ML
B	Aman	Johni	01/07/1994		A + TA	A + TA	A + TA	A + TA
D	Deena	Johnstor	14/08/1994		Abs	A + ext	A + ext	A + ext
C	Charles	Kiler	25/04/1994		A	A	A	ML
A	Petra	Lewis	11/10/1993	School Action	A	A	WT	WT
D	George	Liddle	21/11/1993		A	A	A + ext	A + ext
D	Kristen	Michel	01/08/1994		A + ext	A + ext	A + ext	A + ext
D	Hadyn	Miles	13/04/1994		A + ext	A + ext	A + ext	A + ext

Figure 9.2 Spreadsheet example

The teacher has a code:

A   achieved
ext   extension materials given
WT   working towards
Abs   absent
R   repeat
ML   music lesson
TA   working with teaching assistant support

The codes can be chosen to fit the subject, but A, WT, R, TA and ext, or equivalent will be useful for most records.

The advantage of working electronically is that the basic structure of pages, once a master has been created, can be copied and pasted onto new worksheets and so serve for other subjects and topics. Also using the sort and filter tools, details on groups of pupils can be extracted for analysis. There are many publications and websites that will guide you through the use of Excel. There will also be ICT specialists in your school whom you can ask for support if necessary.

5 Portfolios and e-portfolios

You might also find that your school has a portfolio for each pupil's work. A portfolio is a folder or box into which goes examples of a pupil's achievements, a profile of personal issues, assessments and records. This forms the evidence used to write reports to parents. Your records and work with the pupils will feed into each pupil's portfolio. Growing interest is being shown in e-portfolios, and e-assessment. According to the British Educational Communications and Technology Agency (Becta), within a few years these will be embedded in learning and teaching. Priority 2 of Becta's e-strategy is to 'ensure integrated online personal support for learners'.

The intention is to 'provide a personalised learning space for every learner that can encompass a personal portfolio', and by 2007–2008 for every school and college to have a 'personalised learning space with the potential to support e-portfolios' (http://www.becta.org.uk). Into an individual learner's e-portfolio would go pieces of writing, examples of mathematical problem solving, PowerPoint presentations of humanities projects, video clips of dance and drama, digital photographs, pieces of music, scanned artwork, details of assessments, CVs. The e-portfolio would grow over time, be amended and some items deleted. It will be able to be passed electronically wherever and whenever it is needed. In addition to pupils' developing e-portfolios, you too can create your own to support your professional practice. See Chapter 13 for more information.

Reporting

There is a statutory requirement that schools send at least one written report to parents each year. This report must cover:

*   A summary of the pupil's achievements over the year, including strengths and areas for development in all foundation stage or curriculum areas.
*   Comments on general progress.
*   Details of attendance.
*   A revised Individual Education Plan (IEP) if appropriate.
*   Details of the arrangements the school will be making for parents to discuss their child's report with his/her teacher, the Special Educational Needs Coordinator (SENCO) and the head teacher.
*   The results of any statutory assessment. These are the SATs that take place at the end of Key Stages 1, 2 and 3.

This is regarded as a minimum. End-of-year and half-yearly reports are now common. Many schools include suggested targets, comments by the pupils on their progress and opportunities for parents to respond. Whatever the detail of their content, reports must be focused, constructive and clearly understood. Generalisations like 'Jenny has worked hard this year' are not very helpful. Parents will want to hear how their children are achieving in terms of their perceived abilities. They will also want to know how well they are performing in relation to the class. It is to be hoped that the schools where you have your practical experiences of learning and teaching have held information evenings for parents on assessment for learning and the philosophy that underpins it.

Task 9.4
Developing reporting skills

Imagine you are a parent of a Year 8 pupil. You may in fact be one. Read the following mid-year assessment report on the pupil's achievement in science, taken from an actual report. Does it tell you what you want to know in terms of the pupil's perceived abilities and achievements? How could it be improved to reflect focused judgements on the pupil's learning?

	Always	Usually	Sometimes	Rarely
Subject: Science		*Teacher: Mr. Y*		
Name: Pupil X		*Set: 8R*		
Well organised and prepared		✓		
Behaves sensibly	✓			
I am pleased with the work produced		✓		

Effort: A   B   **C**   D   E

Attainment: A   B   **C**   D   E

Pupil target: I need to work harder in lessons and co-operate more in group sessions.

Teacher comment: Pupil X needs to apply more effort if she is to improve further.

Signature: Teacher Y

SUMMARY

Effective monitoring and assessment is an essential component of teaching and learning. It is based on Assessment for Learning, a synthesis of classroom practice and research. The conclusions of this synthesis are that the integration of the formative assessment, which is AfL, into the culture of schools can improve pupils' summative assessments and tests results. This in turn increases motivation and will go some way to lessening the disenchantment that can affect pupils. You as an HLTA have a crucial role in this process.

The next chapter explores ways to help you develop knowledge and understanding of your specialist area, which may be subject-based or linked to a specific role.

FURTHER READING

Assessment Reform Group (ARG) (1999) *Assessment for Learning: Beyond the Black Box*, Cambridge: University of Cambridge, School of Education. This text is concerned with disseminating understanding of the roles, purposes and impacts of assessment. The ARG was instrumental in shifting focus from summative to formative assessment.

McCallum, B. (2000) *Formative Assessment: Implications for Classroom Practice*, London: Institute of Education. This text considers six research studies on formative assessment and its impact on learning. Discussion on the role of pupils in assessment is particularly useful for practitioners.

WEBSITES

For the final report of the Gillingham Partnership Formative Assessment Project (2001): http://www.aaia.org.uk/pdf/Gillingham3.pdf

For additional publications on AfL: http://www.assessment-reform-group.org

For information on e-portfolios: http://www.becta.org.uk

For details on the Freedom of Information Act: http://www.opsi.gov.uk/ACTS/acts2000/20000036.htm

For the government's approach to self-assessment: http://www.qca.org.uk

For the Primary Strategy: http://www.standards.dfes.gov.uk/primary

10 Developing your Subject Specific Knowledge

Susan Capel

INTRODUCTION

As an HLTA, you provide valuable support for teaching and learning activities. Although you work alongside the teacher, the role you take may vary. You may, for example, work right across the curriculum or be a specialist assistant for a specific subject or department, or help plan lessons and develop support materials. Your specific role in your school is partly as a result of the school's needs, but should also take account of your expertise.

The aim of this chapter is to support you to develop your knowledge and understanding of your specialist area so you can contribute effectively and confidently to support the learning of pupils in the classes in which you are involved. You need to recognise what expertise you bring with you to the role and be able to acquire further knowledge in order to help the pupils you work with make progress with their learning. The knowledge and understanding you need may be subject-based or linked to a specific role (e.g. in support of an age phase or pupils with particular needs).

Other aspects of knowledge and understanding identified in the HLTA standards, such as, how pupils learn, meeting pupils' special educational needs, establishing a purposeful learning environment and promoting good behaviour, use of Information and Communications Technology (ICT), teaching strategies, statutory requirements, the curriculum and testing and examination processes, are addressed in other chapters (see Chapters 6, 7, 8 and 11).

It is not possible in this chapter to cover all aspects of subject specific knowledge for all subjects and different age ranges. Rather, the focus is on helping you to identify what subject specific knowledge you need and providing an introduction from which you can focus on developing the specific knowledge you need to undertake your role.

OBJECTIVES

By the end of this chapter, you should:

- understand what is meant by knowledge and understanding and how subject specific knowledge fits into that;
- recognise what knowledge and understanding you have and know how to acquire further knowledge and understanding in your specialist area;
- be familiar with the school and National Curriculum and their testing/examination frameworks;
- know what ICT you can use to advance pupils' learning, and know how to develop the skills to use ICT tools for your own and pupils' benefit.

This chapter refers to the HLTA standards on developing sufficient understanding of your area(s) of *expertise* to support the learning and progress of children and young people; knowing how statutory *frameworks* for the school curriculum relate to the age and ability ranges of the learners you support; using your area(s) of expertise to plan your role in learning activities and knowing how to *use ICT* to support your professional activities. You can also see Appendix 2 for information on how this chapter maps onto the standards at the time of publication; if these are revised then updated materials will appear on the website supporting this text.

KNOWLEDGE FOR TEACHING

The standards you need to meet to qualify as an HLTA focus on outcomes and therefore present a rather disjointed view of your role and of teaching. So as well as achieving each individual standard, it is important you have a holistic view of teaching and learning and the knowledge base needed to be effective in your role.

One way in which knowledge for teaching has been classified is that by Shulman (1986, 1987), who identified seven knowledge bases needed for effective teaching.

1   *Content (or subject matter) knowledge*
    Knowledge of the content or subject matter, which is the 'stuff' of a subject. This includes the structures of the subject matter: the factual information (substantive structures) and the variety of ways in which basic concepts and principles of the subject are organised (syntactic structures). It also includes the principles of enquiry that help answer two kinds of question: what are the important ideas and skills and what are the rules and procedures of good scholarship and enquiry in this subject?

2   *Curriculum knowledge*
    The materials and programmes that serve as tools of the trade for teachers. In England this is the National Curriculum and its materials and programmes on which teaching is based.

3   *General pedagogical knowledge*
  The broad principles and general strategies of classroom organisation and management that apply to any subject and age range.

4   *Pedagogical content knowledge*
  The distinctive body of knowledge for teaching. It is the blend of content and pedagogy into an understanding of how particular topics, problems or issues are organised, represented and adapted to the diverse interests and abilities of learners and presented for instruction. According to Grossman (1990) this includes knowledge and beliefs about the purposes of teaching a subject to pupils of different ages; pupils' understanding, conceptions and misconceptions of subject matter; knowledge of curriculum materials available for teaching a subject and knowledge of horizontal and vertical curricula for the subject; and knowledge of teaching approaches and representations for teaching particular topics.

5   *Knowledge of learners and their characteristics*
  This comprises two elements: *empirical* or *social knowledge* of learners – knowing what children of a particular age range are like, how they behave in classrooms and school, their social nature, their interests, how factors such as weather or exciting events can affect their work and behaviour and the nature of the pupil-teacher relationship; and *cognitive knowledge* of learners – both general knowledge about child development and specific knowledge about a particular group of pupils, e.g. what kind of knowledge these specific pupils do or do not know and understand. The first informs practice generally, the second develops over time as you teach a specific class or work with particular pupils.

6   *Knowledge of educational contexts*
  The contexts in which teaching and learning take place, which make a significant impact on both teachers and pupils. This includes cultures, communities and the catchment area from which the pupils come, the type and size of school, class size, the amount of support for teachers, the quality of relationships in the school, the expectations and attitudes of the headteacher and how group, classroom, school organisation and governance work.

7   *Knowledge of educational ends, purposes, values and philosophical and historical influences*
  Generally implicit knowledge which underpins and influences classroom activity, e.g. whether education is viewed as being intrinsically valuable or an extrinsic, more utilitarian activity, the purpose of which is to prepare pupils for employment.

Selection of content and materials, teaching approaches and organisational strategies are informed by several of these knowledge bases. These knowledge bases are inter-related and this inter-relationship is complex. For example, a decision requiring subject-specific knowledge may include explicit knowledge from some knowledge bases, e.g. content (or subject matter) knowledge, curriculum knowledge, pedagogical content knowledge, or knowledge of specific learners and their characteristics; but it may also include implicit knowledge from some knowledge bases, e.g. general pedagogical knowledge, general knowledge of learners and characteristics, knowledge of educational contexts or knowledge of educational ends, purposes, values and philosophical and historical influences.

KNOWING WHAT KNOWLEDGE YOU HAVE OF YOUR SPECIALIST AREA TO SUPPORT PUPILS' LEARNING

An HLTA's specialist area is defined generally. It may be, for example, any of the subjects in the school curriculum; or knowledge about pupils and their needs; or the work of a specific age group; or working with pupils/young people outside the classroom. Your specialist area is, however, likely to be an area in which you have some specific expertise. It may be this expertise that helped you decide to become an HLTA or it might be that you do not recognise fully the expertise that you bring to the role. Whatever the specialist area, you need some subject specific knowledge. It is important that you identify any additional subject specific knowledge you need for the role. Task 10.1 is designed to help you to identify this.

> **Task 10.1**
> **Recognising the subject specific knowledge you need for the role**
>
> Use Column 1 in Table 10.1 to list all the subject specific knowledge you can identify as being needed to work effectively as an HLTA in your specialist area. Start by making your own list. However, in order to extend this, discuss with a tutor on your programme or with the teacher(s) with whom you are working in school. Use another sheet if necessary. Leave the remaining columns blank.

Table 10.1 Developing specialist knowledge

Column 1	2	3	4
Knowledge important for the specialist area	Well developed	Further development required	How you are going to develop this knowledge
Knowledge of the National Curriculum for the subject or Key Stage		✓	Read the National Curriculum document for the subject and age range with which working. Discuss this with the teacher. Read school schemes of work and teacher's lesson plans to see how this is translated into practice
Knowledge of the pupils with whom working		✓	Look at class records, discussion with form tutor, subject teachers, SEN coordinator
General pedagogical knowledge			Observe teachers' strategies of classroom management in relation to teaching the subject/Key Stage. Discuss with the teacher(s) effective ways of enabling pupils' learning of curriculum content for your subject/Key Stage.

ACQUIRE FURTHER KNOWLEDGE TO CONTRIBUTE EFFECTIVELY AND WITH CONFIDENCE TO THE CLASSES IN WHICH YOU ARE INVOLVED

Having identified in Task 10.1 the subject specific knowledge that you need to work effectively in your specialist area, you now need to look at your existing knowledge in relation to the knowledge you need. Now complete Task 10.2.

Task 10.2
Developing your knowledge and understanding for your specialist area

Using the table in Task 10.1, complete either Column 2 or 3 according to whether your knowledge is well developed or whether it needs further development. In Column 4, identify how you will develop that knowledge which needs further development.

Discuss your analysis with your tutor or the teacher(s) in the school, to ensure that you have identified appropriate areas for development and means of developing this knowledge and to discuss what is needed to enable you to put this plan into operation to enable you to develop this knowledge.

You might like to return to this task in the middle and towards the end of your HLTA programme to check progress. Before you start, relook at your entry in Column 1 and check if there is any additional knowledge you now identify to undertake your role effectively. Then complete Columns 2 or 3 and 4 for all the aspects of knowledge identified.

Thus far, you have identified knowledge that you need to develop; we have not looked at any subject specific knowledge. The next section aims to provide you with some background for some aspects of subject specific knowledge – as identified in the standards. Inevitably, given the range of specialist areas, subjects and age ranges which you are going to be working with, this section focuses on general aspects of these topics. You will need to undertake further work in relation to the specific area, subject and age range. The further readings and websites at the end of the chapter can help. However, you should also read school documents, talk to the teachers with whom you work, or other staff with responsibility for specific aspects of work in the school, observe teachers and undertake other activities in school.

INTRODUCTION TO SOME ASPECTS OF SUBJECT SPECIFIC KNOWLEDGE

The aspects of knowledge and understanding in this section include the school curriculum – focusing particularly on the National Curriculum and its testing/examination frameworks.

School and National Curriculum

Although the context in which you are working comprises more than the curriculum, the curriculum is an important part of the context within which you work as an HLTA.

Even though you may not always think about it explicitly, it forms a 'frame' to what you are doing.

The curriculum comprises the planned or formal curriculum – the intended content of an educational programme set out in advance. This comprises the school curriculum and subject curriculum. You might think of the school curriculum in terms of a list of names of subjects. However, it could be described in more detail, identifying the content of what is supposed to be taught and learned. The curriculum, in whole or in part, might be compulsory; some of it may be a 'core curriculum', the part of a whole curriculum which is taken by everyone, but around which there is scope for variations; and some of it may be a 'common curriculum', that is, whether or not it is actually compulsory, it is taken by everyone in practice. In some schools or at some ages, particularly in secondary schools, some of the curriculum might be optional.

The curriculum also includes what is known as the hidden or informal curriculum – those things pupils learn as a result of attending school rather than specific learning outcomes of a particular subject/learning experience. This is not covered in the chapter, but it is explained further in Unit 7.2 in Capel, Leask and Turner (2009), which looks at the school curriculum.

When you think about the school curriculum, you probably think about the National Curriculum. This is the structured and assessed framework for pupils ages 5–16 years in all state or maintained schools in England. The National Curriculum is organised into blocks of years called 'Key Stages'. There are four Key Stages as well as a Foundation Stage, which covers children below the minimum compulsory schooling age of five. In Table 10.2 the ages of children and school years for each Key Stage are identified.

Age-related expectations of pupils are clearly specified in the National Curriculum. It is important to recognise that these are related to cognitive, physical/motor and affective changes in children as they grow and develop (see Chapter 7).

Table 10.2 Identifying Key Stages

Key Stage	Age	School Year
Foundation	3–4	
	4–5	Reception
Key Stage 1	5–6	Year 1
	6–7	Year 2
Key Stage 2	7–8	Year 3
	8–9	Year 4
	9–10	Year 5
	10–11	Year 6
Key Stage 3	11–12	Year 7
	12–13	Year 8
	13–14	Year 9
Key Stage 4	14–15	Year 10
	15–16	Year 11

The National Curriculum comprises three core subjects (English, mathematics and science) and 10 foundation subjects. Different subjects are compulsory at different Key Stages. The core and foundation subjects each pupil is taught at Key Stages 1 to 4 are shown in Table 10.3.

The National Curriculum was reformed in 2008 with a QCA review resulting in a new and revised secondary curriculum. The key aims of the secondary curriculum

Table 10.3 The core and foundation subjects of the National Curriculum and the Key Stages in which they are taught

Subject	Key Stage 1	Key Stage 2	Key Stage 3	Key Stage 4
Core subjects				
English	•	•	•	•
Mathematics	•	•	•	•
Science	•	•	•	•
Foundation subjects				
Art and design	•	•	•	x
Citizenship	x	x	•	•
Design and technology	•	•	•	•*
Geography	•	•	•	x
History	•	•	•	x
Information and communication technology	•	•	•	•
Modern foreign languages		x	•	•*
Music	•	•	•	x
Physical education	•	•	•	•

(Adapted from Department for Education and Employment and the Qualifications and Curriculum Authority (DfEE/QCA), 1999, p.16).

Notes:
• = statutory requirement
x = non statutory requirement
*= non statutory requirement with effect from September 2004

review are to raise standards through the design of new qualifications, including the introduction of new specialised vocational diplomas, restructuring A–Levels and the launch of functional skills qualifications in English, maths and ICT. The revised 14–19 curriculum is designed to be less prescriptive and more flexible in order to tailor the curriculum to meet the needs of individual pupils – as part of the government's broader educational drive to personalise learning. These curriculum reforms provide a wider choice of courses for pupils. For further information on the reshaping of the 14–19 curriculum see http://www.dcsf.gov.uk/reforms and http://www.qca.org.uk/qca_12195.aspx

As an HLTA, you need to know how the National Curriculum sets out the knowledge, skills and understanding required in each subject (programmes of study), as well as the standards or attainment targets that teachers can use to measure each child's progress and plan their future learning (attainment targets and level descriptors) and how each child's progress is assessed and reported (assessment arrangements).

Programmes of study are 'the matters, skills and processes which are required to be taught to pupils of different abilities and maturities during each Key Stage' (Department of Education and Science (DES), 1991, p. i). The programmes of study identify the specific knowledge, skills and understanding that pupils should be taught. Detailed information regarding what pupils should be taught is provided through National Curriculum documentation for each subject.

Each National Curriculum subject has specified *attainment targets*. Attainment targets are 'the knowledge, skills and understanding which pupils of different abilities and maturities are expected to have by the end of each Key Stage' (DES, 1991, p. i). For Citizenship there are attainment targets at the end of Key Stages 3 and 4.

Except in the case of Citizenship, for Key Stages 1, 2, and 3 the National Curriculum is accompanied by eight *level descriptions* of increasing difficulty, plus a description for exceptional performance above level 8. At each Key Stage, a range of levels of attainment, which the majority of pupils are expected to work at are identified, along with the level at which it is expected that the majority of pupils will achieve at the end of the Key Stage. For example, by the end of Key Stage 1, most children have reached level 2, and by the end of Key Stage 2, most will be at level 4. These are shown in Table 10.4.

Table 10.4 Levels of attainment and tests and tasks at the end of each Key Stage

Range of levels of attainment which the majority of pupils are expected to work at		Expected attainment for the majority of pupils at the end of the Key Stage		Tests taken at the end of Key Stages 1, 2 and 3 in the core subjects
Key Stage 1	1–3	At age 8	2	National tests and tasks in English, maths and science
Key Stage 2	2–5	At age 11	4	National tests and tasks in English, maths and science
Key Stage 3	3–8	At age 14	5/6	Optional tests and tasks in English, maths and science
Key Stage 4	GCSE or other national examinations	At age 16	GCSE or other national examinations	Some pupils take GCSEs at the end of year 9 or 10. Most pupils take GCSEs or other national qualifications at the end of year 11

(Adapted from: DfEE/QCA, 1999, p. 18).

A description is provided for each level of attainment (see National Curriculum subject documents) which gives an overview of what pupils should be achieving at each level of attainment. Each school reports to parents on the National Curriculum levels their child has reached in both tests and assessments.

ASSESSMENT ARRANGEMENTS

Assessment arrangements comprise *End of Key Stage tests*, which are the national tests pupils must take at the end of each Key Stage – at ages seven and 11, in the core subjects. They show each child's performance in selected parts of a subject on a particular day. They provide the levels of attainment at the end of each Key Stage for each pupil within each of the three core subjects. These tests give an independent measure of how pupils and schools are doing compared with national standards in these subjects. Key Stage 3 obligatory national tests stopped in 2008.

However, in all subjects teachers check each pupil's progress as a normal part of their teaching by looking at their work. In the foundation subjects, the class teacher undertakes a *teacher assessment* based on observations of pupils. They have to decide which National Curriculum level best describes the pupil's performance in each area of learning in that subject to provide the level of attainment.

At the end of Key Stage 4, most pupils sit external assessments, e.g. General Certificate of Secondary Education (GCSE) or other national qualifications. If you are likely to be supporting pupils who are working towards such external assessments, you need to find out more about the awards. Further information about external assessments can be obtained from the awarding bodies' websites (listed at the end of this chapter).

THE SCHEMES OF WORK AND LESSONS IN WHICH YOU ARE INVOLVED

Within the framework of the National Curriculum, schools are free to plan and organise teaching and learning in the way that best meets the needs of their pupils. Being able to support a teacher's work in individual lessons requires that you can see how the general information in National Curriculum documentation is translated into the specific lessons in which you are involved. This requires you to have some knowledge about the scheme of work into which the lesson fits as well as information about the specific lesson. These are covered in Chapter 2. In this section we look at the ICT which you might use to support pupils learning in the lesson.

USING ICT TO SUPPORT YOUR WORK IN THE CLASSROOM

ICT is used to support and enhance teaching and pupils' learning. There is evidence (e.g. The British Education and Communications Technology Agency (Becta), 2003; Organisation for Cooperation and Development (OECD), 2001) that when ICT is effectively deployed, pupil motivation and achievement are raised in a number of respects. As an HLTA, you are expected to know how to use ICT to advance pupils' learning, and be able to use common ICT tools for your own and pupils' benefit. This is a wide-ranging expectation. ICT has been defined as including 'computers, the internet, CD-ROM and other software, television, radio, video, cameras and other equipment' (Teacher Training Agency, 1998, p. 1). You are likely to be involved in using a range of ICT with the pupils with whom you work, e.g. word processing, databases, spreadsheets, printers, scanners, presentation software such as interactive whiteboards, digital cameras, video, DVD, email and the Internet, although the range and types of ICT used with pupils of different ages and in different subjects varies. You might use this to, for example, prepare materials for pupils, help pupils to interact with the materials, complete and analyse pupils' records or obtain information and communicate with others. Table 10.5 shows how ICT can be applied in different subjects, as defined by the English National Curriculum for ICT (finding things out; developing ideas and making things happen; exchanging and sharing information; reviewing, modifying and evaluating work as it progresses).

You are expected to be able to use the ICT that pupils use in lessons you support so you need to identify the range of ICTs you are likely to be working with and then ensure that you have the skills to enable you to work in the relevant areas. Task 10.3 is designed to enable you to audit your ICT skills and identify the areas in which you are competent and those in which you need to develop further competence.

Task 10.3
Auditing your ICT skills

Once you identify areas for development, draw up an action plan which identifies the areas you are going to work on, the ways you are going to develop competence and the time scales you set yourself. To help with this, start by identifying those aspects of ICT most relevant to the age range and/or subject which you are supporting (see Table 10.6). The Becta website is helpful here. You might also want to take the European Computer Driving Licence (ECDL). Both web addresses are given at the end of this chapter.

Further information about why to use ICT, using ICT to support pupils' learning, including motivation and classroom management, and to support your teaching, administration and monitoring, as well as some information about specific ICT applications, e.g. interactive whiteboards, is in Unit 5.7 in Capel, Leask and Turner (2009) *Learning to Teach in the Secondary School*.

SUMMARY

In order to qualify as an HLTA, you have to meet standards related to knowledge and understanding. The aim of this chapter was to help you to identify the knowledge and understanding you possess and what other knowledge and understanding you need to develop. It also aimed to help you become familiar with the school and National Curriculum and their testing/examination frameworks. As HLTAs have different backgrounds and experience, and therefore bring different knowledge, understanding and developmental needs, the focus has been on helping you to identify these for yourself. It is important that you now spend the time and energy developing the knowledge and understanding that you have identified as in need of further development. The next chapter explores ways of using ICT for developing resources to support pupils' learning.

Table 10.5 How ICT can be applied in different subjects

Art and design		Maths	
Finding things out	Surveys (e.g. consumer preferences), web galleries, online artist/movement profiles	Finding things out	Databases, surveys, statistics, graphing, calculators, graphical calculators, dynamic geometry, data logging/ measurement (e.g. timing), web-based information (e.g. statistics/history of maths)
Developing ideas	Spreadsheets to model design specs	Developing ideas	Number patterns, modelling algebraic problems/ probability
Making things happen	Embroidery CAD/CAM	Making things happen	Programming – e.g. LOGO turtle graphics
Exchanging and sharing information	Digital imagery CAD Multimedia for students' design portfolios	Exchanging and sharing information	Formulae/symbols, presenting investigation findings, multimedia
Reviewing, modifying and evaluating	Real world applications – e.g. commercial art	Reviewing, modifying and evaluating	Comparing solutions to those online, online modelling and information sources
Business and commercial studies		Technology	
Finding things out	Pay packages, databases, online profiling	Finding things out	Product surveys, consumer preferences, environmental data
Developing ideas	Business/financial modelling	Developing ideas	CAD, spreadsheet modelling
Making things happen	Business simulation	Making things happen	CAM, simulations (e.g. environmental modelling), textiles, embroidery, control
Exchanging and sharing information	Business letters, web authoring, multimedia CVs, email	Exchanging and sharing information	Advertising, product design and realisation, multimedia/ web presentation
Reviewing, modifying and evaluating	Commercial packages, dot. com, admin systems	Reviewing, modifying and evaluating	Industrial production, engineering/electronics
Performing arts		Physical education	
Finding things out	Online information sources, surveys (e.g. PHSE issues)	Finding things out	Recording/analysing performance, internet sources (e.g. records)
Developing ideas	Planning performance/ choreographing sequences	Developing ideas	Planning sequences/tactics

(Continued)

Table 10.5 How ICT can be applied in different subjects *(continued)*

Performing arts		Physical education	
Making things happen	Lighting sequences, computer animation, MIDI, multimedia presentations	Making things happen	Modelling sequences/tactics, sporting simulations
Exchanging and sharing information	Video, audio, digital video, web authoring, multimedia, animation, DTP posters/ flyers/programmes email	Exchanging and sharing information	Reporting events, posters, flyers, web/multimedia authoring, video, digital video
Reviewing, modifying and evaluating	Ticket booking, lighting control, recording/TV studios, theatre/ film industry	Reviewing, modifying and evaluating	Website evaluation, presentation of performance statistics, event diaries, performance portfolios
English		*Modern foreign languages*	
Finding things out	Surveys, efficient searching/ keywords, information texts, online author profiles, readability analysis	Finding things out	Class surveys, topic databases, web searching/ browsing
Developing ideas	Authorship, desktop publishing (balancing text and images)	Developing ideas	Concordancing software, interactive video packages, DTP and word processing
Making things happen	Interactive texts/multimedia/ web authoring	Making things happen	Online translation tools, interactive multimedia
Exchanging and sharing information	Exploring genres (e.g. writing frames), authoring tools, text/images, scripting, presenting, interviewing (audio/video)	Exchanging and sharing information	Word processing, DTP, web/ multimedia authoring, email projects, video/audio recording, digital video editing
Reviewing, modifying and evaluating	Website evaluation, online publishing, email projects	Reviewing, modifying and evaluating	Internet communication, website/CD ROM language teaching evaluation, translation software
Humanities		*Science*	
Finding things out	Surveys, databases, internet searching, monitoring environment (e.g. weather), census data etc.	Finding things out	Data recording and analysis, spreadsheets and graphing packages, internet searching (e.g. genetics info.)
Developing ideas	Multimedia, DTP, modelling (spreadsheets/simulations)	Developing ideas	Modelling experiments / simulations
Making things happen	Simulations, interactive multimedia/web authoring	Making things happen	Datalogging, modelling experiments, simulations (what if…?)
Exchanging and sharing information	Web authoring, email projects	Exchanging and sharing information	Communicating investigation findings (DTP, web/multimedia authoring, DV)

(Continued)

Table 10.5 How ICT can be applied in different subjects *(continued)*

Reviewing, modifying and evaluating	Weather stations, satellite information, website/CD ROM evaluation, archive information	Reviewing, modifying and evaluating	Accessing information, evaluating for bias on issues (e.g. nuclear power)

Based on: Leask & Pachler, 1999 (with thanks to Dave Maguire).

Table 10.6 ICT skills audit

General skills	*0*	*1*	*2*	*3*
Choosing appropriate software to help solve a problem				
Dragging and dropping				
Having more than one application open at a time				
Highlighting				
Making selections by clicking				
Moving information between software (e.g. using the clipboard)				
Navigating around the desktop environment				
Opening items by double clicking with the mouse				
Printing				
Using menus				
How to change the name of files				
Word processing skills	*0*	*1*	*2*	*3*
Altering fonts – font, size, style (**bold**, *italic*, underline)				
Text justification – left, right and centre				
Using a spellchecker				
Moving text within a document – cut, copy and paste				
Adding or inserting pictures to a document				
Counting the number of words in a document				
Adding a page break to a document				
Altering page orientation – (landscape, portrait)				
Using characters/symbols				
Using find and replace to edit a document				
Using styles to organise a document				
Using styles to alter the presentation of a document efficiently				

(Continued)

Table 10.6 ICT skills audit (*continued*)

	0	1	2	3
Adding page numbers to the footer of a document				
Adding the date to the header of a document				
Changing the margins of a document				
Email skills	*0*	*1*	*2*	*3*
Recognising an email address				
Sending an email to an individual				
Sending an email to more than one person				
Replying to an email				
Copying an email to another person				
Forwarding an incoming email to another person				
Adding an address to an electronic address book				
Filing incoming and outgoing emails				
Adding an attachment to an email				
Receiving and saving an attachment in an email				
Database skills	*0*	*1*	*2*	*3*
Searching a database for specific information				
Using Boolean operators (and/or/not) to narrow searches				
Sorting database records in ascending or descending order				
Adding a record to a database				
Adding fields to a database				
Querying information in a database (e.g. locating all values greater than 10)				
Filtering information in a database (e.g. sorting on all values greater than 10)				
Categorising data into different types (numbers, text, and yes/no (Boolean) types)				
Web browser skills	*0*	*1*	*2*	*3*
Recognising a web address (e.g. www. or co.uk, etc.)				
Using hyperlinks on websites to connect to other website				
Using the back button				
Using the forward button				
Using the history				

(Continued)

Table 10.6 ICT skills audit (*continued*)

	0	1	2	3
Understanding how to search websites				
Using Boolean operators (and/or/not) to narrow down searches				
Creating bookmarks				
Organising bookmarks into folders				
Downloading files from a website				
Spreadsheet skills	*0*	*1*	*2*	*3*
Identifying grid squares in a spreadsheet (e.g. B5)				
Inserting columns into a spreadsheet				
Inserting rows into a spreadsheet				
Sorting spreadsheet or database columns in ascending or descending order				
Converting a spreadsheet into a chart				
Labelling a chart				
Adding simple formulae/functions to cells				
Applying formatting to different types of data including numbers and dates				
Presentation skills	*0*	*1*	*2*	*3*
Inserting text and images on a slide				
Inserting a slide in a presentation				
Adding a transition between slides				
Adding buttons to a presentation				
Using timers in a presentation				

Note:
Each test covers the six types of office software and will contain a balance of the following kinds of skills.
Put a tick beside each skill indicating your level of competence/confidence (0 = no confidence, 3 = very confident).

FURTHER READING

For those working in secondary schools

Capel, S., Leask, M. and Turner, T. (2009) *Learning to Teach in the Secondary School: A Companion to School Experience*, 5th edn, London: Routledge. Further relevant information is also found in the subject specific books in the Learning to Teach series.

For those working in primary schools

Eyres, C. (2005) *Primary Teaching Assistants Curriculum in Context*, London: David Fulton in association with the Open University.

Hancock, C. (2004) *Primary Teaching Assistants Learners and Learning*, London: David Fulton in association with the Open University.

Hayes, D. (2004) *Foundations of Primary Teaching*, London: David Fulton.

Hughes, P. (2008) *Principles of Primary Education*, London: David Fulton.

WEBSITES

Subject associations' websites can be accessed through: http://www.gtce.org.uk/weblinks/subject_associations

Awarding bodies. There are three awarding bodies:

Assessment and Qualifications Alliance (AQA): http://www.aqa.org.uk

Edexcel: http://www.edexcel.org.uk

Oxford and Cambridge Regional (OCR): http://www.ocr.org.uk

Becta (British Educational Communications and Technology Agency): http://www.becta.org.uk

DCSF (Department for Children, Schools and Families) (previously DfES (Department for Education and Skills). For information about the new and revised secondary curriculum 14–19 see:

Department for Children, Schools and Families): http://www.dcsf.gov.uk/14-19/ and http://www. qca.org.uk/qca_12195.aspx

European Computer Driving Licence (ECDL): http://www.ecdl.co.uk

QCA (Qualifications and Curriculum Authority): http://www.qca.org.uk

QCA provides extensive information about the National Curriculum, e.g. *National Curriculum Online* sets out the legal requirements of the National Curriculum in England, provides information to help teachers implement the National Curriculum in their schools, and links every National Curriculum programme of study requirement to resources for teachers (see http://www.qca.org.uk/232.html). *National Curriculum in Action* illustrates standards of pupils' work at different ages and Key Stages and how the programmes of study translate into real activities (see http://www.qca.org.uk/232.html). Subject specific information: http://www.qca.org.uk/2550.html

TDA (Training and Development Agency for Schools): http://www.tda.gov.uk The TDA's website is also very helpful. For example, there are case studies (including videos) illustrating the ways some HLTAs went about meeting specific professional standards. These can be found at: http://www.tda.gov.uk/support/hlta/professstandards/meetingthestandards.aspx

11 Developing Resources and Supporting Pupil Learning using ICT

Sarah Younie

INTRODUCTION

This chapter is about developing resources to support pupils' learning, particularly with ICT, which you can expect to be part of your role. As you work through this chapter, and as your knowledge about the learning process increases, you should develop your knowledge about how to create activities and resources suited to the pupils you support and to use ICT to enhance this aspect of your work.

OBJECTIVES

By the end of this chapter you should:

* have developed an understanding of how to use ICT to support your professional activities;
* have familiarised yourself with how to use ICT to create learning resources;
* be aware of how to contribute to the preparation of resources to support pupils' learning which take account of different learning needs.

This chapter covers aspects of the standards for HLTAs which require you to demonstrate sufficient knowledge and understanding to be able to help the pupils you work with make progress by creating supportive learning activities. Specifically, the standards require that you know how to *use ICT skills to advance learning* as well as *using ICT to support your professional activities*, and that you can contribute to the *selection and preparation of resources.* You can also see Appendix 2 for information on how this chapter maps onto the standards at the time of publication. If these are revised then updated materials will appear on the website supporting this text.

It is the responsibility of the teacher and you, as the HLTA, to enable pupils to access all levels of learning by providing a variety of learning activities. One of your roles is the preparation of resources to support this process and we discuss how you can do this using ICT. We start by considering how ICT can support learning.

USING ICT TO SUPPORT PUPIL LEARNING

All school staff are expected to use ICT as appropriate to support the teaching and learning process. You can expect to be involved in: the use of *particular types of technology*, e.g. digital cameras, computers, interactive whiteboards; the use of *specialist software*, e.g. data logging in science; drawing on expertise from *specialist websites* (see Chapter 13 on developing e-support); making materials available on the *school intranet* for pupils to read before and after lessons or for use during lessons, as well as using ICT for administration and record keeping.

You need to be able to help pupils find resources on the web and ensure they know how to evaluate these by checking who produced the resources, what biases they might have, when the resources were made and for what purpose.

Task 11.1
Expectations of your use of and familiarity with ICT resources

You can expect your school to use ICT resources in a range of ways to support pupils and teachers. Make sure you are familiar with these and make time to learn to use any resources which are new to you. This is an opportunity to check your ICT knowledge and skills and to arrange for training. Following is a guide to help you identify your requirements. You need to know how to:

- Use common software packages such as word processing, spreadsheets and power point presentations; check what other packages your school uses.
- Input data to and print data from your school's intranet.
- Evaluate internet resources for their reliability as learning resources.
- Create digital resources, for example, online worksheets and work with the teacher to check whether these include appropriate differentiated work for pupils with different needs, e.g. through using more or less complex language and through including tasks of different levels of complexity.

Find out what expectations there are for recording and interrogating pupil data in your school. Then make sure you are able to:

- Use pupil assessment data.
- Use ICT for administration purposes.

You also will need to help pupils use ICT as part of their work. Information provided by Becta (British Educational Communications and Technology Agency) and cited by Bennett and Leask (2005) indicates the following educational benefits in using ICT:

> From a learning perspective, the effective use of ICT can lead to benefits in terms of:
>
> greater motivation;
> increased self-esteem and confidence;
> enhanced questioning skills;
> promoting initiative and independent learning;
> improving presentation;
> developing problem solving capabilities;
> promoting better information handling skills;
> increasing time 'on task';
> improving social and communication skills.

More specifically, ICT can enable children to:

- combine words and images to produce a 'professional' looking piece of work;
- draft and redraft their work with less effort;
- test out ideas and present them in different ways for different audiences;
- explore musical sequences and compose their own music;
- investigate and make changes in computer models;
- store and handle large amounts of information in different ways;
- do things quickly and easily which might otherwise be tedious or time-consuming;
- use simulations to experience things that might be too difficult or dangerous for them to attempt in real life;
- control devices by turning motors, buzzers and lights on or off or by programming them to react to changes in things like light or temperature sensors;
- communicate with others over a distance.

Becta defines ICT capability as:

> An ability to use effectively ICT tools and information sources to analyse, process and present information, and to model, measure and control external events. More specifically, a child who has developed ICT capability should:
>
> use ICT confidently;
> select and use ICT appropriate to the task in hand;
> use information sources and ICT tools to solve problems;
> identify situations where the ICT use would be relevant;
> use ICT to support learning in a number of contexts;
> be able to reflect and comment on the use of ICT they have undertaken;
> understand the implications of ICT for working life and society.

Pupils should be given opportunities to develop and apply their ICT capability in the context of all curriculum subjects.

The text for student teachers by Capel, Leask and Turner (2009) *Learning to Teach in the Secondary School* contains a unit by Bennett and Leask on using ICT to support teaching and learning in the classroom and we suggest you read this for further ideas. There are also ICT training courses that you can take, e.g. the ECDL (European Computer Driving Licence), which has international accreditation (see http://www.ecdl.org.) You can discuss your ICT training needs with your mentor and investigate your local training providers.

Chapter 10 in this book includes a self-assessment tool to identify your development needs with respect to ICT, and Chapter 13 discusses forms of professional support available through the Web. One way you can deploy ICT is to help you select and prepare resources suitable for the interests and abilities of the learners you are supporting. The next section outlines some suggestions regarding the ways in which you can do this.

USING ICT TO PREPARE RESOURCES

Part of your responsibility is supporting the ongoing development of the intranet and VLE (virtual learning environment), which is used in your school. You will need to know how to transform learning and teaching resources into an online format for pupils to access electronically, either from computers at school or at home. The advantage of online resources is that they are always available at any time, including 'out of hours' and holidays and can be very useful for pupils for revision periods, or if pupils have missed lessons. Also, if more than one teaching assistant from the same subject area is creating resources on a topic, then it is possible to generate a range of materials and build a bank of activities that support the learning and teaching of your subject – stored on your department's area of the school intranet.

Below we outline activities you should be able to undertake to develop your school's e-resources. This is adapted from Younie and Moore (2005), which we suggest you read for further information and examples.

Activity 1: Upgrade resources into an electronic format

You need to be able to upgrade paper resources into an electronic format, and upload these onto the school intranet site. For example, any worksheets, information booklets or written materials can be put online. If PowerPoint slides have been used in the lesson, these can have annotated notes added and be uploaded also. This will locate all the learning resources for pupils in one place, on the intranet, organised by subject and department. Then if pupils are absent or loose their notes, they can easily retrieve the information and the resources are accessible for pupils at other times, such as revision sessions. Also, by having resources available electronically, this relieves you of the responsibility for printing and photocopying duplicate sets of materials.

Activity 2: Develop online templates and writing frames for pupils to download and work on

A second activity is creating resources for pupils to download onto their network area of the school intranet, which can be used for personalised learning. For example, you can write worksheets that can be downloaded for pupils to add answers to, to edit, or to solve a problem, or you can produce online templates and writing frames to help pupils write a response, or develop a PowerPoint presentation from information provided.

For example, in the lesson or for homework, the pupils save the online template, which from activity one, you have turned into an electronic format and put on the school network. The pupils then download the template into their network area and complete the learning tasks. You can make resources available for pupils to edit or work directly on, as in the case of writing frames or online worksheets. The advantage is that it saves pupils writing out questions, or copying down information. In short, this removes the 'dead time fillers', with pupils instead focusing on writing the answers or solving the problem, or completing the writing frame.

Activity 3: Develop pupil interactivity with the online resources by inserting hyperlinks

As a next activity, you can supplement and extend your school's online resources with links to relevant websites. Pupils are guided directly to the websites selected by you for the topic under investigation. By providing a direct link, you are ensuring that pupils go straight to the site you want. This saves time as pupils do not have to sit and type in a URL from a paper worksheet, which creates room for error. It prevents pupils from being distracted by other sites if they were to do a general search.

The purpose of adding hyperlinks into your e-resources is to generate pupil interactivity as an aid to learning. You could refer to three websites relevant to the topic being studied, which could be differentiated, creating varied learning paths and addressing the issue of diversity. An example from science includes creating an online worksheet with hyperlinks to an external website, in this case an interactive periodic table, so pupils can engage with the interactive model in relation to the questions on the worksheet. Or, you could create access to a pro-blood sports website and an anti-blood sports website to compare the use of evidence. Your role includes selecting relevant websites and reviewing them with respect to their suitability for the topic and learning you are supporting.

Activity 4: Develop more interactivity with online resources

Once you are comfortable with creating hyperlinks in online resources, you can make the learning more interactive by downloading free software programmes that support pupil interactivity. For example, generating word searches, crossword puzzles, interactive quizzes, multiple choice tests, diagram labelling exercises using drop down boxes, mix and match exercises, cloze exercises using drop down boxes and so on. Websites such as 'Hot Potatoes' (http://www.hotpot.uvic.ca) provide software tools for making quizzes, and are free of charge to schools if you make the pages available on the web.

Using free software you can also create interactive tests, which pupils complete and then revisit and complete again, enabling them to monitor their own progression, particularly during periods of revision.

Activity 5: Develop multi-media, for example, simulations and video capture

Further developments could include videoing lesson demonstrations, such as science experiments, for pupils to revisit after the lesson, or capturing activities showing food technology techniques, or painting techniques. Many simulations illustrating key concepts are available on the web for teachers to use. The BBC website provides some examples (http://www.bbc.co.uk).

Activity 6: Develop and use the school's VLE (virtual learning environment) and MLE (managed learning environment)

Becta (2003) describes a VLE as 'a standardised, computer-based environment that supports the delivery of web-based learning and facilitates on-line interaction between students and teachers'. In developing your school's VLE resources, you will find free software, which is available online for you to adapt. Alternatively, there are products available to purchase, which can be adapted. Schools are looking to VLEs to support the personalised learning agenda for each pupil. For more information about VLEs, we suggest looking at *Learning and Teaching with Virtual Learning Environments*, by Gillespie, Boulton, Hramiak, and Williamson, (2007), and Becta (2004) *Virtual and Managed Learning Environments*.

These ICT strategies provide effective ways to enhance the selection and preparation of resources to support pupils' learning. Through ease of access, including the storage and retrieval of resources, you can easily manage and update your learning materials.

Task 11.2
Creating e-resources

Start creating your own electronic resources by adapting paper-based materials that you are currently using or have already written that lend themselves to electronic transfer, e.g. hand-written worksheets that can be word processed. You need to know how to draw and insert pictures, diagrams and graphs into word documents. Other tools include scanners, which convert images and documents into digital data. Next consider following the other activities outlined above to generate interactive learning resources for your subject, which can be stored on the school's intranet and shared with pupils, teachers and other support staff.

Websites like the European Schoolnet (http://www.eun.org) enable schools to find partners for projects from across the European Union and it is this communicative potential of ICT that offers numerous authentic learning opportunities. For example, pupils can engage in online exchanges in a target modern foreign language; experience virtual field trips; visit hyperlinked museums and galleries from around the world; take part in creating a multi-authored newspaper between European schools; or develop collaborative writing exercises. Such interschool exchange enables not only the sharing of knowledge, but also an educationally supportive space where pupils can expand their experiential worlds.

Task 11.3
Exploring educational websites

Visit the European Schoolnet website (http://www.eun.org) and take a virtual tour. As you explore the website and its links, make a note of what resources and learning opportunities present themselves to you. In addition, investigate the other educational websites listed at the end of this chapter and consider how these may support your professional activities.

SUMMARY

After reading this chapter, you should have developed an understanding of the ways in which you can use ICT to support your professional activities, in particular using ICT to aid the selection and preparation of resources to support pupils' learning.

The next chapter examines the role of observation and how this helps you to improve your own practice.

FURTHER READING

In the Routledge Learning to Teach series, all the texts contain chapters about the use of ICT in each specific subject area. You may find further ideas for the application of ICT in your subject areas in these texts. The Routledge text *Learning to Teach Using ICT in the Secondary School* (Leask and Pachler, 2005) also provides detailed guidance.

Gillespie, H., Boulton, H., Hramiak, A.J. and Williamson, R. (2007) *Learning and Teaching with Virtual Learning Environments*, Exeter: Learning Matters. This book provides suggestions for developing learning resources and examples are provided across all subjects and key stages.

Leask, M. and Younie, S. (2001) 'Communal constructivist theory: information and communications technology pedagogy and internationalisation of the curriculum', *Journal of Information Technology for Teacher Education*, 10, 1 and 2: 117–34. This article links Vygotsky's theories of learning to e-learning through the concept of 'communal constructivism'. Pupils, through their use of the Internet, can access current expert knowledge and experience communities outside their own and produce multi-authored/multimedia materials. 'Communal constructivism' conveys the different ways in which 'knowledge is constructed, shared and reconstructed, published and republished by both you, teachers and learners alike' (p. 119).

Younie and Moore (2005) 'Using ICT for Professional Purposes', in Leask, M. and Pachler, N. (eds) *Learning to Teach Using ICT in the Secondary School: A Companion to School Experience*, 2nd edn, London: Routledge. This chapter provides information and illustrations on how to use ICT to create resources for supporting pupil learning.

WEBSITES

BBC: http://www.bbc.co.uk. The BBC website provides a wide range of support materials including simulations and revision questions.

Becta: http://www.becta.org.uk. Becta is a government agency that supports the use of ICT in education. The website provides information and links to government e-learning policy and research evidence about the use of ICT for teaching and learning.

Becta (2004) *Virtual and Managed Learning Environments*, Coventry. Accessible on the Becta website at: http://foi.becta.org.uk/content_files/corporate/resources/technology_and_education_research/v_and_mle.doc

The DCSF (Department for Children, Schools and Families) website provides up-to-date information about legislation and initiatives for schools: http://www.dcsf.gov.uk

ECDL (European Computer Driving Licence): http://www.ecdl.org, for information on the internationally accreditied ICT training course, which is also known as the International Computer Driving Licence (ICDL) outside Europe. This is an end-user computer skills certification programme.

European Schoolnet: http://www.eun.org. This website provides the opportunity to find partners for online school projects across the European Union.

'Global Gateway' by the Central Bureau for Educational Visits and Exchanges: http://www.globalgateway.org.uk

Hot Potatoes: http://www.hotpot.uvic.ca. The website provides software tools for making online quizzes, which are free to schools if they make the pages using the software publically available.

The National Grid for Learning (NGfL) can be found at http://www.ngfl.gov.uk. The Virtual Teachers' Centre is an integral part of the NGfL and can be located at: http://www. vtc.ngfl.gov.uk

Specialist Schools and Academies Trust: http://www.schoolnetwork.org.uk. The website provides case studies of innovative ICT use for learning and teaching. For further information contact the Subject Leader for ICT.

Teachernet: http://www.teachernet.gov.uk. The Teachernet website provides access to a wide range of resources to support learning and teaching in the classroom.

Teachers Training Resource Bank: http://www.ttrb.ac.uk. This website is specifically designed to support the training of teachers and there are many aspects that are relevant to you as an HLTA. For subject specific help, on the front page of the Teacher Training Resource Bank, click on subject resources. This takes you to a list of the major subject association websites.

The Teacher Resource Exchange provides opportunities for teachers and other educators to share lesson plans, teaching materials and ideas: http://tre.ngfl.gov.uk

12 Observing in the Classroom

Elizabeth Marsden

INTRODUCTION

Developing the ability to observe pupils, teachers and the general environment of the classroom takes a considerable amount of time, patience and practice, but it is a vital tool in your professional development survival kit. Observation is more than just watching. It involves preparation and knowledge, focus and attention, recording and reporting, and a willingness to review the whole process in order to improve teaching and learning in the class. Heightman (2005) underlined the importance of observation for educators at all levels: '… there is so much to learn from every invitation you receive to observe …. Lesson observations and the improved professional practice that can be gained from it is an important continual professional development' (p. 63). It is a skill that improves with time and practice once you have a grasp of who/what you are observing; why you are observing and how you are observing. This chapter seeks to supply guidelines to help you with this quest.

Along with evaluation and discussions with colleagues, observation helps you to improve your own practice. Observation is an important skill because it helps you to evaluate pupils' participation and progress by monitoring their responses to learning tasks. This enables you to give constructive support to pupils as they learn, modify your approach accordingly and provide feedback to teachers. It helps if you contribute to maintaining and analysing records of pupils' progress.

OBJECTIVES

By the end of this chapter, you should:

- develop a knowledge of the golden rules for observing in the classroom;
- understand the Observation Cycle;

- try a variety of strategies for observing the teaching, learning and environmental conditions in the classroom;
- suggest ways of recording, reporting and reviewing your observations with your teacher, parents and other adults.

This chapter refers to the HLTA standards on *improving your own knowledge and practice*, through using observation and responding to advice and feedback. See Appendix 2 for information on how this chapter maps onto the standards at the time of publication; if these are revised then updated materials will appear on the website supporting this text.

In essence, your role as an HLTA is similar to that of the teacher's. You both strive to increase pupils' learning by attending to cognitive, emotional, physical, social and spiritual needs. You both seek to improve pupils' sense of well-being, encourage communication and allow them opportunities to develop thinking skills and creativity. One teacher, no matter how experienced or talented, can only observe a certain amount in any one lesson. She also must juggle her teaching and her assessing, and maintain good behavioural control with the whole class. As an HLTA, when working in the classroom with the teacher, you can focus upon specific details and can observe the class at a completely different angle from the teacher's view. You can adopt a different role and status (more informal) from the teacher and you have the opportunity to observe the children in out-of-class activities, which can lead to a more holistic understanding of certain children. An HLTA who is an experienced observer is invaluable to the class teacher.

Task 12.1
What did you see?

Think about the last lesson in which you were assisting and see if you can answer the following:

- Where was the teacher positioned?
- What were the learning outcomes for the lesson?
- How many pupils were successful in reaching those learning outcomes?
- Who was off-task the most? Why?
- Were the lights switched on all lesson?
- How warm was the room?
- What equipment/resources did the teacher use?

Make a note to observe these points in your next lesson. Then compare your recorded notes with your remembered notes; what can you conclude from this comparison?

As you learn more about how to observe, you will begin to remember more details and eventually you will notice important things subconsciously. But when you are just beginning, focus, attention and concentration are priorities. The following 'golden rules for observing' can be very useful as you begin to practise this new skill.

GOLDEN RULES FOR OBSERVING IN THE CLASSROOM

1   *Be unobtrusive.* Do the dynamics of the class change when you enter? If you are working in a class with a teacher, she sets the *feel* of the class. An experienced teacher has a certain *presence* in the class which determines the ethos. Your role, at this point, is to support the teacher and maintain that ethos. Burnham and Jones (2002) refer to this as not being a distraction: '(Teaching) assistants should make sure that when they are observing pupils, their presence is not a distraction to the children and that they are acting as a supporting role to both pupils and teacher' (p. 129). If, however, you are covering for a teacher, your role and *presence* is totally changed. You cannot now be unobtrusive. The pupils need to know that *you* are in charge.

2   *Know what your main focus is to be.* In order to be useful in assisting learning, you need to be fully informed through discussion with the teacher at the preparation and planning stage so that you know what the learning outcomes are, how the work is differentiated and what the lesson structure looks like. Your teacher will collaborate with you to determine your role in this specific lesson period. You can then work out what your priorities are for observing. It is so important that the task is reasonable to achieve in the time you have. Good observations are clearly focused.

3   *Pay attention to your positioning.* As in golden rule 1, you do not want to be intrusive, but once you know what your focus is to be for the lesson/activity, you do need to think about the best place to be in order to observe. You get a completely different set of observations if you are sitting at the back of the class unconnected to any group or individual compared with sitting in a group or even sitting at the front of the class where you can see all of the pupils' facial responses. Your focus may indicate that you need to move around the class or to remain sitting. You do need to be able to see clearly what you have decided to observe. Occasionally, it is difficult to do this and remain unobtrusive and your positioning needs to be thought about carefully before you begin. However, matters in a classroom do change quite quickly sometimes, so you do need to be prepared to move in order to continue your observations.

4   *Know what kind of framework to use for recording.* Can you record your observations easily, quickly and clearly? Is a chart/table the best way to record or are post-it notes better? If, for example, observing pupil talk is the task, the easiest method of whole class observation might be to have a list of pupils' names and four different coloured pens. Each time a pupil answers a teacher question, a blue tick can be inserted next to the relevant name; if a pupil asks the teacher a question, a red tick is inserted; if pupils speak to each other in on-task discussion, insert a green tick and if pupils speak to each other but are off-task, a black tick might be inserted next to their names.

Following is an example of a simple table that you could use if you were observing different types of pupil talk for a 20-minute period. This example shows observations of the whole class responses minute by minute for the first four-minute period. It is hard work to continue such intensive observation of the whole class over 20 minutes so it is best to allow yourself a rest in the fifth, 10th and 15th minutes.

Table 12.1 Pupil talk in the classroom

Real time – minute intervals	Pupils initiating questions	Pupils answering teacher's questions	Off-task talk with peers	On-task discussion with peers	Other notes about the class activity or other events
9.10	John B Fred B Julie O				Tony W staring out of window
9.11		Rose D	Liam M and Reece C		
9.12	Alan M	Philip N and Rose D			Tony W dreaming
9.13				90% of class	Melissa and Tricia kicking each other under the table

If you are in a practical class, such as PE, where activities are changing rapidly, you may need to think of a very different strategy to record adequately what you have seen. Many PE teachers use post–its which they stick onto the walls as they move around the space; others may occasionally use a camcorder, but experienced PE teachers will tell you that it is virtually impossible to observe the whole class in detail. For the purpose of assessing whether their learning outcomes have been met, they tend to observe a small group of pupils in more detail. Observations of whole classes, even when they are relatively still and sitting in a classroom, are really quite taxing to the novice observer and it is usually advisable to start with small group observations. Other strategies for assessing, monitoring and recording pupils' progress are given in Chapter 9.

5   *Report succinctly, keeping to the focus.* One of the biggest temptations during observing, recording and reporting results to others is going off track and losing focus. This is why frameworks or criteria are used in observing and recording. Similarly, when you need to report your observation findings to your class teacher, parents or others, it is important that you spend some time studying the results beforehand and summarising them succinctly. Results and recordings need to be treated confidentially and not left lying around. If you have used a checklist or table for recording, you have the evidence there, but most teachers' time is pressured and they need you to be very focused in your reporting. Preparing beforehand what you should say in occasional delicate situations helps you avoid being indiscreet.

6   *Compare your observations with others.* From time to time, it is a very good idea to work collaboratively with another observer (maybe a special educational needs co-ordinator (SENCO), a teacher, visiting specialist or another teaching assistant) using the same observation/recording schedule and the same agreed focus. Whilst each individual has their own view on various occurrences, there should be

'Well Mr & Mrs Pratt, considering Walter has a brain the size of a walnut ...'

Figure 12.1 How not to give feedback to parents

Source: Cartoon by Jon Bird, http://www.jonbirdpix.yahoo.co.uk.

general agreement on the observations. If there are wide discrepancies, then a discussion should take place to decipher the differences. This is an exercise in standardisation to which all professionals are subject from time to time and does, in part, contribute to continuous professional development.

7   *Strive to be consistent.* There is no disputing that observing, especially over a period of time, is hard work. In order to do it well, however, you need to be consistent in the amount of effort you put in to it. You also need to be consistent in keeping to the agreed focus, in the detailed recording of your observations and in the way you report to others. Collaborating with others and support from your class teacher also help you remain consistent. Do not be afraid to ask for feedback from others as you do need to know you are doing a consistently effective job.

WHAT DOES A TEACHING ASSISTANT NEED TO OBSERVE?

The golden rules for observation present a strategy for *how* you might approach observation but exactly *what* might you need to observe? There are three major observable areas that you need to understand in order to become an effective HLTA: the teacher, the pupils and the environment.

Observing the teacher

Chapters 2, 9 and 10 give you an insight into the mechanics of lesson construction, delivery and evaluation. They should help you to understand why it is necessary for you to have a good working knowledge of the subject area(s) and Key Stages in which you are involved. Your experience has already imprinted the fact that every teacher is unique and the relationship that is developed between any one class and its teacher is also unique. In order to assist a teacher, you need to be aware of how that teacher establishes his or her routines, behaviour strategies, teaching styles and assessment procedures with each class s/he takes and what role s/he wants you to take in developing an excellent learning environment. It is also important that you are confident with their methods so that on those occasions when you are covering their class, you are able to continue similar routines.

Also, your duties involve working with small groups or maybe occasionally with individual pupils and it is a great opportunity to observe how a specialist might work with particular pupils, such as those with behavioural difficulties or those pupils with additional learning needs. When such experiences lend themselves, well-practised observing techniques become invaluable.

Task 12.2
Observing the lesson

Choose a lesson in which the teacher agrees for you to carry out the following observations. Use a notebook for recording observations and remember that you may need to move around in order that you can answer all the questions.

- What are the Learning Outcomes of the lesson?
- Were these explained to the pupils?
- How did the teacher introduce the lesson?
- What learning activities did the pupils undertake?
- Did the teacher use any behavioural strategies to get all pupils on-task?
- Was there any group work or pair work during the lesson?
- How did the teacher maintain motivation?
- Did s/he change the pace of the lesson?
- How did s/he manage any transitions?
- What resources did s/he use?
- Was any work differentiated for pupils?
- Which pupils received the most attention and why?
- Was the lesson successful in meeting the learning objectives?

In order to focus in more detail on how the teacher is working, a similar activity can be undertaken to that in Table 12.1 where pupil talk was being observed. Task 12.3 looks more closely at how the teacher uses verbal stimuli.

Task 12.3
Observing teacher use
of talk

Complete the following checklist for a section of the lesson or the entire lesson.

Teacher talk	What was said	Effect on pupils
Giving academic information		
Correcting errors		
Praising		
Questioning to check understanding		
Questioning to encourage pupil thinking and problem solving		
Asking pupils to focus on specific aspects		
Summarising learning		
Encouraging pupil reflection		
Coaching in skills		
Answering pupil questions		
Correcting poor behaviour		
Guiding pupils back on-task		
Outlining next learning tasks		

After the data collection, arrange a time for you to discuss the observations with the teacher in order to deepen your own understanding of how s/he is working and why s/he chose to work the way they did with that specific class.

Observing the pupils

When you are not engaged in actually covering the teaching of a class or even a small group, you are in an ideal position to observe pupils and the way they respond to the teacher, each other and the environment. You are in the enviable position of seeing pupils out of the class in other areas such as the dining room, the playground, the sports field or in after-school activities. You are also more likely than the teacher to really get to know some pupils as you might be working individually with them and they are more likely to confide in you as you often have a less formal role than the teacher. In Chapters 6, 7 and 8 you have learned about the way pupils learn, the different learning styles they adopt and the differences you may find between pupils of the same age and sex. It is possible to use a checklist or proforma for many areas involved with pupil learning such as whether they are on- or off-task; whether they are answering oral questions correctly or problem solving with their peers. But the actual process of learning is so complex that there is no observation proforma for recording it. The best way to find out about pupil learning is to ask the teacher if you may see the work that the pupils have completed and discuss it with the teacher.

Your observations of pupils' states of mind, relationships with one another and sharing of resources and equipment with each other can be of vital importance in assisting the learning process. When in a non-participant observation role, you can more easily and quickly recognise if a pupil, such as Jack (Figure 12.2), is on-task, because his apparent vacant stare is actually the way Jack looks when he is problem-solving. To a teacher who turns round from writing on the whiteboard, this stare may look like Jack is dreaming and definitely off-task.

By discussing Jack's learning style with the teacher, you may be facilitating the well-being of both teacher and Jack.

Pupils who are new to the class or those from a cultural minority or those whose first language is not English may all show signs of difficulty in adapting to the rules, ethos and routines of their new school. You might notice particular difficulties some pupils have at lunch times when they have no friends yet in the school or where their eating customs or language differences make social interaction problematic. Discussions with teachers, certain responsible pupils and other adults present at these break times can help you to think of ways to make integration quicker and less painful.

It is often the HLTA who recognises changes in pupils' behaviour before anyone else sees it and steps can be immediately taken to curb an emerging disruption. It is important that you have read and understood the school's behaviour policies and that you are aware of the accepted strategies for dealing with behavioural problems. If a disruption does occur in class, it is useful to ask the following questions:

Figure 12.2 Is Jack concentrating or dreaming?

Task 12.4
Observing pupil
disruption

- What seemed to be the precursor to the disruption?
- Which pupils were involved and had you noticed any changes in their mood or behaviour previously?
- What actually happened?
- How did the teacher react and how did this affect the situation?
- How did the other pupils react/cope?
- How was the disruption resolved?
- How long did it take to restore a learning environment?
- Were there any consequences for those involved in the disruption?

Trying to understand the background to any disharmony is very important to the long-term well-being of the class. Information that you share with your teacher and vice versa must remain confidential in order for pupils to build confidence and trust in you.

Observing the environment

Often the environment is taken for granted and little attention paid to it and yet it can have a very powerful effect on all those within it. The following task should focus your attention on your surroundings and you should see many things you had not previously noticed.

**Task 12.5
Observing familiar
surroundings**

In your own classroom, sit near the back of the class and note:

- Can you hear the teacher clearly at all times even when there is background noise?
- Can you see the whiteboard, the blackboard and any other visual aids your teacher is using?
- Are you warm or cold? Is there enough ventilation? Do you need the lights on/off?
- Is the work challenging or too hard?
- Is the class motivated to work or bored? Are you?
- Do you have any resources/equipment to help you learn?
- Can all the pupils use the resources? Does the equipment work? Is anyone having trouble with it?
- Are there any wall/table displays? Are they up-to-date and smart? What percentage is the pupils' work?
- Do they feel they have ownership of it, i.e. do they look at it and use it? Are they proud of it?
- Can you remember what the learning objectives are for this lesson?

Now take a 5–10 minute walk around the corridors of the school and make a note of notices or wall posters or table displays and ask yourself if they are eye-catching, up-to-date, useful for pupil learning (or safety) and appropriate. Is the school well lit, warm, tidy? Are the colours fresh and positive and contribute to a good 'feel' in the school? Is the space used well or is there rubbish/out-of-date equipment cluttering the corridors? Do people acknowledge each other/smile/greet each other as they pass in the corridors? Is there a positive ethos? How could things be improved? With whom could you discuss new ideas for improvement?

When our surroundings are familiar to us, it is easy to ignore the subconscious effect that colour, temperature, lighting, ventilation, cramped space, noise, smell and untidiness can have on our mood, physical comfort and cognitive focus. Each of these has an effect on pupils' readiness to learn.

Even the way the seating is arranged in class can have a marked effect on pupils' on- and off-task behaviour. Some pupils find it difficult to stay on-task when seated next to others in a group situation, but can stay on-task for most of the lesson when seated alone without distraction (Lucas and Thomas, 2000). Similarly, some pupils need to work in silence for full concentration while others work better with music in the background.

'Er, Mr Winterbottom, do you think we could shut the window just a wee bit? Billy seems to have frostbite.'

Figure 12.3 Adjusting the environment for optimum learning conditions

Source: Cartoon by Jon Bird, http://www.jonbirdpix.yahoo.ac.uk.

Some pupils become drowsy and unmotivated if the room temperature climbs above a certain temperature while others cannot concentrate if they are feeling chilled. It is obviously impossible to get the class environment perfect for every child all of the time, but being aware of the power of the environment on optimum learning is useful in trying to achieve the best possible conditions for the maximum amount of time.

As an observant HLTA you may be more aware than the pupil that s/he is sitting in a position where s/he cannot hear properly, especially if they are answering the question incorrectly or are completing the wrong page of problems. The pupil can easily be moved to a better position and one where there is less interference from either outside (close the window) or inside the classroom (move to quiet spot where there is no interference from chatter). Similarly, as an observant HLTA, you realise that a pupil who is normally bright is unable to follow the process of solving a maths problem on the board and/or who may be able to throw a ball well in PE but be unable to catch it, may have a sight problem. Simple steps can be taken to make learning more accessible whilst she is having her sight reviewed by the medical authorities. She could be moved closer to the board and adjustments made to colour contrasts with the whiteboard or the blackboard. In PE, a larger and different coloured ball can be tried for catching. In ICT, different backgrounds and fonts can be used. These are simple adjustments to the environment, but they make the difference between a pupil struggling or being able to learn in comfort.

Similarly, you may notice some pupils struggling with, or avoiding altogether, certain pieces of equipment. This may be because the equipment is the wrong size or not working properly. It may be because the pupil does not know how to use it or is afraid of it. In other situations, there is not enough equipment and some pupils are not willing to share it with others. All of these situations are potentially frustrating and may lead to serious disruptions. If equipment is not prepared in advance or placed for easy access, the lesson can be spoiled by wasting too much time trying to access it. Knowing the lesson plan, preparing thoughtfully and examining the environment beforehand with the teacher can avoid these situations arising. The following task should remind you how useful various resources and aids can be for assisting learning.

Task 12.6
Complete this grid over a five-day period

The resource	Pupil activity	Learning benefit
Text book		
Prepared study guide or worksheet		
Pictures, mind maps, graphics		
Video, CDs, DVDs		
Computer programmes including internet		
Tape recording		
Television programme or film		
Experiment		
Games, puzzles, models and activity cards		
Whiteboard/electronic whiteboard		
Digital camera		

Did you notice which pupils tended to use visual resources and which used aural or kinaesthetic ones? Did their choice match what you know of their learning styles? A good teacher knows the preferred learning styles of her pupils and tries to supply resources to include all pupils. Creating a good learning environment depends largely on planning, knowledge and observation skills twinned with imagination and leads to much happier and more efficient classes and teachers.

THE OBSERVATION CYCLE

Your role as an HLTA in education is flexible, varied and vital. The skill of observation is probably one of the most important skills you will need to do this job well. Some of the time you are covering a class in the teacher's absence and most of the time you are assisting so you really need to be able to see what is happening so that you can react appropriately. The planning and preparation of a lesson and its environment should always link back to the observed evaluations of the previous lesson in order to progress learning. Your role, during the lesson, is to observe the pupils, teacher and the environment closely in order to assess how things are going and what needs to be adjusted. After the lesson, work is evaluated by reading pupils' completed submissions and talking with the teacher. It is then time to review plans, strategies and decide on the next steps. The reviewing of the lesson goes hand in hand with assessing and evaluating pupil learning and leads on to planning the next lesson. It is important that you and the teacher take time to review all the factors involved, including behaviour management, classroom organisation and access and usage of equipment. It is also important that you can review your role as HLTA in any specific class with the class teacher at a regular interval.

The observation cycle is more clearly represented in the observation cycle diagram. Here it can clearly be seen how important skilled, critical observation is to the learning process, that is, of the pupils', the teacher's and your own learning. Hence observation should be a reflective ongoing practice that you endeavour to continually implement in your professional development.

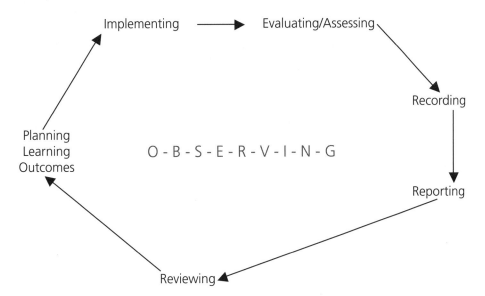

Figure 12.4 The observation cycle

SUMMARY

You should now appreciate the importance of developing the ability to critically observe the pupils, teacher and the environment of your class(es) and even more widely within the school. Your role as observer of the pupils' readiness and motivational state to learn, and of setting optimum environmental conditions for learning, is of vital importance to the teacher's ability to implement the planned lesson. You should have understood the golden rules for observing and have recognised some strategies for carrying out realistic observations in the time available. You should also realise the importance of confidentiality and discretion when reporting observations. Finally, you should now seek to work collaboratively with the teacher and other classroom adults in improving your observation practice.

The next chapter examines your professional development needs and looks at ways in which you can support your professional activities so you can improve your own knowledge and practice.

FURTHER READING

Burnham, I. and Jones, H. (2002) *The Teaching Assistant's Handbook S/NVQ Level 3*, Oxford: Harcourt, pp. 129–67. This chapter on observing and reporting on pupil performance is full of ideas, tips and practices for improving how, what and why observation of pupils is vital in the learning process. It also provides examples of spotting covert bullying and suggests ideas for improving pupil behaviour.

Clipsom-Boyles, S. (2000) *Putting Research into Practice in Primary Teaching and Learning*, London: David Fulton, pp. 13–47. These chapters outline various pieces of research concerned with pupil behaviour, classroom organisation and a method of assisting pupils who are struggling academically. The classroom organisation project shows pupils' behaviour change in two pieces of action research carried out by practitioners. By changing the organisation of the classroom, pupils' work output and ability to concentrate increased by marked amounts. It is useful for helping you see how changing your environment can powerfully affect pupil learning.

Tilstone, C. (ed) (1998) *Observing Teaching and Learning: Principles and Practice*, London: David Fulton. This book is for those who want to study this subject in much greater depth. It is very comprehensive and provides a theoretical underpinning of observation in both teaching and learning.

13 Your Professional Development

Sarah Younie and Ken Powell

INTRODUCTION

Being aware of your own professional development needs is an important part of your growing ability to be reflective so that you can improve your own practice through self evaluation. As an HLTA, you may wish to expand your work to other areas within the school, or you may wish to consider going on to train as a teacher. This chapter outlines how to use ICT to support your professional development; how to identify appropriate training programmes and qualifications by using the career development framework and also explores the various routes into teaching.

You need to be aware that if you want to become a teacher in a state-maintained school in England, you will need to achieve Qualified Teacher Status (QTS). This is awarded when you have successfully completed an Initial Teacher Education (ITE) programme either through an academic or employment-based route and have achieved the professional standards for QTS, which is a formal set of skills, knowledge and understanding required to be an effective teacher.

OBJECTIVES

By the end of this chapter, you should:

- understand how to use ICT to support your professional development through creating an e-portfolio and e-support network;
- have an awareness of the career development framework that will enable you to identify appropriate training programmes and qualifications to enhance your career;
- have an overview of the different routes progressing to Qualified Teacher Status.

This chapter touches on those HLTA standards that refer to ICT, in particular knowing how to *use ICT* to support your professional activities and those that refer to *professional development*, in particular knowing how to improve your own practice through your own initiative and self-evaluation. You can also refer to Appendix 2 to see how this chapter maps onto the standards at the time of publication; if these are revised then updated materials will appear on the website supporting this text.

USING ICT TO SUPPORT YOUR PROFESSIONAL DEVELOPMENT

As part of the standards, you are required to know how to use ICT to advance pupils' learning and, importantly, demonstrate that you can use ICT to support your work for your own and pupils' benefit (see Chapter 10 and 11 for more information). This chapter illustrates how to use ICT to support your professional development. It outlines how to create an e-portfolio and find e-support for yourself as your career progresses.

An e-portfolio allows you to collate your professional development experiences and to showcase examples of your best practice of working with pupils. Similarly, developing your own e-support in the form of a list of online contacts for professional advice provides you with a network that can be accessed and built on across the course of your career.

e-support

As part of your professional development you may want to develop e-support links on your web browser.

To support your professional practice you can list links to websites, online communities and contacts that offer information and advice. For example, you can bookmark educational websites – subject associations and/or government education sites such as the TDA (Training and Development Agency), DCSF (Department for Children, Schools and Families – previously DfES (Department for Education and Skills)), QCA (Qualifications and Curriculum Authority), Becta (British Educational Communications and Technology Agency) and Teachernet. This chapter will outline a number of websites relevant to your professional development and provide a list at the end of the chapter for your consideration. You may want to explore those most relevant to you and bookmark them.

In developing your own e-support, you can also create your own email address book, with key contacts to facilitate your professional practice. You can make links to educational forums and online discussions, which offer the opportunity to pose questions, have answers from a range of practitioners in the field, with experience and expertise, thereby enabling you to be in contact with a community of practice that offers insights and support in your Key Stage and subject area.

Advantages of developing your own e-support network include keeping up-to-date with government initiatives and developments in your specialised field. For example, from 2007 the reshaping of the 14–19 curriculum will bring a raft of reforms that will need to be understood in terms of their impact on the pupils you are supporting. For example, will the pupils you work with be studying one of the new specialised vocational diplomas? Are any of these in your subject area? If you have a specialism in literacy, numeracy or ICT, you will need to be aware of the new functional skills qualifications. For further information on the changes to the 14–19 curriculum see http://www.dcsf.gov.uk/14-19 and http://www. qca.org.uk/qca_12195.aspx.

e-portfolio

The aim of developing your own e-portfolio is to equip yourself with a record of your professional development in an online format. Your e-portfolio is simply a collection of relevant materials, which you may choose to have on your computer or your work space on the school intranet. Your e-portfolio can contain sections that you update throughout your career. You could choose to have this as a webpage. Your e-portfolio may have a section for a short CV, a section for training courses you have attended and may also contain a list of websites that you find useful for your professional practice, as discussed above. These different sections can be put as links across the top of the webpage, with a photo of yourself.

Importantly, you can select and store examples of your work supporting pupils to reflect your best practice, through video or screen shots of lesson activities, examples of pupils' work and examples of resources you have developed for facilitating pupils' learning. With your e-portfolio, you are the author and you select the evidence that you feel best reflects your professional practice. You could create a section for your continuing professional development (CPD), which contains your observations, discussions with mentors and what you consider to be your training needs. You would then be demonstrating your initiative and ability to be reflective and self-evaluative as the standards require.

Pupils can also create an online portfolio for their school work, as a place to record their learning and achievements. See Chapter 9 for further information.

The advantages of creating your own e-portfolio are to showcase your best practice, which you can store on a CD-ROM, or put online. You would then be able to send this to prospective employers, whilst clearly demonstrating your level of ICT competence to support your development and that of pupils. Creating an e-portfolio provides an opportunity for the structured and systematic collection of evidence, with accompanying critical reflections, which form an important part of your developing professionalism and can be used to demonstrate that you have achieved the standards. Your e-portfolio can be easily updated and revised as its creation is underpinned by initiative and self-evaluation. Your e-portfolio can form the basis of any professional review by supplying access to a wide range of evidence and stimulate discussion with your line manager.

Task 13.2
Creating an e-portfolio

Find out if the school where you are working has a set format for staff e-portfolios. If they have, you may like to compare their approach to the one outlined in this chapter. In fact, some countries are developing a national e-portfolio framework. Also, look at http://www.eportfolios.ac.uk and the Becta website for more information on e-portfolios at http://www.becta.org.uk. What would you want to put in your e-portfolio?

With regards to your professional development, you will need to identify the skills and knowledge that need extending for you to progress in your career. This means being able to identify training programmes and qualifications that support your development, and to help you do this the TDA has created the career development framework.

CAREER DEVELOPMENT PLANNING

We suggest that on your own and with your mentor you examine the career development framework, which sets out national training programmes and qualifications so that you can identify development opportunities that will help you advance your career. For example, you should have achieved a nationally recognised qualification at level 2 or above in English/literacy and mathematics/numeracy. You then need to examine which other qualifications and programmes will support your professional needs.

As the TDA outlines, the career development framework maps the support staff roles found in schools against 'commonly-used qualifications and national training programmes and shows opportunities for lateral transition (role conversion, multi-skilling and/or career changes) as well as progression within a job role' (TDA, 2007).

The framework has been produced to help you identify appropriate training and development by illustrating progression opportunities and enables you to consider potential career pathways. It is designed to aid you in discovering clear career progression routes for yourself. You can use the information to make informed decisions about training and development. See the TDA website for the guidance materials to help you use the career development framework.

As the TDA stresses, it is important to choose qualifications and training that are right for you, your role and the needs of the school. You may be reflecting on what you need to do or where to start to achieve this. The framework can help you find the information you need to evaluate whether a qualification or training programme will meet your needs.

You need to be aware that the government has introduced a common core of skills and knowledge for all those working with children and a set of vocational qualifications for accrediting support work in schools. Both these advancements may produce development needs for you which you may be required to identify. We will briefly explain these developments here for you and suggest you discuss these further with your mentor.

A common core of skills and knowledge

The government is developing a single framework of qualifications for all those who work with children, young people and families and is examining all national occupational standards (NOS) and qualifications with a view to incorporating a common core.

The TDA has already developed and incorporated this common core into induction training for teaching assistants (see http://www.tda.gov.uk/partners/supportstafftraining/inductionmaterial). The qualifications in the framework will be updated periodically, and you can check the online database for the latest information on nationally accredited qualifications and awarding bodies at http://www.openquals.org.uk.

Support work in schools qualification

There are new vocational qualifications for support work in schools. These are both knowledge-based and competency-based and are achieved through training and on-the-job assessment and form part of the national qualifications framework (NQF). The qualification includes mandatory and optional units and you select the units that best match your role and your development needs. You can choose from the list of units by searching for support work in schools in the national qualifications database (see http://www.openquals.org.uk).

The national qualifications framework for England, Wales and Northern Ireland and the framework for higher education qualifications (FHEQ) sets out the levels at which qualifications can be recognised. These provide broad descriptions of learning outcomes at each level and are designed to help you compare the levels of different qualifications and identify clear progression routes.

Performance review

The career development framework can also support your performance review or appraisal by identifying the qualifications or training programmes which are relevant to your current role and those that can help you progress in the future.

Once you have identified your training and development needs, you can plan your career progression. To help you do this, you can visit the Skills4Schools website and use the online 'journey planner', and access examples of how others have approached their training and development. See http://www.skills4schools.org.uk.

You can also use the career development framework to help you identify higher level qualifications as it enables you to compare the knowledge and skills you already have against those that you would need to develop your career. For example, you may explore the possibility of completing a foundation degree, which is an intermediate higher education qualification equivalent to level 5 of the national qualifications framework.

Importantly, there are some foundation degrees specifically designed for support staff and these include foundation degrees in classroom support, learning support and early years. A foundation degree can lead to a full honours degree if you should wish to continue with your academic study. For a full list of providers and their foundation degree subjects, see the UCAS website (http://www.ucas.com). You can also find out more about foundation degrees from the foundation degree website (http://www.foundation degree.org.uk).

- Take some time to reflect on your professional development needs and consider the skills and knowledge you would like to extend.
- Discuss with your mentor or line manager how you could develop professionally and how you might progress your career.
- Explore the career development framework to identify where your skills and knowledge need developing and find training programmes and qualifications identified by the TDA as relevant to your professional development.

Be aware that although the framework focuses on national qualifications, not all will be available locally. Many local authorities have adapted the framework to suit their needs. Contact your local authority or talk to your mentor and line manager about training and development opportunities in your area.

CHOOSING TO BECOME A TEACHER

If you would like to become a teacher, then the next step is to gain qualified teacher status (QTS), which means completing a programme of initial teacher education (ITE). ITE is also sometimes referred to as initial teacher training (ITT) and is conducted in universities, colleges and schools throughout the UK. ITE has options to suit everyone, whatever your qualifications, experience, preferences or personal circumstances.

This section looks at the various routes available to you to train to be a teacher and there are more routes now than ever before. These are all recognised as leading to QTS and it is important to choose the one that suits your needs best. The variety and flexibility available warrant explanation here though we recommend that you take the time to explore the TDA website for further information when considering which route would be most appropriate for you. The information is correct for England in the 2007–2008 academic year; other regions of the UK may differ. For more details, and the ability to search for training institutions in particular areas, please visit http://www.tda.gov.uk.

The two main strands of ITE are undergraduate and postgraduate, with the latter split between employment and non-employment based routes. Undergraduate routes usually involve undertaking a full degree (usually over three years), which combines degree courses and teaching practices to give a BA or BSc with QTS. There is also the registered teaching programme (RTP) if you have less than a full degree, which allows you the completion of degree credits and attainment of QTS, whilst working in a school. Postgraduate courses are available to those who already have a degree equivalent. There are also overseas trained teacher (OTT) routes available for people who already hold a teaching qualification from a country whose qualification is not automatically recognised in England.

Your next step then is to choose a route, check the entry requirements and make an application. To do this, you need to explore the range of courses and training providers that lead to qualified teacher status. Next identify the factors you need to consider when choosing your route, for example, by investigating the financial support available for each, alongside your experience and qualifications.

To train as a teacher, on any programme, you must achieve a standard equivalent to a grade C in GCSE English language and mathematics. If you want to teach primary or Key Stage 2/3 (ages 7–14), you must also have achieved a standard equivalent to a grade C in a GCSE science subject. Many training providers offer equivalency tests in these subjects if you do not meet the minimum requirements, which would then allow you to train as a teacher.

You can choose various routes into teaching as outlined in Table 13.1 below.

UNDERGRADUATE ROUTES INTO TEACHING

With the undergraduate route, you are able to study for an honours degree and train to be a teacher at the same time. The undergraduate routes are offered at universities and colleges throughout the UK and applications are made through the Universities and Colleges Admissions Service (UCAS). See http://www.ucas.ac.uk. You can take a Bachelor of Education course, which incorporates QTS, or a Bachelor of Arts with QTS, or Bachelor of Science with QTS.

Degree with QTS

A Bachelor of Education (BEd) course enables you to study for your degree and complete your initial teacher training simultaneously. Course content may vary according to the university or college providing it, but all BEd graduates receive

Table 13.1 Routes into teaching

Undergraduate options		You can train to be a teacher while completing a degree	
Bachelor of Education courses		BEd	
Bachelor of Arts with Qualified Teacher Status or Bachelor of Science with Qualified Teacher Status		BA + QTS BSc + QTS	
Postgraduate options		If you already have a degree, you can train to be a teacher in 1–2 years	
Non-employment-based routes		Employment-based routes	
Postgraduate Certificate of Education	PGCE	Graduate Teacher Programme	GTP
School-centred Initial Teacher Training	SCITT	Registered Teacher Programme	RTP
Teach First Programme	Teach First		
		OTTP (Overseas Trained Teacher Programme) Holders of overseas teaching qualifications	

QTS in addition to their degree. Courses generally take three or four years full-time or four to six years part-time. However, if you have undergraduate credits from previous study you may be able to complete a course in two years. Entry requirements vary according to the specific course, so to find out more you need to contact your individual course providers. Applications for BEds are made through UCAS.

Bachelor of Arts with QTS

By taking a Bachelor of Arts (BA) or Bachelor of Science (BSc) degree with QTS, you can study for a degree and incorporate initial teacher training at the same time. Entry requirements vary according to the specific course although a minimum of two A-levels or equivalent is usually required. You should check with individual course providers for details. Again, applications are made via UCAS.

Partial degree route: registered teacher programme

The registered teacher programme (RTP) may be for you if you already have some credits towards a degree. The RTP route allows you as a non-graduate to complete studying for your degree and qualify as a teacher at the same time, by providing a blend of work-based teacher training and academic study. The RTP route will lead you to qualified teacher status.

To be eligible, you first need to be working in a school as an unqualified teacher. In order to ensure that you can extend your subject knowledge to degree level, your training provider will also work with a local higher education institution (HEI) and your training will be tailored to your own individual needs. The RTP route usually takes two years, but may be less, depending on your prior teaching experience.

You can complete the RTP in any English school, as long as they are prepared to employ you as an unqualified teacher for the duration of the programme. However, this does exclude schools that OfSTED has placed under 'special measures' and pupil referral units. To undertake the RTP you must have a grade C in English and maths at GCSE and if you wish to teach primary or Key Stage 2/3 you must also have a GCSE in science or an equivalent (see Table 13.2). For more information about the RTP route see the TDA website.

Postgraduate routes into teaching

All postgraduate routes require you to meet certain basic requirements. Although these are stated in terms of UK qualifications, equivalents from other countries will be accepted. Remember many providers also offer equivalency tests in subjects if you do not meet the basic requirements which, if passed, will allow you to continue into ITE.

Once the basic requirements above have been met, there are a variety of postgraduate routes into teaching. These include (listed alphabetically):

- GTP (Graduate Teacher Programme)
- PGCE (Post/Professional Graduate Certificate Education)

Table 13.2 Basic qualification requirements for entry

Qualifications	Minimum grade needed
A GCSE in English	C
A GCSE in mathematics	C
A UK degree	Pass
A GCSE in science only if applying for primary or Key Stage 2/3 courses	C

- SCITT (School-centred Initial Teacher Training)
- Teach First

Each of these routes will now be considered in more detail.

Graduate Teacher Programme

The Graduate Teacher Programme (GTP) involves on-the-job training provided by a school, allowing people to gain QTS while being employed as an unqualified teacher. Schools usually advertise places in the local press, but you can also approach schools directly to see if they have places available or apply to the GTP provider, which covers the area you are interested in. These GTP providers are either DRBs (designated recommended bodies) or EBRITTPs (Employment-based Route Initial Teacher Training Providers) and are listed on the TDA website.

As an unqualified teacher, you can expect to be paid at least £14,751 (taxed) for the year. Many GTP places are offered by schools that receive a grant from the TDA to cover some of the costs associated with employing a trainee teacher (known as salary grant places). However, schools can also offer places that they fund directly (known as training grant places).

The GTP route allows you to train to teach either primary or individual secondary subjects. DRBs are allocated places to give to schools in three strands: primary, priority secondary and other secondary. In general, there are more salary grant places available for priority secondary subjects than for other secondary subjects. The school that employs you is responsible for your training, so most will interview candidates for each salary grant post available. Competition can be very high for these posts.

Post/Professional Graduate Certificate of Education

PGCE programmes involve an ITE provider educating you to become a teacher and achieve QTS. Most focus on educating you to teach rather than subject knowledge so a degree, or a component of your degree, in your chosen specialism is usually required. However, this is not always essential, and it is advisable that you discuss with your ITE provider their requirements as there are ways to top up or enhance your specialism. PGCEs offered by schools are covered in the SCITT section following.

There are many varieties of PGCE. Both primary and secondary courses are offered. Many courses are one-year (full-time) but there are also part-time, flexible and modular courses, which will take longer. In addition, there are extended courses for people who wish to teach mathematics, physics or chemistry at secondary level, but who require additional subject knowledge education. These courses will last between 18 months and two years. All PGCE courses involve spending at least 120 days in a school or educational setting.

Grants are provided for students on a PGCE. All students are entitled to a grant of £2700 from their local authority, of which £1200 is not means tested. You may receive an additional grant of £9000 (for secondary maths, science, English, ICT, D&T, MFL, RE and music teachers) or £6000 (all other subjects). Grants do not have to be repaid and are tax free. In addition, you may be entitled to a golden hello, paid at the start of your second year of teaching in secondary school. Maths and science teachers receive £5000, while English, ICT, D&T, MFL, RE and music teachers receive £2500. These payments are subject to tax.

ITE providers are entitled to charge student fees on PGCE courses. At present, these are a maximum of £3000. Fees can be paid back through salary, like an undergraduate loan, so do not need to be paid up front. PGCEs are applied for through the GTTR (graduate teacher training register) which is available online at http://www.gttr.ac.uk.

School-centred Initial Teacher Training

SCITTs are local schools that have formed consortia to offer teacher education courses across the group. They are treated as PCGEs with respect to funding arrangements (details in the preceding section). All SCITTs provide QTS as an outcome and many also award a PGCE. SCITTs are applied for through the GTTR (http://www.gttr.ac.uk) as is the case with PGCEs.

With an SCITT, you will spend almost all your time in the consortia schools whereas PCGEs will have a component of the year (about one-quarter to one-third in many cases) in a university environment. GTP courses are different again in that the SCITT is awarded by a group of schools whilst a GTP course is focused almost entirely in one school. The funding arrangements for GTP students are also different. See the TDA website for further advice about financial support for these routes.

Teach First

Teach First is a training route, run by an independent organisation, that enables top graduates to complete a two year programme working in challenging schools in cities around the country that awards QTS and also provides leadership training and work experience with leading employers. Teach First is only available in secondary schools and aims to recruit top graduates.

The minimum requirements are different to the other ITE programmes in that a potential trainee must meet the following requirements: an upper second degree, 40 per cent of which relates to a National Curriculum subject; 300 UCAS tariff points (equivalent to BBB at A level) and an ability to show high levels of competency in areas such as leadership, teamwork, resilience, critical thinking, communication skills, initiative and creativity, respect, humility and empathy.

You will be paid at point 3 on the unqualified teacher scale during the first year of the programme and as an NQT during the second year. In addition, your food and accommodation will be paid for during the summer institute at the start of the Teach First course. Teach First only accepts applications through the online form at http://www.teachfirst.org.uk.

OVERSEAS TRAINED TEACHERS

If you are a qualified teacher from within the European Union you can access teaching positions in the same way as 'home' trained teachers with QTS. From outside the European Economic Area (EEA), however, the Overseas Trained Teachers Programme (OTTP) applies.

OTTP allows people with teaching qualifications from outside the EEA to gain QTS. It must be gained within four years of starting to work as an unqualified teacher. You must gain an unqualified teaching position in an English school before you can start the OTTP. In addition you will require a qualification equivalent to a UK bachelors degree, a qualification equivalent to a GCSE grade C in maths and English, or a qualification equivalent to a GCSE grade C in science if you plan to teach primary or Key Stage 2/3. The National Academic Recognition Centre (http://www.naric.org.uk) allows equivalent qualifications to be identified.

The OTTP is individualised, so the length of the training and the requirements are decided through an initial assessment. It is possible that you will only require QTS assessment. Your school will continue to pay you as an unqualified teacher until you have passed the QTS assessment; in addition, if further training is required, the TDA will cover the cost up to £1250.

Once you have gained a teaching post and are certain you meet the other criteria, you should apply directly to a DRB in your area. If you trained in the EEA or Switzerland, you may be eligible for QTS without further assessment. Contact the GTCE (http://www.gtce.org.uk) for details.

Task 13.4
Selecting a route into teaching

In order to become a teacher, you will need to examine your initial teacher training options before making your application. Deciding on which training course to do can be challenging, so you need to identify which factors are important to you (for example funding) when choosing your ITE course. Find out more information about the QTS routes and funding opportunities by examining the TDA website in more detail. You can also register for more information on the website. Consider in the first instance, which route would be best for you?

Next, find out what ITE providers and courses are available in your local area and be aware of other options, such as studying at a distance, or part-time, which may be offered by ITE providers further away. Next contact your selected ITE provider for further information.

Once you have chosen a course, make sure you have checked the entry requirements, then verify whether you meet these or need to make arrangements through equivalency tests to satisfy these requirements. Next, you need to make an application and check when the applications must be made by.

SUMMARY

This chapter has outlined how to use ICT to support your professional practice through the creation of an e-support network and online portfolio, which can capture your best practice and collate your professional development experiences. We have also outlined the career development framework that is designed to help you identify where your skills and knowledge need developing and find training programmes and qualifications relevant to your professional development. For those who wish to become teachers, we have outlined the different progression routes into teaching: the undergraduate route, in which you train to be a teacher while completing a degree; the postgraduate route, where if you already have a degree you can train to be a teacher in a year; and the employment-based route, in which you can train and qualify as a teacher while working in a school.

FURTHER READING

QCA (Qualifications and Curriculum Authority) has a national database of qualifications that allows you to check the online database of nationally accredited qualifications, units and awarding bodies at http://www.openquals.org.uk

Skills4Schools is an online resource to help school support staff access learning opportunities at work. The website has a journey planner and examples of how people have approached their training and development: http://www.skills4schools.org.uk

TDA (Training and Development Agency for Schools): http://www.tda.gov.uk

For advice about career progression see the TDA website and the career development framework at http://www.tda.gov.uk/support/careerdevframework.aspx. For information on the common core of skills and knowledge for the children's workforce, see http://www.tda.gov.uk/partners/supportstafftraining/inductionmaterial

For advice about meeting specific professional standards for HLTAs, see the TDA website, which contains case studies (including videos), at: http://www.tda.gov.uk/support/hlta/professstandards/meetingthestandards.aspx

For advice about meeting the needs of all children and young people with respect to special educational needs (SEN) and disabilities, we recommend that you read the TDA publication '*Special educational needs in mainstream schools: a guide for the beginner teacher*'. This leaflet is available online and will help you to support learners in accessing the curriculum in accordance with the SEN code of practice and disabilities legislation. See http://www.tda.gov.uk/about/publicationslisting/TDA0202.aspx

WEBSITES

Becta (British Educational Communications and Technology Agency) for information on e-portfolios: http://www.becta.org.uk

Children's Workforce Development Council (CWDC): http://www.cwdcouncil.org.uk

Children's workforce qualifications: http://www.dcsf.gov.uk/childrenswfqualifications

Classroom 2.0: http://classroom20.ning.com

Common core: http://www.dcsf.gov.uk/commoncore

DCSF (Department for Children, Schools and Families): http://www.dcsf.gov.uk/14-19

e-portfolios: http://www.eportfolios.ac.uk

Foundation degree: http://www.foundationdegree.org.uk

Futurelab: http://www.futurelab.org.uk

GTC (General Teaching Council for England): http://www.gtce.org.uk

GTTR (Graduate Teacher Training Register): http://www.gttr.ac.uk

Higher education courses including degree, foundation degree and access courses: http://www.ucas.com

HLTAs (higher level teaching assistants): http://www.tda.gov.uk/support/hlta

NARIC (National Academic Recognition Centre) allows equivalent qualifications to be identified: http://www.naric.org.uk

NOS (National Occupational Standards) directory: http://www.ukstandards.org

NQF (National Qualifications Framework): http://www.qca.org.uk/493.html

QCA (Qualifications and Curriculum Authority): http://www.qca.org.uk

School workforce advisers: http://www.tda.gov.uk/partners/workforceadvisers

Subject associations' websites: http://www.gtce.org.uk/weblinks/subject_associations

Teachernet: http://www.teachernet.gov.uk

Teach First: http://www.teachfirst.org.uk

UCAS (Universities and Colleges Admissions Service): http://www.ucas.ac.uk

UK Education Evidence Portal: http://www.eep.ac.uk/Main/Default.aspx

Appendix 1

HLTA professional standards

The HLTA set of professional standards which follow are from the TDA website (TDA Standards for HLTAs, 2008).

PROFESSIONAL ATTRIBUTES

Those awarded HLTA status must demonstrate, through their practice, that they:

1   Have high expectations of children and young people with a commitment to helping them fulfil their potential.
2   Establish fair, respectful, trusting, supportive and constructive relationships with children and young people.
3   Demonstrate the positive values, attitudes and behaviour they expect from children and young people.
4   Communicate effectively and sensitively with children, young people, colleagues, parents and carers.
5   Recognise and respect the contribution that parents and carers can make to the development and well-being of children and young people.
6   Demonstrate a commitment to collaborative and cooperative working with colleagues.
7   Improve their own knowledge and practice including responding to advice and feedback.

PROFESSIONAL KNOWLEDGE AND UNDERSTANDING

Those awarded HLTA status must demonstrate, through their practice, that they:

8   Understand the key factors that affect children and young people's learning and progress.

9 Know how to contribute to effective personalised provision by taking practical account of diversity.

10 Have sufficient understanding of their area(s) of expertise to support the development, learning and progress of children and young people.

11 Have achieved a nationally recognised qualification at level 2 or above in English/ literacy and mathematics/numeracy.

12 Know how to use ICT to support their professional activities.

13 Know how statutory and non-statutory frameworks for the school curriculum relate to the age and ability ranges of the learners they support.

14 Understand the objectives, content and intended outcomes for the learning activities in which they are involved.

15 Know how to support learners in accessing the curriculum in accordance with the special educational needs (SEN) code of practice and disabilities legislation.

16 Know how other frameworks that support the development and well-being of children and young people impact upon their practice.

PROFESSIONAL SKILLS

Teaching and learning activities must take place under the direction of a teacher and in accordance with arrangements made by the headteacher of the school.

PLANNING AND EXPECTATIONS

Those awarded HLTA status must demonstrate, through their practice, that they:

17 Use their area(s) of expertise to contribute to the planning and preparation of learning activities.

18 Use their area(s) of expertise to plan their role in learning activities.

19 Devise clearly structured activities that interest and motivate learners and advance their learning.

20 Plan how they will support the inclusion of the children and young people in the learning activities.

21 Contribute to the selection and preparation of resources suitable for children and young people's interests and abilities.

MONITORING AND ASSESSMENT

Those awarded HLTA status must demonstrate, through their practice, that they:

22 Monitor learners' responses to activities and modify the approach accordingly.

23 Monitor learners' progress in order to provide focused support and feedback.

24 Support the evaluation of learners' progress using a range of assessment techniques.

25 Contribute to maintaining and analysing records of learners' progress.

TEACHING AND LEARNING ACTIVITIES

Those awarded HLTA status must demonstrate, through their practice, that they:

26   Use effective strategies to promote positive behaviour.
27   Recognise and respond appropriately to situations that challenge equality of opportunity.
28   Use their ICT skills to advance learning.
29   Advance learning when working with individuals.
30   Advance learning when working with small groups.
31   Advance learning when working with whole classes without the presence of the assigned teacher.
32   Organise and manage learning activities in ways which keep learners safe.
33   Direct the work, where relevant, of other adults in supporting learning.

(TDA Standards for HLTAs, 2008).

Appendix 2
Map of chapters to standards

The professional standards for HLTAs, like those of other educational professionals, such as teachers, are subject to periodic updating and revision. However, whilst these may alter the numbering and wording of specific standards, the generic knowledge and skills required are likely to remain, albeit with some amendments. It is part of your professional duty to keep up to date with government changes in education, including the standards, and we suggest you review relevant websites, in particular the TDA website, and consider which revisions are relevant to you and impact upon your role and responsibilities. In the future, when the HLTA set of standards become updated, a revised version of this appendix will appear on the website that accompanies this book.

The degree to which each chapter refers to the standards identified in the righthand column of the following table varies. Whilst some explicitly cover the standard identified in detail, for example, Chapter 9 on monitoring and assessment, others may touch upon a standard, but cover more than one, or may only refer to part of a standard. The aim of each chapter is to support your professional development in relation to a particular area, defined by the chapter title, and for you to work on this whilst being aware of how this relates to the standards.

The current set of professional standards for HLTAs is organised around professional attributes; professional knowledge and understanding and professional skills, which include reference to planning and expectations; monitoring and assessment; and teaching and learning activities.

	Chapter	Standards 2008	Standards
1	Your role as a higher level teaching assistant	1, 3, 5, 13, 16, 32, 33	Professional attributes regarding your general role and responsibilities; having *high expectations* of children and young people, demonstrating *positive values*; you *recognise the contribution that parents and carers can make*; you have a knowledge of *statutory and non-statutory frameworks for the school curriculum* that relate to the learners you support; you know about how *other frameworks that support children impact on your practice*; you understand your responsibilities with respect to health and safety, in particular, organising and managing the learning environment in ways that *keep learners safe*; you can *direct the work of other adults in supporting learning*.
2	Collaborative working with the teacher	6, 9, 14, 21, 23, 25, 32	Demonstrate collaborative and cooperative *working with colleagues*; taking account of *diversity* through understanding differentiation; contribute to the preparation of *resources*; understand the *objectives, content and intended outcomes* for the learning activities in which you are involved; understand the processes of *monitoring and assessment*, specifically monitor learners' progress and maintaining records of learners' progress; an awareness of *keeping learners safe*.
3 and 4	Developing your communication skills: non-verbal and verbal	2, 4, 29, 30	Develop your communication skills to help establish supportive and *constructive relationships* with children and young people; to *communicate effectively* and sensitively with children, young people and colleagues; to advance learning when working with *individuals*; to advance learning when working with *small groups*.
5	Understanding pupil diversity	1, 9, 27	You know how to contribute to effective personalised provision by taking practical account of *diversity*; you are able to *recognise and respond appropriately to situations that challenge equality of opportunity*.
6	Pupil behaviour and teaching styles	2, 4, 9, 26	You are able to *establish relationships* with children and young people that are respectful, trusting, supportive and constructive; you can *communicate effectively* and sensitively with children and young people; know how to contribute to effective *personalised provision* by taking practical account of *diversity*, through different teaching strategies; use effective strategies to promote *positive behaviour*.
7	Understanding how pupils learn	8, 9, 15, 19, 20	You understand the *key factors that affect children and young people's learning* and progress; you are able to contribute to effective *personalised provision* by taking practical account of *diversity*; know about the need to support learners in accessing the curriculum in accordance with the *special educational needs* (SEN) code of practice; understand factors affecting motivation so you are able to *motivate* learners and advance their learning; be able to plan how to support the *inclusion* of the children and young people in the learning activities.

	Chapter	Standards 2008	Standards
8	Understanding learning theories and strategies	7, 8	You are able to *improve your own knowledge and practice*, through understanding how children and young people learn; understand the *key factors that affect children and young people's learning*, e.g. different learning styles and strategies.
9	Monitoring and assessing pupils	10, 22, 23, 24, 25	You know how to *use ICT* to support your professional activities; you are able to *monitor* learners' responses to activities and modify the approach accordingly; monitor learners' progress in order to provide focused support and feedback; support the evaluation of learners' progress using a range of *assessment* techniques; contribute to maintaining and analysing records of learners' progress.
10	Developing your subject specific knowledge	10, 12, 13, 17, 18	You have sufficient understanding of your area(s) of *expertise* to support the development, learning and progress of children and young people; know how to *use ICT* to support your professional activities; know how statutory and non-statutory *frameworks* for the school curriculum relate to the age and ability ranges of the learners you support; use your area(s) of *expertise* to contribute to the planning and preparation of learning activities; use your area(s) of expertise to plan your role in learning activities.
11	Developing resources and supporting pupil learning using ICT	12, 21, 28	You know how to use *ICT to support your professional activities* as well as *using ICT to advance learning*. You can contribute to the *selection and preparation of resources*.
12	Observing in classrooms	7	You are able to *improve your own knowledge and practice*, through using observation and responding to advice and feedback.
13	Your professional development	7, 10, 11	You know how to *use ICT* to support your professional activities; you can *improve your own knowledge and practice*. You have achieved a *nationally recognised qualification at level 2 or above in English/literacy and mathematics/numeracy*.

Appendix 3

Glossary of terms, acronyms and abbreviations

Education provision in the UK has developed specialised terms, acronyms and abbreviations. A list of those used in the chapters is included here for reference. These provide a shorthand way for those involved in the education profession to talk about their work to each other. You will need to become familiar with a wide range of terms specific to education. In addition there are a number of useful glossaries which will provide explanations of terms you come across. Most professional educational websites will have glossaries of terms to help you understand the specific material being referenced. Some of the items in the following table have been adapted from Capel, Leask and Turner (eds) (2009) *Learning to Teach in the Secondary School: A Companion to School Experience*.

Attainment Targets The knowledge, skills and understanding that pupils of different abilities and maturities are expected to have by the end of each Key Stage (qv). Except in the case of citizenship Attainment Targets consist of eight level descriptions (qv) of increasing difficulty, plus a description for exceptional performance above level 8. See also Level Descriptions and Programmes of Study (PoS).

BA/BSc with QTS Bachelor of Arts/Bachelor of Science with QTS (qv). A route to QTS.

Becta British Educational Communications and Technology Agency

BEd Bachelor of Education (a route to QTS (qv)).

CDF Career Development Framework: developed by the TDA, this has advice about career progression and can be accessed on the TDA website.

Common core of skills and knowledge for the children's' workforce The government is developing a single framework of qualifications for all those who work with children, young people and families and is examining all national occupational standards (NOS (qv)) and qualifications with a view to incorporating a common core. The TDA has already incorporated this common core into induction training for teaching assistants.

CWDC Children's Workforce Development Council

DCSF Department for Children, Schools and Families (previously DFES)

DFES Department for Education and Skills

Differentiation This refers to the need to consider pupils' individual abilities when planning work so that all pupils, whatever their ability, are challenged and extended by the work, i.e. work is differentiated for each pupil.

EAL English as an Additional Language

EBRITTP Employment-based Route Initial Teacher Training Provider: these are listed on the TDA website

ESL English as a Second Language

Formative Assessment Assessment linked with teaching; describes pupils' progress and used to identify the next stage of teaching and learning; it uses diagnostic approaches, employing a wide range of methods, including formal and informal methods.

GTC General Teaching Council

GTP Graduate Teacher Programme. This involves on-the-job training provided by a school, leading to QTS (qv) while being employed as an unqualified teacher.

GTTR Graduate Teacher Training Register

HEI Higher Education Institution

HLTA higher level teaching assistant

HMCI Her Majesty's Chief Inspector of Schools in England

HMI Her Majesty's Inspectors of Schools in England

ICT Information and Communications Technology

IEP Individual Education Plan

ITE Initial Teacher Education; provides accredited programmes that lead to QTS (qv) and these are conducted in universities and colleges throughout the UK.

ITT Initial Teacher Training. See Initial Teacher Education (ITE (qv)).

KS Key Stage: the periods in each pupil's education to which the elements of the National Curriculum apply. There are four Key Stages, normally related to the age of the majority of the pupils in a teaching group. They are: Key Stage 1, beginning of compulsory education to age 7 (Years R (Reception), 1 and 2); Key Stage 2, ages 7–11 (Years 3–6); Key Stage 3, ages 11–14 (Years 7–9); Key Stage 4, 14 to end of compulsory education (Years 10 and 11). Post-16 is a further Key Stage.

LA Local Authority – have a statutory duty to provide education in their area.

Learning Objectives These are specific statements which set out what pupils are expected to learn from a particular lesson in a way that allows school staff to identify if learning has occurred.

Learning Outcomes These specify the expected pupil outputs. For example, a learning objective might be for pupils to know how to write a formal letter. The learning outcome for the lesson may be a letter to an employer in application for an advertised post.

Lesson Plan The detailed planning of work to be undertaken in a lesson. This follows a particular structure, appropriate to the demands of a particular lesson. An individual lesson plan is usually part of a series of lessons in a unit of work (qv).

Levels of Attainment Eight levels of achievement, plus exceptional performance are defined within the National Curriculum Attainment Targets in England. These stop at KS3. In deciding a pupil's level of attainment teachers should judge which description best fits the pupil's performance (considering each description alongside descriptions of adjacent levels).

Level Descriptions Of the National Curriculum for England. A statement describing the types and range of performance that pupils working at a particular level should characteristically demonstrate. Level descriptions provide the basis for making judgements about pupils' performance at the end of Key Stages 1, 2 and 3. At Key Stage 4, national qualifications are the main means of assessing attainment in National Curriculum subjects.

LSA Learning Support Assistant: gives additional support for a variety of purposes, e.g. general learning support for SEN (qv) pupils, ESL (qv). Most support is given in-class although sometimes pupils are withdrawn from class.

NARIC National Academic Recognition Centre: this enables equivalent qualifications to be identified.

NC National Curriculum – the core and other foundation subjects and their associated Attainment Targets (qv), Programmes of Study (qv) and assessment arrangements of the curriculum in England.

NFER National Foundation for Educational Research. Carries out research and produces educational diagnostic tests.

NOS National Occupational Standards

NQF National Qualifications Framework. This sets out the levels at which qualifications can be recognised and provides broad descriptions of learning outcomes at each level.

NSG Non-Statutory Guidance (for National Curriculum). Additional subject guidance for the National Curriculum but which is not mandatory; to be found attached to National Curriculum Subject Orders.

NVQ National Vocational Qualifications

OFSTED Office for Standards in Education. Non-Ministerial government department established under the Education (schools) Act (1992) to take responsibility for the inspection of schools in England. Her Majesty's Inspectors (HMI) (qv) form the professional arm of OFSTED. See also OHMCI.

OHMCI Office of Her Majesty's Chief Inspector (Wales). Non-Ministerial government department established under the Education (schools) Act (1992) to take responsibility for the inspection of schools in Wales. Her Majesty's Inspectors (HMI) (qv) form the professional arm of OFSTED. See also OFSTED.

Openquals Refers to the QCA (qv) national database of qualifications that allows you to check the online database of nationally accredited qualifications, units and awarding bodies.

PANDA Performance and Assessment Reports (used by OFSTED (qv)).

PE Physical education

PGCE Post Graduate Certificate in Education. The qualification for secondary school teachers in England and Wales recognised by the DCSF (qv) for QTS (qv).

PoS Programmes of Study (of National Curriculum for England). The subject matter, skills and processes which must be taught to pupils during each Key Stage (qv) of the National Curriculum (qv) in order that they may meet the objectives set out in Attainment Targets. They set out what pupils should be taught in each subject at each Key Stage and provide the basis for planning schemes of work (qv).

Progression The term used in lesson planning to describe the planning of the development of knowledge, skills, understanding or attitudes over time, with the learning outcomes for each lesson building on the lesson before.

PSHCE Personal, Social, Health and Citizenship Education

QCA Qualifications and Curriculum Authority: formed as a result of the Education Act in 1997. Its remit is to promote quality and coherence in education and training. Duties include an overview of the curriculum, assessment and qualifications across the whole of education and training, from pre-school to higher vocational levels.

QTS Qualified Teacher Status. This is usually attained by completion of a Post-Graduate Certificate in Education (PGCE) (qv) or a Bachelor of Education (BEd) (qv) degree or a Bachelor of Arts/Science degree with Qualified Teacher Status (BA/BSc (QTS) (qv)). There are other routes into teaching.

RPA Regional Provider of Assessment

RTP Registered Teacher Programme. This enables non-graduates to study for a degree and qualify as a teacher at the same time, by providing a blend of work-based teacher training and academic study. The RTP route will lead to qualified teacher status (QTS (qv)).

SATs Standard Assessment Tasks: externally prescribed National Curriculum assessments, which incorporate a variety of assessment methods depending on the subject and Key Stage. This term is not now widely used, having been replaced by 'Standard National Tests'.

Scaffolding Scaffolding learning refers to the process of building pupils learning on the foundation of their existing knowledge, skills, capabilities and attitudes (see also constructivist learning theories in Chapters 7 and 8).

SCITT School-centred Initial Teacher Training: this refers to collections of local schools that have formed consortia to offer teacher education courses across the group.

SEN Special Educational Needs: referring to pupils who for a variety of intellectual, physical, social, sensory, psychological or emotional reasons experience learning difficulties, which are significantly greater than those experienced by the majority of pupils of the same age.

SENCO Special Educational Needs Coordinator

Skills4Schools This is an online resource to help school support staff access learning opportunities at work. The website has a journey planner and examples of how people have approached their training and development.

SoW Scheme of work: this represents long-term planning as it describes what is planned for pupils over a period of time (for example a Key Stage (qv) or a year). It is derived from the Programme of Study (qv) and Attainment Targets (qv) and should contain the knowledge, skills and processes required for each area of activity.

Summative Assessment Assessment linked to the end of a course of study; it sums up achievement in aggregate terms and is used to rank, grade or compare pupils, groups or schools. It uses a narrow range of methods which are efficient and reliable, normally formal, i.e. under examination conditions.

Support Work in Schools Qualification There are new vocational qualifications for support work in schools, which are part of the national qualifications framework (NQF). The qualification includes mandatory and optional units and you select the units that best match your role and your development needs. You can choose from the list of units by searching for support work in schools in the Openquals (qv) national qualifications database.

TDA Training and Development Agency for Schools: in 2005 the TDA superseded the TTA (Teacher Training Agency) with an extended remit for overseeing standards and qualifications across the school workforce.

UCAS Universities and Colleges Admissions Service

Unit of work Medium-term planning: this describes what is planned for pupils over half a term or a number of weeks. The number of lessons in a unit of work may vary according to each school's organisation. A unit of work usually introduces a new aspect of learning. Units of work derive from schemes of work (qv) and are the basis for lesson plans (qv). The number and length of units of work varies from school to school. (QCA recommend units of work are 12 weeks long.)

Appendix 4
Websites

The following educational websites provide a comprehensive list for you to consult during the course of your professional development.

Awarding bodies. There are three awarding bodies:
  Assessment and Qualifications Alliance (AQA) (http://www.aqa.org.uk)
  Edexcel (http://www.edexcel.org.uk)
  Oxford and Cambridge Regional (OCR) (http://www.ocr.org.uk)
BBC: http://www.bbc.co.uk. The BBC website provides a wide range of support materials for learning and teaching, including simulations and revision questions.
Becta (British Educational Communications and Technology Agency): http://www. becta.org.uk/. The website provides information and links to government e-learning policy and research evidence about the use of ICT for teaching and learning; see for information on e-portfolios.
Children's Workforce Development Council (CWDC): http://www.cwdcouncil.org.uk
Children's workforce qualifications: http://www.dcsf.gov.uk/childrenswfqualifications
Classroom 2.0: http://classroom20.ning.com
Common core: http://www.dcsf.gov.uk/commoncore
DCSF (Department for Children, Schools and Families) (previously DfES (Department for Education and Skills)) http://www.dcsf.gov.uk
For information about the new and revised secondary curriculum 14–19: http://www. dcsf.gov.uk/14-19/ and http://www. qca.org.uk/qca_12195.aspx
European Computer Driving Licence (ECDL): http://www.ecdl.co.uk
European Schoolnet http://www.eun.org. This website provides the opportunity to find partners for school-based projects across the European Union and is a portal providing access to European government supported educational websites.
Foundation degree: http://www.foundationdegree.org.uk

Futurelab: http://www.futurelab.org.uk

Global Gateway, by the Central Bureau for Educational Visits and Exchanges: http:// http://www.globalgateway.org.uk

GTC (General Teaching Council for England): http://www.gtce.org.uk

GTTR (Graduate Teacher Training Register): http://www.gttr.ac.uk

Higher education courses including degree, foundation degree and access courses: http://www.ucas.com

HLTAs (higher level teaching assistants): http://www.tda.gov.uk/support/hlta.

Hot Potatoes: http://www.hotpot.uvic.ca. The website provides software tools for making online quizzes.

ITTE (Information Technology in Teacher Education): http://www.itte.org.uk. ITTE is the national subject association that promotes ICT in Initial Teacher Education and the continual professional development of teachers with ICT.

NARIC (National Academic Recognition Centre) allows equivalent qualifications to be identified: http://www.naric.org.uk

NGfL (The National Grid for Learning): http://www.ngfl.gov.uk

NOS (National Occupational Standards) directory: http://www.ukstandards.org

NQF (National Qualifications Framework): http://www.qca.org.uk/493.html

OFSTED (The Office for Standards in Education). This website not only provides reports on school inspections, it provides subject summary reports and reports on educational issues: http://www.ofsted.gov.uk

QCA (Qualifications and Curriculum Authority): http://www.qca.org.uk

QCA has a national database of qualifications that allows you to check the online database of nationally accredited qualifications, units and awarding bodies at http:// www.openquals.org.uk

QCA provides information about the National Curriculum. e.g. *National Curriculum Online* sets out the legal requirements of the National Curriculum in England, provides information to help teachers implement the National Curriculum in their schools, and links every National Curriculum programme of study requirement to resources for teachers (see http://www.qca.org.uk/232.html). *National Curriculum in Action* illustrates standards of pupils' work at different ages and Key Stages and how the programmes of study translate into real activities (see http://www.qca.org. uk/232.html).

Subject specific information: http://www.qca.org.uk/2550.html

School workforce advisers: http://www.tda.gov.uk/partners/workforceadvisers

Scottish Consultative Council on the Curriculum: http://www.claudius.sccc.ac.uk

Skills4Schools: http://www.skills4schools.org.uk. An online resource to help school support staff access learning opportunities at work. The website has a journey planner and examples of how people have approached their training and development.

Specialist Schools and Academies Trust: http://www.schoolnetwork.org.uk. The website provides case studies of innovative ICT use for learning and teaching.

Subject Associations' websites can be accessed though: http://www.gtce.org.uk/ weblinks/subject_associations

TDA (Training and Development Agency for Schools): http://www.tda.gov.uk

For advice about career progression see the TDA website and the career development framework: http://www.tda.gov.uk/support/careerdevframework.aspx

For information on the common core of skills and knowledge for the children's workforce see http://www.tda.gov.uk/partners/supportstafftraining/inductionmaterial

For advice about meeting specific professional standards for HLTAs, see the TDA website which contains case studies (including videos) at: http://www.tda.gov.uk/support/hlta/professstandards/meetingthestandards.aspx

Teachernet: http://www.teachernet.gov.uk. The teachernet website provides access to a wide range of resources to support learning and teaching in the classroom and provides information on professional development.

Teach First: http://www.teachfirst.org.uk

The National Curriculum online: http://www.nc.uk.net

TRE (Teacher Resource Exchange) provides opportunities for teachers and other educators to share lesson plans, teaching materials and ideas: http://www.tre.ngfl.gov.uk

TTRB (Teachers Training Resource Bank): http://www.ttrb.ac.uk. This website is specifically designed to support the training of teachers and there are many aspects that are relevant to HLTAs.

UCAS (Universities and Colleges Admissions Service): http://www.ucas.ac.uk

UK Education Evidence Portal: http://www.eep.ac.uk/Main/Default.aspx

VCN (Voice Care Network): http://www.voicecare.org.uk

VTC (The Virtual Teachers' Centre) is an integral part of the NGfL: http://www.vtc.ngfl.gov.uk

References

Argyle, M. (1978) *The Psychology of Interpersonal Behaviour*, Harmondsworth: Penguin.

Arthur, J., Grainger, T. and Wray, D (eds) (2006) *Learning to Teach in the Primary School*, London: Routledge.

Assessment Reform Group (1999) *Assessment for Learning: Beyond the Black Box*, Cambridge: University of Cambridge, School of Education.

Association of Teachers and Lecturers (2002) *Achievement for All: Working with Children with Special Educational Needs in Mainstream Schools and Colleges*.

Ausubel, D. P. (1968) *Educational Psychology: A Cognitive View*, New York: Holt, Rinehart and Winston.

Ball, S. (2003) *Class Strategies and the Education Market: the Middle Classes and Social Advantage*, London: RoutledgeFalmer.

Bandura, A. (1989) 'Social cognitive theory', in R. Vasta (ed.), *Annals of Child Development: Vol 6; Six theories of child development*. Greenwich, CT: JAI Press.

Bartlett, S. J. and Burton, D.M. (2007) *Introduction to Education Studies*, 2nd edn, Sage/PCP.

Becta (2004) *Virtual and Managed Learning Environments*, Coventry: Becta.

Bee, H. and Boyd, D. (2004) *The Developing Child*, 10th edn, London: Allyn and Bacon.

Bennett, R. and Leask, M. (2005) 'Teaching and learning with ICT: an introduction', in S. Capel, M. Leask, and T. Turner (eds) *Learning to Teach in the Secondary School: a companion to school experience*, London: Routledge.

Bernstein, B. (1977) *Class, Codes and Control: Vol 3; Towards a theory of educational transmissions*, 2nd edn, London: Routledge and Kegan Paul.

Biggs, J. B. (1993) 'What do inventories of students' learning processes really measure? A theoretical review and clarification', *British Journal of Educational Psychology*, 63: 3–19.

Bligh, D. (2000) *What's the Point in Discussion?* Exeter: Intellect Books.

Bouffard, T. and Couture, N. (2003) 'Motivational profile and academic achievement among students enrolled in different schooling tracks', *Educational Studies*, 29, 1: 19–38.

Bourdieu, P. (1974) 'The school as a conservative force: scholastic and cultural inequalities', in J. Egglestone (ed.), *Contemporary Research in the Sociology of Education* (pp. 32–46). London: Methuen and Co Ltd.

Bourdieu, P. (1989) 'How Schools help Reproduce the Social Order', *Current Contents/Social and Behavioural Science*, 21(8): 16.

Briggs, A. (1983) *A Social History of England*, London: Book Club Associates.

Burnham, I. and Jones, H. (2002) *The Teaching Assistant's Handbook S/NVQ Level 3*, Oxford: Harcourt.

Burton, D. (2005) 'Ways pupils learn', in S. Capel, M. Leask, and T. Turner (eds) *Learning to Teach in the Secondary School: A Companion to School Experience*, London: Routledge.

Burton, D. M. (2007) 'Psychopedagogy and Personalised Learning', *Journal of Education for Teaching*, 33, 1: 5-17

Burton, D. (2009) 'Developing teaching and learning strategies', in S. Capel, R. Heilbronn, M. Leask and T. Turner (eds) *Starting to Teach in the Secondary School: A Companion for the Newly Qualified Teacher*, London: RoutledgeFalmer.

Capel, S., Leask, M. and Turner, T. (eds) (2009) *Learning to Teach in the Secondary School: A Companion to School Experience*, 5th edn, London: Routledge.

Child, D. (2003) *Psychology and the Teacher*, 7th edn, New York, London: Continuum.

Clarke, S. (2003) *Enriching Feedback in the Classroom*, London, Hodder and Stoughton.

Cooper, B., and Dunne, M. (2000) *Assessing Children's Mathematical Knowledge: social class, sex and problem solving*. Buckingham: Open University Press.

Coopersmith, S. (1967) *The Antecedents of Self-esteem*, San Francisco: W.H. Freeman.

Crystal, D. (1971) *Linguistics*, Harmondsworth: Penguin.

Davies, N. (2000) *The School Report: Why Britain's Schools are Failing*, London: Vintage Books.

Davis, B. and Sumara, D. J. (1997) 'Cognition, complexity and teacher education', *Harvard Educational Review*, 67: 105–121.

DES (Department of Education and Science) (1985) Education for All: the Final Report of the Committee of Inquiry into the Education of Children form Ethnic Minority Groups, Cmnd. 9469. London: HMSO (The Swann Report).

DES (Department of Education and Science) (1981) *Education Act*, London: HMSO.

Dewey, J. (1938) *Experience and Education*, New York: Macmillan.

DfEE (Department for Education and Employment) (1998) *The National Literacy Strategy*, London: HMSO.

DfES (Department for Education and Skills) (2005) *Youth Cohort Study: the activities and experiences of 16 year olds* (England and Wales 2004). London, Department for Education and Skills. http://www.dcsf.gov.uk/rsgateway/DB/SFR/s000560/SFR04-2005v4.pdf, accessed 1/10/2008.

DfES (Department for Education and Skills) (2004) *Five Year Strategy for Children and Learners*, London: HMSO. http://www.dcsf.gov.uk/publications/5yearstrategy

DfES (Department for Education and Skills) (2004) *Pedagogy and Practice: Teaching and Learning in Secondary Schools, Unit 2: Teaching Models*, London HMSO.

DfES (Department for Education and Skills) (2003) *England's Success*, London: HMSO.

DfES (Department for Education and Skills) (2003) *Every Child Matters*, London: HMSO.

DfES (Department for Education and Skills) (2003) *Excellence and Enjoyment: A strategy for primary schools*, London: Crown Ref, DfES 0377/2003.

DfES (Department for Education and Skills) (2003) *Guidance on Bullying*, London: DfES.

DfES (Department for Education and Skills) (2003) *Key Stage 3 National Strategy, Assessment and Learning*, London: DfES.

DfES (Department for Education and Skills) (2003) *Key Stage 3 National Strategy, Behaviour and Attendance*, London: DfES.

DfES (Department for Education and Skills) (2003) *Key Stage 3 National Strategy, Pedagogy and Practice*, London: HMSO.

DfES (Department for Education and Skills) (2003) *Primary National Strategy, Social, Emotional and Behavioural Skills*, London: DfES.

DfES (Department for Education and Skills) (2003) *Teaching and Learning in Secondary Schools: Pilot Unit 3: Modelling*, London: Crown Ref, DfES 0343/2003.

DfES (Department for Education and Skills) (2003) *Teaching and Learning in Secondary Schools: Pilot Unit 4: Questioning*, London: Crown Ref, DfES 0344/2003.

DfES (Department for Education and Skills) (2003) *Teaching and Learning in Secondary Schools: Pilot Guidance. Units 4–7*, London: Crown Ref, DfES 0347/2003.

DfES (Department for Education and Skills) (2003) *Teaching and Learning in Secondary Schools: Pilot Unit 10: Learning Styles*, London: DfES.

DfES (Department for Education and Skills) (2003) *The Code of Practice*, London: HMSO.

DfES (Department for Education and Skills) (2003) *The Induction Support Programme for Newly Qualified Teachers*, London: HMSO.

DfES (Department for Education and Skills) (2003) *Time for Standards*, London: HMSO.

DfES (Department for Education and Skills) (2002) *Supporting Pupils Learning English as an Additional Language*, London: Crown Ref, DfES 0239/2002.

DfES (Department for Education and Skills) (2001) *Special Educational Needs Code of Practice*, London: HMSO.

DfES (Department for Education and Skills) (2004) *Five Year Strategy for Children and Learners*, London: HMSO. http://www.dcsf.gov.uk/publications/5yearstrategy

DfES (Department for Education and Skills) (2004) *Pedagogy and Practice: Teaching and Learning in Secondary Schools, Unit 2: Teaching Models*, London HMSO.

DfES (Department for Education and Skills) (2005) *Youth Cohort Study: the activities and experiences of 16 year olds* (England and Wales 2004). London, Department for Education and Skills. http://www.dcsf.gov.uk/rsgateway/DB/SFR/s000560/SFR04-2005v4.pdf, accessed 1/10/2008.

Diamond, K. (2002) 'Social competence in children with disabilities', in P. Smith and C. Hart (eds) *Handbook of Childhood Social Development*, Oxford: Blackwell.

Dillon, J. and Maguire, M. (eds) (2001) *Becoming a Teacher: Issues in Secondary Teaching*, 3rd edn, Buckingham: Open University Press.

Doherty-Sneddon, G. (2004) 'Don't look now…I'm trying to think', *The Psychologist*, 17, 2: 82–5.

Dryden, G. and Vos, J. (2001) *The Learning Revolution: To Change the Way the World Learns*, Network Educational Press in association with Learning Web.

Ekman, P. and Friesen, W. (1972) 'Hand Movements', *Journal of Communication*, 22: 353–74.

Entwistle, N. J. (1981) *Styles of Learning and Teaching*, Chichester: Wiley.

EOC (Equal Opportunities Commission) (2001) *Women and Men in Britain: Sex Stereotyping – from School to Work*, The Equal Opportunities Commission. Retrieved 2/7/04 from http://www.eoc.org.uk/cseng/research/wm_sex_stereotyping.pdf

EOC (Equal Opportunities Commission) (2003) *Facts about Men and Women in Great Britain 2003*, The Equal Opportunities Commission. Retrieved 2/7/04 from http://www.eoc.org.uk/cseng/research/factsgreatbritain2003.pdf

Erikson, E. H. (1995) *Childhood and Society*, 2nd edn, London: Vintage.

Fawcett, A. and Nicholson, R. (1996) 'Impaired performance of children with dyslexia on a range of cerebellar tasks', *Annals of Dyslexia*, 46: 259–83.

Fitzgerald, R., Finch, S., and Nove, A. (2000) Black Caribbean Young Men's Experiences of Education and Employment, Report Number RR186. London: DfEE.

Gage, N. L. and Berliner, D. C. (1984) *Educational Psychology*, 3rd edn, Boston: Houghton Mifflin.

Gagne, R. M. (1977) *The Conditions of Learning*, New York: Holt International.

Gallahue, D. L. and Ozmun, J. C. (1995) *Understanding Motor Development: Infants, Children, Adolescents, Adults*, 3rd edn, Iowa: Brown and Benchmark Publishers.

Gardner, H. (1993) *Frames of Mind: The Theory of Multiple Intelligences*, London: Fontana.

Gardner, H. (2006) *Multiple Intelligences: New Horizons in Theory and Practice*, New York Basic Books.

Garhart-Mooney, C. (2000) *Theories of Childhood: An Introduction to Dewey, Montessori, Erikson, Piaget and Vygotsky*, Minnesota: Redleaf Press.

Gauvain, M. (2001) *The Social Context of Cognitive Development*, New York: Guildford Publications.

Gillborn, D. and Gipps, C. (1996) *Recent Research on the Achievement of Ethnic Minority Pupils*, London: HMSO (OFSTED: views of research).

Gillborn, D. and Mirza, H. S. (2000) *Educational Inequality: Mapping Race, Class and Gender; A Synthesis of Research Evidence*, London: OFSTED.

Gillespie, H., Boulton, H., Hramiak, A. J. and Williamson, R. (2007) *Learning and Teaching with Virtual Learning Environments*, Exeter: Learning Matters.

Gold, K. (2003, 7/3/2003) Poverty is an excuse, *Times Educational Supplement*, p. 22.

Good, T. and Brophy, J. (2000) *Looking in Classrooms*, 8th edn, New York: Addison-Wesley Longman.

Gould, S. J. (1984) *The Mismeasure of Man*, London: Pelican.

Green, S. K. (2002) 'Using an expectancy-value approach to examine teachers' motivational strategies', *Teaching and Teacher Education*, 18: 989–1005.

Gross, R. (2001) *Psychology: The Science of Mind and Behaviour*, 4th edn, London: Hodder and Stoughton.

GTC (General Teaching Council) (2002) *Code of Professional Values and Practice for Teachers*, The General Teaching Council for England. Retrieved 2/7/04 from http://www.gtce.org.uk/gtcinfo/code.asp

Hatcher, R. (1998) 'Class Differentiation in Education: rational choices?', *British Journal of Sociology of Education*, 19(1), 5–24.

Hay McBer (2000) *Research into Teacher Effectiveness*, DfEE: London.

Heightman, S. (2005) 'Reading classrooms', in S. Capel, M. Leask, and T. Turner (eds) *Learning to Teach in the Secondary School: A Companion to School Experience*, London: Routledge.

Henry, M. (2004) 'Developmental needs and early childhood education: evolutionary, my dear Watson', *Early Child Development and Care*, 174, 3: 301–12.

Jackson, C., and Warin, J. (2000) 'The importance of gender as an aspect of identity at key transition points in compulsory education', *British Educational Research Journal*, 26(3), 375–91.

Kennan, T. (2005) *An Introduction to Child Development*, London: Sage.

Klein, G. (1993) *Education Towards Race Equality*, London: Cassell.

Lave, J. and Wenger, E. (1991) *Situated Learning: Legitimate Peripheral Participation*, Cambridge, UK: Cambridge University Press.

Leadbetter, C. (2004) *Personalisation Through Participation: A New Script for Public Services*, London: DEMOS/DfES Innovations Unit.

Leask, M. and Pachler, N. (eds) (2005) *Learning to Teach Using ICT in the Secondary School: a companion to school experience*, 2nd edn, London: Routledge.

Leask, M. and Younie, S. (2001) 'Communal constructivist theory: information and communications technology pedagogy and internationalisation of the curriculum', *Journal of Information Technology for Teacher Education*, 10, 1 and 2: 117–34.

Lloyd, S. (1992) *The Phonics Handbook*, Chigwell: Jolly Learning.

Lucas, D. and Thomas, G. (2000) *Organising Classrooms to Promote Learning for All Children: Two Pieces of Action Research* in S. Clipson-Boyles (ed) *Putting Research into Practice*, London: David Fulton.

McCallum, B. (2000) *Formative Assessment: Implications for Classroom Practice*, London: Institute of Education.

McCormick, J. and Leask, M. (2005) 'Teaching styles', in S. Capel, M. Leask, and T. Turner (eds) *Learning to Teach in the Secondary School: a companion to school experience*, London: Routledge.

Mehrabin, A. (1972) *Non-verbal Communication*, New York: Aldine Atherton.

Mercer, N. (2000) *Words and Minds: How We Use Language to Think Together*, London: Routledge.

Miles, T. (1993) *Dyslexia: The Pattern of Difficulties*, London: Whurr.

Montgomery, D. (1996) 'Differentiation of the curriculum in primary education', *Flying High*, 3: 14–28, Worcester: The National Association for Able Children in Education.

Mosston, M. and Ashworth, S. (2002) *Teaching Physical Education*, 5th edn, Cummings, San Francisco.

Muijs, D. and Reynolds, D. (2001) *Effective Teaching, Evidence and Practice*, London: Paul Chapman (Sage).

Myers, K. (1987) *Genderwatch!* Cambridge: Cambridge University Press.

Myers, K. (1990) *Sex Discrimination in Schools*. London: Advisory Centre for Education.

Noyes, A. (2003) 'Moving schools and social relocation', *International Studies in Sociology of Education*, 13(3), 261–80.

Paechter, C. (2000) *Changing School Subjects: Power, Gender and Curriculum*: Open University Press.

Piaget, J. (1976) *The Child and Reality*, New York: Penguin Books.

Piaget, J. (1954) *The Construction of Reality in the Child*, New York: Basic Books.

Piaget, J. (1932) *The Moral Judgment of the Child*, New York: Macmillan.

Power, S., Edwards, T., Whitty, G. and Wigfall, V. (2003) *Education and the Middle Class*, Buckingham: Open University Press.

(QCA) Qualifications and Curriculum Authority (2001) *Planning, Teaching and Assessing the Curriculum for Pupils with Learning Difficulties*, QCA/01/759.

Raiker, A. (2002) 'Spoken language and mathematics', *Cambridge Journal of Education*, 32, 1: 45–60.

Riding, R. J. (2002) *School Learning and Cognitive Styles*, London: David Fulton.

Riding, R. J. and Cheema, I. (1991) 'Cognitive styles – an overview and integration', *Educational Psychology*, 11: 193–215.

Riding, R. J. and Rayner, S. (1998) *Learning Styles and Strategies*, London: David Fulton.

Robertson, J. (1996) *Effective Classroom Control: Understanding Teacher-Student Relationships*, 3rd edn, London: Hodder and Stoughton.

Ruddock, J. (2004) *Developing a Gender Policy for Secondary Schools*, Open University Press.

Ruel, G. and Bastiaans, N. (2003) 'Free-riding and team performance in project education', *International Journal of Management Education*, 3, 1: 26–37.

Sage, R. (2000a) *Class Talk*, Stafford: Network Educational Press.

Sage, R. (2000b) *The Communication Opportunity Group*, Leicester: University Press Leicester.

Scanlon, M. and Buckingham, D. (2004) 'Home learning and the educational marketplace', *Oxford Review of Education*, 30(2), 287–303.

Scottish Consultative Council on the Curriculum (1996) *Teaching for Effective Learning*, Dundee: SCCC.

Scott-Gibson, E. (1992) *The Dictionary of British Sign Language*, London: Faber and Faber.

Shayer, M. and Adey, P. (eds) (2002) *Learning Intelligence: Cognitive Acceleration Across the Curriculum from 5 to 15 Years*, Buckingham; Philadelphia: Open University Press.

Shulman, L. S. (1986) 'Those who understand: knowledge growth in teaching', *Educational Researcher*, 57: 4–14.

Shulman, L. S. (1987) 'Knowledge and teaching: foundations of a new reform', *Harvard Educational Review*, 57: 1–22.

Smith, A. and Call, N. (2002) *The ALPS (Accelerated Learning in Primary School) Approach*, London: Accelerated Learning in Training and Education (ALITE).

Smith, P. K., Cowie, H. and Blades, M. (1998) *Understanding Children's Development*, 3rd edn, Oxford, London: Blackwell Publishers.

Stones, E. (1992) *Quality Teaching: A Sample of Cases*, London: Routledge.

Tilstone, C. (ed) (1998) *Observing Teaching and Learning: Principles and Practice*, London: David Fulton.

Timerley, H. S and Philips, G. (2003) 'Changing and sustaining teachers' expectations through professional development in literacy', *Teaching and Teacher Education*, 19, 6: 627– 41.

TTA (Teacher Training Agency) (2002) *Qualifying to Teach: Professional Standards for Qualified Teacher Status and Requirements for Initial Teacher Training*, London: DfES/TTA.

Tuckman, B. (1965) 'Developmental sequences in small groups', *Psychological Bulletin*, 63, 6: 384–99.

Vygotsky, L. S. (1978) *Mind in Society: The Development of Higher Psychological Processes*, London: Harvard University Press.

Vygotsky, L. S. (1994) 'The development of concept formation in adolescence', in R. van der Veer and J. Valsiner (eds), *The Vygotsky Reader*, Oxford: Blackwell Publishing.

Wersky, G. (1988) *The Visible College: A Collective Biography of British Scientists and Socialites from the 1930s*, London: Free Association Books.

West Burnham, J. (2004; 2nd edn 2007) 'Understanding learning' in *Leadership Development and Personal Effectiveness*, Nottingham: NCSL.

Wheldell, K., Bevan, K. and Shortall, K. (1986) 'A touch of reinforcement: the effects of contingent teacher touch on the classroom behaviour of young children', *Educational Review*, 38, 3: 207–16.

Willis, P. (1977) *Learning to labour: how working class kids get working class jobs*, Aldershot: Gower.

Willis, P. (1983) 'Cultural production and theories of reproduction', In L. Barton and S. Walker (eds), *Race, Class and Education* (pp. 107–38), London: Croom-Helm.

Woodward, W. (2003, 21/4/2003) Poverty Hits Exam Scores, *The Guardian*, p. 8.

Wragg, E. and Brown, G. (2001) *Questioning in the Secondary School*, London: RoutledgeFalmer.

Younger, M., Warrington, M., and Williams, J. (1999) 'The Gender Gap and Classroom Interactions: reality and rhetoric?', *British Journal of Sociology of Education*, 20(3), 325–41.

Younie, S. and Moore, T. (2005) 'Using ICT for professional purposes' in M. Leask and N. Pachler (eds) *Learning to Teach Using ICT in the Secondary School: a companion to school experience*, 2nd edn, London: Routledge.

Index of names

Subject index